SPIT
POLISH
DISCIPLINE

LIFE IN THE AUSTRALIAN ARMY
AS A NATIONAL SERVICE RECRUIT
1967–1969

PETER THOMAS COLLINS
Service No. 1733569

WITH JANINE CHIPPERFIELD

Published in Australia by Sid Harta Books & Print Pty Ltd,
ABN: 34632585293
23 Stirling Crescent, Glen Waverley, Victoria 3150 Australia
Telephone: +61 3 9560 9920, Facsimile: +61 3 9545 1742
E-mail: author@sidharta.com.au

First published in Australia 2024
This edition published 2024
Copyright © Peter Thomas Collins 2024
Cover design, typesetting: WorkingType (www.workingtype.com.au)

The right of Peter Thomas Collins to be identified as the Author of the Work has been asserted in accordance with the Copyright, Designs and Patents Act 1988.

All rights reserved. No part of this publication may be reproduced, stored in a retrieval system, or transmitted, in any form or by any means without the prior written permission of the publisher, nor be otherwise circulated in any form of binding or cover other than that in which it is published and without a similar condition being imposed on the subsequent purchaser.

ISBN: 978-1-922958-93-8

DEDICATION

To my friend, colleague and mate who suffered the supreme sacrifice in the line of duty in Vietnam on 11 December 1969. Thank you, Robert (Robbie) "Jock" Buchan, for your companionship and friendship all those years ago as we trained and served together as members of D Company 6RAR.

ACKNOWLEDGMENTS

I thank my current wife of twenty-three years, Karen, for recognising and assisting me through the trauma of post-traumatic stress and for her patience with me as I wrote this book over a long period of time.

I am forever indebted to Janine Chipperfield, my first wife of twenty-three years, for agreeing to edit my rough and ready manuscript and shape it into something resembling a book.

I am proud to have served with 6th Battalion, Royal Australian Regiment, and grateful to them for bringing me home safely and for the continued association with current and past members through the Battalion Association.

To my fellow soldiers of the tenth National Service intake, I thank you for the continued association and friendship all these past fifty-plus years. A particular thank you to Frank Douglas, a sig (radio operator) with me in Vietnam, who, after fifty-seven years, continues to care about me as we celebrate our mutual birthdays each year.

I acknowledge and thank Peter Cullen, a well-known historian, for his historical piece about the first National Service in the 1950s.

I thank my friend Dennis Youngberry for the poem *The Cross* and for his continued support of the veterans of the war.

Photos other than those from my personal collection are in the public domain and cited as they appear throughout.

DISCLAIMER

Written from memory, this work is wholly my own except where indicated by references and acknowledgments and I take full responsibility for the book's content. While my memory is imperfect, facts have been checked where possible, and events, places, people and organisations are recorded as I remember them. I apologise to my mates, friends and family members named if what I have written offends in any way. The situations referred to are my recollections of many years ago. I have included these in my story as an indication of the value these relationships held for me during a difficult time of my life.

CONTENTS

Introduction: Here we go — 1
1. The news — 3
2. Leaving on a jet plane, er, bus — 20
3. 3TB Singleton — 32
4. Are you fit? Are you ready, Pete? — 44
5. Mean and nasty training tactics: Teaching discipline? — 48
6. Let the good times roll — 58
7. How do I get "outa" this place? Christmas leave — 66
8. Infantry Corps — 69
9. Moving on: The real deal — 81
10. Lavarack Barracks — 95
11. Life in the tropics: Partying — 105
12. Training an Army battalion — 110
13. On the battalion parade ground — 121
14. Back to training: Serious stuff & good stuff — 126
15. Home again: Another long trip — 145
16. Preparation and departure — 170
17. Leaving on a jet plane: For war in Vietnam — 177
18. Vietnam. A life-changing experience! — 182
19. Settling in: First night in Vietnam — 194
20. Another day in paradise — 210
21. The 6th arrives: Work begins — 219
22. A holiday on the South China Sea — 231
23. Army transport: A love-hate relationship — 243
24. A new adventure: The Cambodian border — 249
25. The real deal — 259
26. Preparation for RTA — 269

27.	"Freedom Bird" awaits	273
28.	Coming home: Not so easy!	278
29.	Entering the financial world	288
30.	Big changes ahead	296
31.	Starting a new life	301
32.	One last battle	308
33.	Robert (Jock) Buchan	313
34.	The 6th Battalion	319
35.	The thorny question of conscription	321
36.	Positives and negatives	326
37.	Spit polish discipline: How does it all end?	330

Appendix 1. National Service memories by Peter Cullen	332
Appendix 2: A poem by a special friend	336
Bibliography	338
Glossary of Terms	340

INTRODUCTION: HERE WE GO

This book is a recollection that may be a little bit off the mark as far as time, dates and names are concerned, but the essential memories of fifty-seven years ago are correct. Several books have been written about Vietnam, but this is essentially about my National Service commitment for two years from 1967 to 1969. I hope to show the impact of this on a twenty-year-old male plucked out of "civvie" life to serve two years in the Army and also the impact it had on family. I hope to recall the funny stuff, the difficult stuff, the frustrating stuff, the ridiculous stuff, the scary stuff and other stuff that comes to me as I travel back through this period of my life.

It is a memory of my call-up into the Australian Army, the induction, recruit training at 3rd Training Battalion (3TB), Singleton, New South Wales, and battle efficiency training at Lavarack Barracks, Townsville in north Queensland with the 6th Battalion, Royal Australian Regiment (6RAR).

As an integral part of 6RAR, myself and others of my intake were unexpectedly sent to Vietnam in 1969. It will be necessary to finish this book, not only with a recollection of my time in Vietnam, but with the later effects of that deployment.

This version is a second attempt following the loss of a previous manuscript to computer malfunction, or perhaps it was an operator malfunction.

My hope is that this will satisfy my wish to write a book on a subject that is important to me and had a dramatic effect on my life. I also hope it will sell a million copies and I can forget the Lotto.

I must warn you, though, that it contains coarse language

and culturally offensive idioms for which I apologise in advance. I am writing about a completely male environment where all involved are young and participating in a new and strange life. I don't believe I can relate the story properly without this coarse and offensive language. Our Army trainers used this type of language to emphasise the Army point and as an attention tool. I hope you understand. It was very much part of the life I am attempting to describe.

I hope you enjoy my story.

1. THE NEWS

I gently slid my beige Morris 1100 down the wide grassy verge in front of number eighty-three Curzon Street, climbed out of the little beast and opened the letter box. One letter addressed to me. I opened it, read it, climbed back into the Morris and drove to the pub. The place was Toowoomba, Queensland; the date was July 1967.

'Give me a pot please, Anne.'

'There ya go, Pete. Eighteen cents, please.'

'While you're at it, Anne, give me another pot. Here's the dough.'

'Another pot please, Anne. Ah! Here's Bill and another pot with a dash please, luv.'

'Hey Bill, what's with him, that's his third in no time flat.'

Bill looked at me quizzically, so I handed him the letter.

'Well bugger me! Hey, you blokes, Pete here has been called up.'

'Yeah, bloody good riddance, I say.'

'They'll sort you out in no time.'

'Don't let the "noggies"[1] get you.'

'You'll look the duck's nuts in a uniform.'

'Hey Pete, which end of a gun do you hold onto?'

'The same as you, stupid: the long skinny end.'

Huge laughter from my mates as they sang a version of *You're in the Army now*, 'Here we go, here we go, off he goes, he's in the Army now.'

Bill said, 'Did you get this in today's mail? Wonder if I got one?'

'Another two pots please, Anne, one with a dash.'

Ron Davy, owner of the White Horse Hotel, walked into the bar in response to the noisy rabble. Ron knew us all very well and was a

---

1 A racist derogatory term for people from Southeast Asia in use at the time.

good friend of mine. He looked after us as most of us were under the legal drinking age of twenty-one. 'Who's in the Army now?'

'It's Pete,' they all yelled. 'Stiff shit for him, hey, Ron?'

Anne delivered our beers. Ron said, 'I'll get those. What a blow Pete. When do you have to go?'

'Probably early October, if my medical tests are okay.'

'You couldn't pass wind, Pete, let alone a medical test.'

Sick bastards, I thought.

Had a couple more pots with Bill before going home. It won't be a lot of fun telling my dad and my three sisters the news.

'Give me a bell, Bill, and let me know your fate.'

'Bye, mate. See you here tomorrow arvo.'

*

Dad and I were very close, perhaps because I was the only boy in his family of four kids. Three of us—Sandra, myself and Jill— were all born in the same week in February, two years apart. Wendy was a surprise late arrival a few years later.

Dad had supported me in everything I wanted to do. He got me my job at the ANZ Bank in 1964. I was able to start work full-time two weeks after my senior year at high school finished. Earlier in my life he played cricket with me when he got home from work in the backyard until it was too dark to see. When he finally went inside, Mum would say, 'You're late again tonight, Gordon.'

He would reply with a smirk on his face, 'Been a bit busy, Rene. Sorry.' They had a good relationship; we were a happy family.

Dad was a very hard and responsible worker and was a foreman at the Toowoomba Foundry during World War II. Designated as an "essential person" by the government, he was unable to enlist as had his three brothers, Bill, Charlie and Ron. The foundry produced many military defence items, including artillery shells, for the war effort.

Dad met my Mum in that machine shop. Irene English was from a large Toowoomba family which had many serving members in the war effort. She operated a large "lathe" machine which, for the uninitiated, spins fast and shapes metal. Mum had long dark hair. One day her hair caught in the machine. The ever-vigilant foreman saved the moment and her hair, pre-workplace health and safety, obviously. A loving relationship had begun. Dad left the foundry after the war and worked for a machine shop, Muller Bros, for a few years where he perfected a way to repair cracked cylinder heads. By placing the head in a furnace fire and heating it until it was glowing red, he would then enter the extremely hot furnace to affect the repair. By melting pure cast iron into a groove he had previously created, the crack would be filled. Once cooled naturally, the head would be surface machined, reseated and reassembled. This procedure was highly successful. Many expensive or unavailable items were successfully repaired to customers' delight.

Dad was to later open his own business, Collins Welding and Engineering Service. He employed three or four tradesmen and ran a very successful business. I enjoyed using his equipment to complete "hot up jobs" on mine and my mates' cars. Dad was supportive of this and sponsored me in my first motor racing venture in an FJ Holden. I rewarded him by winning many races at Echo Valley under his sponsorship. In fact, he kept on helping and paying for my cars for some years. He died in 2016 at the age of ninety-six.

My Mum had died in a single-car accident in 1966. On her way to collect Wendy from school, she crashed into a telegraph pole and died instantly. Mum's granddaughter, Debbie (Sandra's sixteen-month-old daughter), who was a passenger, was presumed to be unhurt, but a week later was found to have a broken leg. My call-up was barely a year later and our family, especially Dad, was still suffering the loss. She was only forty-two years old. The news of my call-up would be a significant blow to my family. How would Dad react? Mum had cried and was sad when I was transferred to

Brisbane a year before she died. She wrote every week even though I was home every weekend. God bless her, she won't need to worry.

*

When I arrived home, Dad said, 'Where have you been, young fella? We were worried.'

'Sorry Dad, I had something to think about away from home and needed a drink or three.'

'I can see that, Son. What is it? Can I help?'

I handed him the letter. He read it and said, 'Now I want a drink. Get me a beer, mate, and one for yourself.'

Dad was not a drinker. He concentrated on his work. I remembered Canon Ralph Wicks (later Bishop Wicks) coming to see us after Mum died carrying two XXXX tallies (750 ml beer bottles) so I guessed this was okay. We sat down, side by side. Dad put his hand on my leg and said in a faltering voice, 'I have lost my wife. I don't want to lose my only son. Can we get you out of this?'

'Don't know about that, Dad.'

He said, 'Can I have one of your Marlboros, mate?'

I was shocked. I had been smoking very lightly for a few weeks but didn't take cigarettes home. I was wearing a fashionable (for the time) black cardigan; in the right pocket were the cigarettes.

'Ah! Yeah Dad, here ya go.'

'Got a light?' he said quietly, 'Aren't you having one?'

'Dad, I have one a day, Monday to Friday.'

'How come?' he said.

'Well, as you know, I'm number two teller at the bank. Norm, who's number one teller, sits down under his counter at closing time and has a smoke. He says it relaxes him before the daily drama of balancing his cash for the day. Norm saw how nervous I was at balance time and offered me a cigarette.' After a week I'd purchased my first packet of twenty Marlboro Red at the expensive price of twenty-three cents.[2]

Dad said, 'I'll speak to Norm about this.' And he did!

*

The daily cash balance at the bank was such a trauma because if the cash was short and an independent recount didn't locate the error, the teller was responsible and had to repay the money. This was usually done by fortnightly pay deductions. After it was repaid in full, the teller could apply for the bank to stand the loss and be reimbursed for all payments. This was usually granted provided there had not been other losses. I had two significant cash losses. One was $1000 on a Friday. I was a gibbering mess after I had checked everything three times with no joy.

Old mate Norm asked, 'Wadda problem, li'l mate?'

'I'm short a thousand, Norm. Double-checked and once again with no result.'

'Let me have a look,' he said. 'Start with all big transactions of cash paid out.'

I said, 'Norm, there was only one, the Bellevue Hotel, one of my last transactions today.'

'Okay,' said Norm, 'I know them very well. I'll ring and see if they can help.'

Norm came back and said the hotel was balancing its cash now and would ring back. Norm and I sat down under the counter and had a smoke while we waited. The office manager, Ted, came up to the counter, 'Hey, what are you two doing?'

Norm said, 'Looking for a thousand. Pete here is short.'

---

2   Sadly, one a day didn't last long. By 1977 I was smoking sixty a day, every day. All to do with the pressure of work as a District Credit Manager for Australian Guarantee Corporation (AGC) in a large office. Thankfully, one night at the pub my boss, myself, and two other staff smokers decided to stop. I did stop and haven't had a cigarette for forty-seven years.

'Fuck me!' said Ted, 'Do you think it's on the floor?'

Just then Norm was called to the phone. He came back and said, 'No, Ted, we found it at the Bellevue.' Norm hugged me and said, 'Let's go and get it li'l mate,' and we did!

My second, and thankfully last, loss was $200. By this time, I was number one teller and responsible for ensuring the branch had sufficient coins of each denomination on hand. Our branch was the recipient of the Toowoomba City Council's parking metre collection on a daily basis. Consequently, we had an oversupply of five and ten-cent pieces which I would swap for twenty-cent pieces with other banks. Coins in bags are heavy so we used the boss's car to pick-up and deliver. On one occasion the car was unavailable, so I used my own.

Though the bulk was coin holding, notes too were part of my cash and included in the daily count and balance. I was $200 short, and the error was in the coin holding. I checked and double-checked, rang other banks with no joy. I searched my car without result. I reported it to the manager and the process of repayment began.

Two or three weeks later I had a flat tyre in the Morris. When removing the spare wheel I had a surprise. There lay a bag of twenty-cent coins— $200 worth. Good stuff.

*

I did have a smoke with Dad that evening and another beer before the nosy sisters wanted to know what was going on. Dad told them, 'Your brother has been called up in the Army for the next two years. It is the law. He has to go.'

Scream, scream, scream, all three went in unison, on and on and on. 'Oh no, Pete!' said Sandra the oldest, two years older than me, 'When? When do you have to go?'

'I have to have a medical exam. If I pass the medical, about the first week in October.'

'Maybe you'll fail the medical and can stay home.'

Dad said, 'He'd have to be nearly dead to fail, I think, if I know the Army system.'

Everyone was in tears, even my dad. I said, 'My mates reckon I couldn't pass wind let alone pass a medical.' This little joke eased the tension, and we all had a good laugh and went to bed.

That night, alone in my bed gave me space to think, and think and think some more. How did I feel about this? So far it had been something of a joke with the mates and I hadn't thought about it seriously. My first thoughts were of family and my girlfriend, Karen. We did have future plans. What would become of those plans? Two years, twenty-four months, ninety-six weeks, 662 days away from home and those you love is a long time. Army— what will it be like in the Army? Can I handle what they have in mind for me? I have had a good and carefree life so far which will obviously change dramatically. I am concerned about my dad. He has been my rock, and I will miss him immensely. Will he be proud of what I do in the next two years? I am apprehensive and yes; yes, I think I'm scared. I did fall asleep eventually, alcohol-induced mostly, and woke up to the alarm to get to work. The world as it is now goes on.

At the morning tea break before the bank opened, I went to see the branch manager, my boss Graham White. I told him my news. He said, 'Thanks, Pete, for telling me so soon. Your dad rang me earlier.' Good on ya, Dad. 'I told your dad: "Gordon, Pete's job at the bank will be here for him when he comes back."

'I also told him the ANZ will pay the difference in Army pay and the applicable bank entitlement fortnightly. I'll be very sorry to lose you as my employee for two years, especially since you lost your mother not so long ago. I personally wish you well. Come, we'll tell your staff mates who I know are going to miss you and your expertise.'

*

When Mum was killed, I was working in Brisbane as a savings bank teller at the ANZ Queen and Wharf Streets branch, affectionately known as the "Old People's Home" by ANZ staff. On that day, the branch manager came to me at 3:15 pm and said, 'Pack it in, Pete. You are to go home to Toowoomba immediately. I will look after your cash.' I never went back. The ANZ thought I should be with my family and instigated a transfer back home. The bank gave me two weeks paid leave with more time if necessary. I wish to this day that I had not left the bank for the Australian Guarantee Corporation (AGC) in 1970.

There were, as I recall, three reasons for doing so. (1) I was transferred to a boring little ANZ branch at Crows Nest, near enough to home to daily commute. (2) The ANZ took over the English, Scottish & Australian (ES&A) Bank which had Esanda as a finance arm offering hire purchase as a form of lending. I was very interested in this when introduced by an Esanda representative. I told him of my interest and was informed I could transfer. (3) The ANZ Crows Nest manager refused a transfer, so when an opportunity to go to AGC came, I took it!

*

Out in the main office area, the staff were already waiting when the manager and I arrived. The boss told them my news and assured them I would be back, albeit in two years.

There were shouts of: 'It's not fair, Pete.'

'Don't go, stay here.'

'We won't let you go.' Many hugs, kisses, handshakes and some tears.

Up at the counter as our first customers came in Norm said, 'I am going to miss you, little friend, and our Monday pontoon club will miss your money.' During the day, Norm was telling the news to his regulars and mine. We both had our special customers who would wait for us to be free. My favourite was a beautiful young girl from the chemist shop. She came in every day close to three pm and would wait for me to serve her, much to Norm's chagrin. Rachel was visibly upset and wished me good luck, gave me a peck on the cheek and whispered, 'I'll miss you, Pete.' I had tears in my eyes back behind the counter.

'Don't worry, Pete. I'll look after her.'

'Yeah Norm, thought so!'

This being a Friday, the closing time was five pm and, as usual, several of us were anxious to get to the pub, especially today. It was the usual rush in spades to get everything balanced. The REMS (remittance of cheques to other branches and other banks) were the real bugbear. They had to balance with the deposits received. Often they did not! Usually, it was a machining error. Clerks operated adding machines recently converted to decimal currency (introduced in February 1966) to total those many cheques. It was the REMS that didn't balance on this particular Friday. 'Bugger,' said Ted, 'I hope your fix works, Pete.'

Being something of a numbers whizz, I had worked out that if the error amount was divisible by nine, the error was most likely a reversed figure. For example, if the error was forty-five dollars under, there is a machining error where seventy-two has been entered as twenty-seven. The task is then simplified to examining all the figures ending in twenty-seven. It often worked and saved a lot of time. The boss thought I was a genius and said so every time it worked. 'How are we going to survive these afternoons without our whizz kid?' Having balanced the REMS, the boss said to everyone 'Pete, Norm and I are going to the pub, the White Horse private bar. See you there when you finish.'

I gained a title in the three ANZ branches as "Fix It" and was called on to help find balancing errors. At that time, 1964–1967, there were no electronics at all, everything was mechanical and subject to human error. One branch had a ledger error of $200 that had existed for some time and was now a problem. I found the error in a few hours by examining all $200 transactions. It was a double entry where the second entry, due to machine malfunction, printed perfectly over the first. The slightly darker print was the clue. Just bloody brilliant, hey what, Watson!

The boss bought a couple of beers before the staff arrived. Every last one of them was there, plus a couple from the other two branches, including both managers. My boss said he had spoken to state office who asked him to wish me all the best and a safe return. The state manager had authorised some funds— within reason— for drinks and nibbles. I really felt like a king. Everyone was slapping me on the back and buying me drinks, making comments like, 'Have a drink, Pete, maybe your last on two legs.'

The singing started somewhere in the bar and spread to our party; 'You're in the Army now; off he goes; he's in the Army now.' They all thought it funny, and I played along, but it hit me like a ton of bricks. Soon and for two years I won't be here, they will all be having a fun Friday night. Where the hell will I be? And what will I be doing?

The boss was leaving, being the responsible bank manager he was, so I took the opportunity to say some thanks and goodbyes and go home earlier than usual for a Friday. Dad was home and waiting for me. He never went to the pub, only occasionally had a beer at home. He said, 'Feel like a drink, mate? Let's go out on the veranda and have a beer. I have something to talk about.'

*

Number eighty-three was a 1900s Queenslander, a large home with verandas on three sides. Some of it was in need of TLC, but Dad had revitalised the kitchen, bathroom, lounge and bedrooms. It was on a big block of land and I loved it. I had lived there since I was one year old. The neighbours were the Hodgsons, a chemist shop proprietor, and the Lawrences, a Japanese prisoner of war and his wife, bless his heart. Oh, and their cat, a pure black cat named Snowy who once was stupid and ran in front of my archery target. Well! Yes, I shot him. Not dead, but he ran off with my arrow. I went to Mrs L and asked if I could have my arrow back. A bit bewildered she said, 'Of course, Peter. Where is it?'

'Stuck in Snowy,' I said. 'He's in the laundry.'

The cat was not injured, no blood, nothing, so I retrieved my arrow and left to a, 'Ah, you kids, I don't know!'

*

Dad and I went out to the front veranda with a beer. He said he had spoken to a few influential people who said because of Mum's death fairly recently, I could get excused on family compassionate grounds. I thought fuck me, that's putting me in a shit of a position. I go away and upset my father and sisters; I stay home by getting out of it like this— how will I feel about myself in the future? What a bind! I said, 'Thanks, Dad. Can we both think about this over the weekend and have a family talk on Sunday at dinner?'

Wendy came out and said, 'Pete, Bill rang.'

'Why? Did he ask you out?'

'I wish,' said Wendy. Bill had this caring thing about Wendy because she was the youngest and she had confessed to Bill her deep-down sorrow for the loss of our mother. 'He says give him a bell at home when you get here.' So, I did.

'What's happening, Bill?'

'Ah Pete,' Bill said, 'how about meeting at Zach's at 7:30? We'll drink the shelves.'

'Okay mate, see you there.'

Bill and I had this stupid thing (wasn't stupid then) we called "drinking the shelves". In Zach's lounge bar, there were shelves of liqueurs, spirits and assorted alcohol mixes. Our clever trick was to have a drink of every bottle on the shelves in one sitting. If we really liked one, we might have two or three before moving on.

Bill was waiting with a fresh pot in his hand. 'Another pot for Pete please, Anne.' She was the same Anne as at the White Horse because Ron owned Zach's too. 'Got something to tell you, Pete. I got the call-up letter today.' Silence fell upon us.

'Recruit Bill, let's get pissed!'

'With ya, recruit Pete. Shelves, here we come. Anne, you know the drill, love. Start at the top and keep it going until we fall off the stool or off our legs.'

Bill was happy. His dad had been in the Royal Navy in World War II and was awarded the British Empire Medal. His oldest brother was in the Australian Navy and his older brother was in the Army with the rank of Warrant Officer Class One (WO1). Bill would be able to continue the family's service tradition. This pleased him greatly.

Some hours later, we fell off our legs. The hotel staff put us in a room and closed the door on a night of friends, laughter and tears. It was great and it felt bloody good that my best friend, who I had known since Grade One at primary school, would be entering into this new life challenge with me. *We'll show them a few things hey what!* I thought. Bill was fairly short but had arms on him like Popeye. He was a motor mechanic at the Ford dealer, where both his girl, Debbie, and my girl, Karen, also worked. Bill was a renowned boxer. He introduced me to the sport, but after three, three-round fights, I earned the name "Canvas Back". So be it! And so endeth the boxing career!

Saturday boomed into life just in time to meet the team at the White Horse for darts practice at 10 am. 'Hiya Anne! A pot and one with a dash if you would.' Bill was up and running, to the toilet that is, but soon he was back up fighting fit and ready for another session. As young males, we lived for our grog and the company of our mates. We had a wonderful carefree life in the 1960s. We drank but never caused any trouble; we were friends with the police detectives and knew the traffic cops pretty well. Sergeant Dank, the top motorcycle cop, was kept busy with us in our cars, but he was a fair-minded bloke who said many years later he'd enjoyed the chase.

After staring at my beer for some time, I asked Anne for another.

'Pete, you haven't drunk the first one.'

'Yeah, Anne. You know what they say, the second one always tastes better.'

'Not surprised you're a bit off the boil after what you and Bill did last night.'

'Do not remember, Anne. Sorry if we played up.'

The rest of that weekend was full of fun, laughter and tears.

Decision time was now.

On Sunday night I was home early and sober as a judge. Sandra cooked a terrific lamb roast, and the family enjoyed a great meal and had a good time together. Over a cup of tea, Dad said, 'Son, have you thought about this call-up business? I want to say now I don't want you to go and neither do your sisters. However, it is your life and your decision.'

At that moment in my life, I was politically naive. I did not know nor understand what it was my government was asking me to do. I did not understand, nor even know, the reasons for this government action of forcing young men like me to spend two years in the Army. This was not in a citizens' military force nor any sort of reserve; it was twenty-four hours a day, seven days a week, for two years, in the regular Australian Army. I would be joining seasoned, experienced soldiers.

I was cognisant of the fact that at ages nineteen and twenty in 1966–1967 I was unable to vote, could not drink alcohol legally, and was considered not yet an adult in many legal and social aspects. Despite my not having any say at all, the government could conduct a ballot based on birthdays and force the "winners" to give up two years of their life in military service. Was this a democratic process? Was it fair? Democracy is supposed to be fair, is it not? So, to force an individual to do something under threat of imprisonment— is that fair? What if that person is considered to be a minor and not entitled to vote— is that fair? Of course, it is NOT fair. Yet under the National Service legislation, every nineteen-year-old male had to register for these ballots. The punishment for not, or for refusing to register, was imprisonment for two years. Looking back, two years behind bars might have been a better option!

According to the Australian Government and the then prime minister, Menzies, our country was under threat from the communists of the north. He said we Australians needed to be armed, trained and ready for a communist invasion. "Communists"— what are they, aliens from Mars or beyond? The Vietnam War was happening somewhere. Where the hell is Vietnam? What has it to do with me? I did not know about it, did not care about it, and I had not thought of ever being involved in it.

I said to Dad, 'Whenever I'm not at work I think of nothing else, even at work on the counter I'm constantly reminded of it. I've already been treated like a hero by the bank staff and some customers. I've had cheers and tears. The truth is I haven't made a decision one way or the other. I still have the medical to go through, maybe something will make me unsuitable for what the Army has in mind for me. If my mother was still here, I wouldn't feel I was leaving you alone without the support you need. I do keep returning to two questions.

'One is leaving you and my family. The other is a concern about how I might feel about myself in the future if I use this "excuse" to not go. Will other people think ill of me? I'm not afraid of two years in the Army, but not going might be with me forever. I hope you Dad, you Sandra, you Jill, and you Wendy, understand, that I will go with whatever happens. The other news is that, as you know, I have been absent since Friday night. Sorry about that, but Bill and I have been celebrating— or commiserating— as he has been called up too. Bill is very happy about it and has helped me mull it all over. It would be good to have a trusted mate with me. What will be, will be.'

ARMY MEDICAL SCIENCE

Notice to attend a medical examination arrived promptly. I was to report to the Returned Soldiers Memorial, (RSL) Hall Anzac Room at 7:30 pm.

Outside the RSL, there was a small crowd of young guys talking among themselves, some looking concerned, others being raucous dickheads. Moving among them were a few clipboard-carrying people dressed in white coats. There were no Army or other service uniforms to be seen. A half dozen police stood around in pairs, seemingly uninterested. Mostly the call-up "winners" or "victims" were on their own, but there were a few parents present.

Before I left home, Dad was watching a TV show called *You Can't See Round Corners*. It was, as I recall, about authorities trying to catch draft dodgers, one in particular who seemed pretty smart.

Dad said with a smirk, 'I'll make a few notes about this so you can escape to the bush.'

'Good stuff, Dad. Don't wait up. I'll probably go to the White Horse clinic after this is over.'

'See you tomorrow, Son.'

Here we go, here we go; off to the Army, we go!

The mood outside the RSL was jovial. Everyone was giving advice. 'Tell 'em ya blind'; 'Tell 'em you're deaf'; 'Tell 'em you're a Russian spy'; 'Tell 'em you're a poofter'; 'Tell 'em you've got a wooden leg'; 'Yeah, and a wooden dick, ya wanker.' The laughter increased, the jokes came thick and fast. Nervous humour maybe. Until …

'Righto you lot, listen up! When I call your name, get over 'ere quick.' The noise, it was a big noise, and it came from a nurse five feet tall and five feet round, a booming voice and dressed to kill.

Silence … then someone up the back yelled, 'Righto, bitch!'

Miss Bitch clattered across the room in the direction of the voice, 'Righto, who was it? Car'n, own up or you'll all be here all night.'

'Pig's arse we will,' came from the other side of the room. A tall guy in a white coat came to Miss Bitch's aid. 'Okay guys settle down, when Sister (Bitch) calls your name go to the table she directs you to, let's get this done.'

'Peter Thomas Collins,' that would be me, 'Table Three.'

Here we go! My last hope of a reprieve! *Don't get your hopes up for that, Pete,* I said to myself. *You are walking on two legs; probably sufficient for this lot.*

'Good evening, Mr Collins, may we call you Peter?'

'Please do. It's my name.'

'Peter, we need you to strip off in a few minutes. Any objection?'

'None.'

They did a sight test, hearing test, height, weight, teeth, eye, hair and complexion colour.

'Strip off, please.' No obvious marks, feet, legs, arms, hands; two of each.

'Bend over. Cough. Good!' Whack, whack with the rubber stamp. 'All done, Pete. You will hear from us soon.'

This was the tenth intake of National Service recruits. One would expect that after nine previous intakes, the authorities would have all bases covered and be aware of all the tricks these blokes might try on. The medical was the obvious place to try something. There were, of course, some brave or maybe desperate souls who tried it on, with very little success.

Eyes and ears; hearing and sight were the abilities thought to be the most likely to pull off a scam. Some blokes would start the act right from when their name was called. Ignoring the call time and time again until a mate explains it to him. They would continually say, 'Sorry, could you repeat that,' or, 'What did you say?' Or they would answer a question that wasn't asked. Like 'What is your blood group?' 'Oh, my family is all Australian born.' The doctor would just smile a little and move on. These guys were just too perfect. At the end of the interview, the doctor would say quietly as the subject or sucker walked away, 'Ah, Rod! You've left your car keys, mate!' Nearly always the guy would stop and turn around. The doc would say, 'In the next few days you will get a referral for a full hearing test. Good night.'

Eyes were a little easier. Misread the chart lines with one eye but remember the error you made when doing the same test again later. A different reading the second or third time was a red light to the doctor. As the person left the table the doc would raise a black cotton drape across the door space. Everyone except the genuinely sight-challenged would duck the drape. 'Ah, mate!' the doc would say, 'You'll get a referral for a professional eye test soon. Good night, mate.'

These people were professionals. It would take an expert to fool them. Why bother trying?

I passed the medical with flying colours as expected and sat back and awaited the next communication.

2. LEAVING ON A JET PLANE, ER, BUS

THE FIRST DAY IN ARMY CAPTIVITY

received confirmation of my medical results and was informed I would be advised shortly of a departure date. It was not long in arriving.

Seven am, 2 October 1967, Dad is driving me to McCafferty's bus station in Neil Street for an eight am departure to Brisbane. Not much is being said. We are both lost in our own thoughts. There are a lot of people at the bus station, families and friends and the young men who are leaving.

When I received the movement letter about a week before, the reality of what was happening really hit me, hit me pretty hard. Dad was home with me when I opened the letter. My reaction was a bit of a shock to him, I think.

'Holy shit, this is for bloody real. I am in the fuckin' Army, for the next two long fuckin' years!'

Dad said, 'Don't use that language, Son. You are better than that.'

'Am I? I have to leave you, my sisters and my friends and my home for what sort of life?'

*

Dad was not a prude; he could swear with the best. One day at number eighty-three my mate Dennis and I were sitting in my post-box red 1953 FJ Holden and one of us said, 'Fuck.'

Dad came over to the passenger's side window and said that was not swearing and launched into a soliloquy of swear words that went on for several minutes after which he said, 'THAT is swearing. If you are going to do it, do it well!' He explained that his father had been a bullock team driver in the Maleny forests, pulling large logs out of the steep forest terrain then loading them on a dray and carting them to the mill. His dad could swear at the twelve-strong bullock team for half an hour without repeating a word.

*

'I am proud of you,' he said, 'It may be tough, but you'll handle whatever. Be yourself. Keep your mouth shut, try hard, listen, learn and support your mates. I know you; you'll do it well and you'll come back to me a man, a man proud of himself.'

In hugs and tears, I said, 'I will do that for myself and for you, Dad.'

Dad said, 'What about your sisters?'

'Ah, fuck them; they are girls, hey!'

My reply is not how I feel about my sisters. Though I often refer to Sandra, Jill and Wendy as my "sugly isters" (ugly sisters), be assured they are in no way ugly. The bond we formed in our early childhood is unbreakable,[3] although surely tested when Sandra forced Jill and I to eat her mud pies. These three wonderful people are the love of my life. I trust they will understand my attempted humour in the text.

The bank had given me paid leave immediately. The boss had personally thanked me for my contribution to his branch and the bank, saying, 'I've had many comments on the excellent service given by you, Pete and Norm up there on the front line. Ted (the office manager) is devastated to lose his number one problem-solver. Good luck from all of us, see you back here for Christmas 1969.'

---

3 Distance now means my sisters and I rely on our love and respect for each other to continue this special relationship. Sadly, we lost Wendy, our youngest, in 2024, but the love and bond remains unbroken.

It was very quiet at the bus station, lots of hugs, kisses and tears. Mums, dads, brothers and sisters all gathered around their boys. It was surprising to me that there were a couple of wives. A couple of guys had decided to marry their sweethearts before leaving. To me this was a bit silly, a bloody lot could change in two years. After all, we were still very young. Too much to expect a young girl to hibernate for two years. I do remember discussing the issue with my Karen. We agreed to leave things as they were but do our own thing and see what happened in a couple of years. A good idea as it turned out. I'll get to that later.

Karen and I had been together the night before. It was a sad time for us. This gorgeous, long dark-haired to-die-for striking girl had been my steady girlfriend for a while. I didn't think I was in the hunt as I had admired her from afar. Finally, I'd asked her to dance (which I could not do, dance that is) one night at the Bowl, a former movie theatre converted to a rock'n'roll music venue. Karen was a ballet dancer of note but accepted my invitation. I was astounded when she agreed to let me drive her home and again to go for a drive the following Sunday afternoon in my little Morrie. It was hard, hard to leave her. I hoped she would be there for me whenever I came home. She said she would be there to see me off the next morning.

Barry, brother-in-law, salt of the earth, "Bazza", was there to see me off. He would be good support for Dad once I was gone; not just that day, but whenever needed. Barry was Sandra's husband. Karen arrived a bit late and a bit breathless. She'd woken up a bit late, hurriedly dressed and put on her makeup, and had run all the way down from Station Street to McCafferty's bus depot. We couldn't say very much. We were both sad and depressed. All we knew was two years of National Service was about to begin. We would write to each other, and I'd be home on leave from time to time and we'd be together again. The time came for us to say our goodbyes. We embraced and kissed. I got on the bus and sat by a window. I was in a daze. I didn't smile or wave. I just sat there and looked out at Dad, Barry and Karen. Then the bus was gone. Little did we know what was to come in the next two years.

As our bus drove off people were waving and shouting. The blokes were doing the same. As we turned the corner, and the people were out of sight, the bus went totally silent; only the engine could be heard. My recollection of that trip to Brisbane that day is that the silence prevailed until we arrived at our destination at Frasers Paddock, Enoggera Army Barracks, in Brisbane. Maybe others spoke but I was consumed by my own thoughts. I think I was thinking of what I had just left not what I was going to. The trip took two or so hours. Our last two hours of freedom as civvies.

When the bus stopped an Army officer climbed aboard. At least he looked like an officer, but who cares? Ah! Look out. You will care. A lot. 'Righto (again with the righto stuff), listen up and pay attention. You will be processed alphabetically.' This was the Army's basic organisational process. We would see it time and time again. I am being processed, what the fuck is that supposed to mean? Like in a factory? What will I look like after being processed?

'You will be issued your service number. Remember it— for your own sake, stick it in your little brain—and remember it; remember it for the rest of your life.' Yeah, fifty-seven-plus years on, it's 1733569!

'You will be signed onto the Australian Army Military Force as a recruit. You will be addressed as "Recruit numnuts" and, when called, you will reply, "Present Sa!" You will be on parade here at 0600 hours sharp!' Oh goodie, my first parade and at six fuckin' am! 'Be there or suffer the WO's very bad humour!,' WO being a Warrant Officer.

WOs came in all shapes and sizes. There were Warrant Officer Ones (WO1s) and Warrant Officer Twos (WO2s), but all were considered arseholes and all of them had a fuckin' loud voice. They all wore an officer's cap to confuse us newbies. Because they were non-commissioned officers, they did not have to be saluted but had to be addressed as, "Sir!" How many newbie recruits were to be caught out saluting a WO? Probably every last one of us at some stage over the next three months.

*

I got caught out a few days after arriving at 3TB Singleton recruit training base. Marching up a path— we had to march everywhere as opposed to walk— I came across this spit-polished orificer (no misspelling) approaching in a clatter of marching boots. Without looking for rank insignia I saluted! *Wrong! Wrong—he is a WO you dickhead*, I recognised immediately. 'Halt! Right there, soldier,' he bellowed. 'Fuck me, mate, I am only five feet away, keep it down buddy,' I mumbled as well as, 'Oh! Fuck me, here we go.'

'Don't you know an officer when you see one? They have shiny bits on their shoulders. Can you see anything on my shoulders?'

Only an ugly angry bull head with a big mouth, I thought. No, but I wish! 'No,' I said.

'No fuckin' what?'

Ah! 'No, sa!'

'Righto! Soldier, see that tree over there? I want you to salute that tree one hundred times!'

Dumb fuckin' lookin' tree, probably more intelligent than an officer. Pleased to meet you, Sir Tree!

Ninety-nine, one hundred …. See ya later, Sir Tree.

*

'Righto! (Obviously Army tough talk.) When I call your name, reply loud and correct.' *You mean loudly and correctly, don't you?* I felt like saying but didn't dare.

'Adams, Brendan J.'— ten seconds, no response. It seems Brendan, a country boy, was more used to being called Bren, and didn't respond.

Again, 'Adams, Brendan J.'

Kicked by a mate, Brendan replied, 'Yeah.'

'Okay, let's try once more. Adams, Brendan J.'

'Yes, sa! Present, sa!'

'Adams, you will be in Hut 1, Cubicle A. Do you think you can remember that?'

'Yeah, sa!'

And so, we were all allocated a bed for the night.

'Go to your assigned quarters, drop your gear and be on parade here at 1100 hours.'

'Righto! Listen UP!' How many times do I have to hear this shit? Only day ONE of 730!

'On parade NOW!!!!'

Some uniformed blokes grabbed a few guys and shoved them into position, 'Four ranks on these men, move it!'

'Ca'rn! ("come on" in Army speak), I don't have all day to be fucked around by you dickheads.' The "voice" was a big sergeant, ugly and angry. Sorry we upset your day, Sarge. 'NNOOWW! Listen Up! When your name is called, if you know your name, reply, "Present, sa!" And go to the table allocated.'

'Collins, Peter T.'

'Present, sa!'

'A1.'

This was the formal identification, sign-on and issue of service number 1733569. Remember it, eat it, digest it, never, never forget it. From now on you will be known by your service number. We were given the lunch, dinner and breakfast times and parade time for the next morning prior to departure to Eagle Farm Airport. Parade time was 0600 hours. Shit, and that was *after* breakfast. Be late, be sorry!

We were directed to lunch by a couple of uniformed guys who informed us they were at the bottom of the pile as privates. 'But you guys aren't even in the pile yet. When you finish recruit training at 3TB Singleton, you'll join us down here at the bottom.' Their advice:

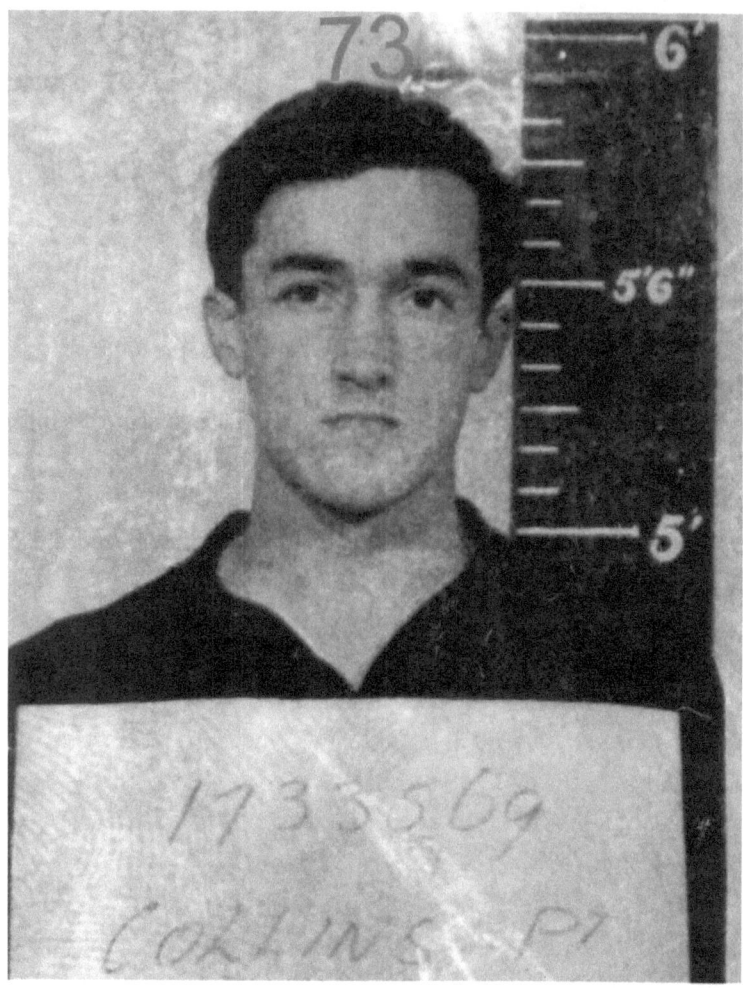

Formal sign-on and issue of service number, October 1967

'Keep your head down. These sadistic bastards love to make your life hell. They will pick on the weak or slow until they win.'

Geez! Guys, thanks for your advice and pep talk. Fuck me! What am I in for?

'Here is where lunch will be served soon. Hope you enjoy this lunch. It will be your last of this sort,' the privates told us as they left.

Well, look at this!!!!! The dining room was set with tables of six. Not unusual but these tables were set with white linen tablecloths, silver cutlery, glasses, side plates, cold water jugs, all the condiments, a menu, napkins and even bread rolls. There must be some mistake. Those two privates must be taking the piss, surely.

Then a guy in a white coat and black trousers appeared and asked us to come in and take a seat of our choice. One of us said, 'This can't be for real, the next thing a waiter will turn up.' We all had a laugh and poured a glass of water each.

'Good afternoon, gentlemen, I will be your waiter today. When you are ready, I will take your lunch order. Be back shortly guys, the menu is on the table.'

Well, I'll be a monkey's fuckin' uncle. Is this really the Army? I bet my cods this is a one-off. Not quite, but pretty close to the mark.

Lunch was very nice, two courses including dessert. We relaxed for the first time that day and went to our quarters for a rest. There was nothing to do until 1800 hours when dinner was scheduled. Will dinner be like lunch? I slept for a couple of hours and caught up on last night's lack of sleep. Tomorrow will be a biggie methinks.

Six o'clock came around quickly. All showered, shaved and in new gear, we headed to the mess. Did not know what to expect. I thought *no way will it be all bells and whistles like lunch*. Well, it was. The Army can do amazing things when it wants to impress new arrivals (lambs to the slaughter?). We were again greeted at the door, this time by an officer, who introduced himself as Captain somebody (name escapes me) who asked our name and regimental number and checked us off his list. Probably our first "roll call" to see if anyone had done a runner since lunch.

'Gentlemen, welcome to the mess. Have a seat and enjoy your dinner.'

Yeah, mate, our last in the real world I bet, I thought

This same officer appeared again when all were seated. 'Welcome (to paradise) to Enoggera Army Base and to our sergeants' mess. Tomorrow at 0600 you will be on parade prior to departure for Eagle Farm Airport. From the airport, you will be flown to the Australian Air Force Base at Williamtown, New South Wales. From there you will travel by bus to 3TB at Singleton. Remember 0600; 6 am in the morning. Do not be late and start your day on the wrong foot. The WO can be mean on any slow movers. Please remember that and be on time. Okay, fellas, enjoy your dinner.'

OH SHIT – HERE WE GO

Fucking hell, what is happening!!!!!!! Bang! Crash! Thump! Some asshole with a tin drum beating the fuck out of it. Yeah, it was! Someone we would see very often in the future. Not the same person but a corporal clone. Spit polished (will get to that later), perfect in every way and wide awake, enjoying his early morning treat of making our life hell. If these bastards did not make our life miserable, they were not doing their job. And these bastards were bloody good at their job as we would find out over the next few weeks. More of them later; much more.

'Ca'rn you slack Nashos (National Service conscripts), get out of the fart sack (bed). Parade is in ninety. Breakfast in thirty. Be there or miss out, now move those slack little arses.'

'Nice blokes, don't you think, Pete?'

'Yep, Mick. I think my life just went down the gurgler. You coming with me?'

'Do I have a choice?' said Mick.

'Fraid not, mate. Let's get over to breakfast. I bet your arse there won't be any waiters this time.'

'I think my arse is safe,' said Mick.

'There's a queue over there, Pete. That must be breakfast.'

'Bet your own arse, Mick.'

Of course, it was a fuckin' queue. The Army invented queues, they use them for every bloody thing imaginable. One got nothing or nowhere in the Army without a fuckin "Q", nothing! I was to learn about "Qs" and the "Q" order was always A to Z. If I was a W, X, Y or Z I reckon I would have gone over the wire. Being a "C" was good. It meant getting to eat earlier, get paid quicker, get a leave pass, gear issue, mail call, haircut, needles, you name it. The poor bastards at the end of the alphabet just waited and waited. I never saw a reversal in two years, but I heard some great friendships were formed down the back.

'Your arse is safe, Mick.' There were NO waiters, just a row of cooks serving the food. Pick-up a tray, place on a plate, two if cereal is your choice, and follow the leader. The food was not too bad; eggs fried, bacon burned, beans and tomatoes, and a slice of toast. Mick's cereal was a gluggy white something.

I finished my food, got a coffee from a big urn. Mick was still eating something.

'We had better make a move, Mick.'

'Yeah, mate. I'll have a coffee and be with you.'

I left him to have his coffee and went to the barracks to collect my stuff in readiness for the parade. I did notice how disorganised Mick had left his bed. I did some rearranging, but packing was up to him. Please Mick, for once in your life, be on time.

Nine o'clock, 9 am, 0900, whatever, parade deadline was approaching, and where was he? Mick was very intelligent, but took his own time about everything, even his first day in the real Army. Come on mate for fuck's sake. Ah! A bit of movement out front, not Mick but the pair of spit-polished corporal bastards had arrived with chests out and scowling faces ablaze with happiness. Here we go again.

'Attenshun (more Army speak) you lot!' in the loudest voice possible, 'Fall in!' Where? Into what do we fall? Into five ranks, lines, stupid, one behind the other. No political correctness in 1967!

'Move it! I haven't got all day.' It's okay, mate, take as long as you like. We're in no hurry to go anywhere. Oh, Mick! Where are you, mate? I can't imagine what will happen if you're late.

The Cs take a backward step, and an impressive, slightly-built officer stands before us.

'I, I am the Regimental Sergeant Major (RSM— top dog in the non-commissioned ranks) of this Army base. I will conduct this parade. PARADE! Attenshun! Corporal X, please call the roll. I, I require a loud response of, "Sa, present sa".'

Blah blah blah blah. 'Mick Y.' No response. Oh shit, Mick, where are you? I couldn't see him in the parade. I should have stayed with him; he just dithers and takes forever to do whatever. But then I would be in the shit too. I had made up my mind to not ruffle the feathers of these Army blokes no matter what; keep your nose clean, as they say.

Then, 'Are you Mick Y? You are late for parade. Ca'rn get in line. Noooowww!' Well, Mick walked with a sort of a limp and a little bit stooped and was not very quick on his feet. 'Hey Y, the whole fuckin' parade is waiting on you.'

'Sorry, mate,' says Mick, 'I am very tired.'

Suddenly the WO got involved, 'Mister, I am sorry to inconvenience you. Perhaps you would like to sit a while? Listen up, Mister. Run— and I mean run— up to the orderly room and get yourself a chair and run— I mean run— back here with your chair. GOT IT, Maatey?' Away went Mick with the WO calling the pace. 'Faster, faster, dickhead, come on, get that chair back here nooww!'

Mick got back with his chair with the instructions to place it in line on the front row. 'Now sit!'

The parade was all about the move to the airport and the boarding procedure. There would be two planes and we were given our allocation of aircraft and seat number. Mick, please pay attention.

'Parade atttennn-shunnn! Move off to your allocated transport in an orderly manner.'

The WO said, 'Mister Y, please give me back our chair before you leave.'

'Sa!'

Well, fuck me, Mick is awake and paying attention. Off he went to take the chair back up the hill to the orderly room. He returned puffing and wheezing. The bus was loading the last few when in a bellow 'Mister Y, where is my chair? I said bring it to me. GET IT and bring it here to me, on the double or you will miss the bus and be my guest for the night.'

Poor Mick, off he ran up the hill, got the chair or, as it was, the nearest chair and back to the WO.

'You will remember this day, young fella, as will all the others. Don't be late again, okay?'

'Yes, saah!!'

I have often wondered what Mister Mick said under his breath.

And so, we took the ride to Eagle Farm Airport to fly into our future life. What awaited us we could never have imagined. As a bunch of undisciplined young civvies, we were about to find out.

3. 3TB SINGLETON

This was my first flight, something of a new and exciting experience, but it was a bit lost in the hubbub of what was actually happening. We were boarding an Ansett ANA Viscount aircraft which was chartered to fly us to Williamtown Airforce base near Newcastle, New South Wales. I must admit I remember little of that flight except that it was a noisy plane. We landed and were transferred to buses. We must have been as my next memory after the Viscount landed was being on a bus and being told, 'This is 3rd Training Battalion Singleton, your new home for the next few months. Enjoy your stay with us!' No, they definitely didn't say that!

The bus rolled to a stop beside a sergeant and two corporals eagerly waiting for their new victims. Some of our guys were smoking. In those days of the 1960s, one could smoke anywhere, but not so in the Army.

'Righto! Let's have ya off the bus quick smart, three ranks.' The corporals sprung into action and ushered, maybe pushed, us into three straggly lines. 'Attten-shunnn! That, my precious recruits, means feet together, arms by the side, head up, stand still and look to the front. Put those fuckin' smokes out and don't throw the butts on the ground or your butt will be on the ground with it, got it?'

Some brave soul called out, 'Well, where do we put them?'

'In ya fuckin' pocket,' came the reply.

That reply is my enduring memory of Singleton 3TB. Any crumby feeling in my pockets brings back the memory. I spent months with cigarette butts and old tobacco in my pockets. It was a very effective reminder about littering of any kind. Camp tidiness was obsessive and any untidiness punished severely without hesitation. Punishment usually involved cleaning something or somewhere that didn't need cleaning. But more of those "dirty tricks", as we called them, later.

'Righto, listen up!' (Listen up? What about listen down? Sideways?) 'Your name will be called allocating your hut number one or two. I expect a loud and instant reply of "Yes, sa!".' Several names were called then Collins, 1733569.

'Yes, sa!'

'Hut One. Everyone called for Hut One form two ranks on this pathway. Corporal K will take you to your hut. The rest of you listen UP!'

'Hut One, attention, quick march, follow this path to its end and turn left.' Away we marched to our new life and existence for the next two years: less one day, I pleaded. I was feeling totally alone, afraid and very apprehensive. I wanted to be back home with my family, even if there were three sisters. We arrived at Hut One.

'Squad halt. Okay, move on in and claim your bed for the next three months or so. Stow your personal gear under the bed or in the bedside locker. Nothing is to go in the tall locker. Get back out here in two ranks. You have five minutes.'

I was last in and got the last bed. They were in sections of four and there were four sections. If you are a math expert like I am, there were sixteen in the hut, although there was one guy missing. I threw my bag under the bed and went back outside.

Corporal Kropinyeri, of Indigenous descent, was waiting. 'Hi there, fella. What's your name?'

'Collins, sa!' I replied.

'What Collins?' he asked.

'Peter,' I replied.

Corporal K held out his hand and said, 'Pleased to have you on the team, Pete!'

Fuck me, I thought, *what does he want from me?* The rest of the guys filed out of the hut.

'Form two ranks on Collins as right marker. Move it. We have a lot to do today to get you lot settled. Collins, when I give the order, follow this path, first right, first left and onto the Q store. Okay, squad by the left, Quiiick March.' At the quartermaster's store, he called, 'Halt. You will be issued your initial kit here, including bedding, greens, boots, etcetera, etcetera. Collins, move off to the counter, Staff Sergeant Taylor is waiting to load you up. Follow on from behind Collins when he leaves the store. Parade will be at 1730 outside the hut.'

At the wide, long counter the quartermaster was waiting. 'G'day, young fella. Welcome to Singleton. Okay, let's go.' He threw a big green hutchie (all-weather cover) on the counter and spread it out. He and an assistant then began piling stuff on the hutchie. Blanket, pillow, sheets, towels, uniform bits, boots, gaiters, belt and heaps of other stuff. At the end, they said, 'There you go.' They pulled the four corners together, tied them with a rope, and said, 'Good luck, mate. See ya again.'

I pulled the load off the counter and the weight of it spreadeagled me on the ground. Amid much laughter, I picked it up and half carried, half dragged it back 50 km to the hut. Felt like 50 km. At the door of the hut, I found the bag would not fit through the door. My bed was at the other end of the hut. Rather than carry individual bits through the hut, why don't I go around the back? Sounds like a plan.

So off I went up the grass side of the hut. I was just about there when someone yelled, 'Get off my fucking grass you fucking idiot!' I covered the rest of my little journey rather quickly and miraculously pulled my load inside. I sat exhausted and waited for someone to appear. No one did.

Having gotten away with that little venture, I turned my attention to stowing away all this stuff in the tall two-door locker. I figured the Army would want an equipment locker to be packed neatly and with some user-friendly organisation. There are a few hangers in the narrow drop space, so the great coat, shirts and trousers will go there. Exactly the number of hangers. Good. Might be a correct call. Little things on the top, neatly folded, followed in descending size. *Make it neat, stupid, your life may depend on this.* I unpacked my personal stuff and neatly placed everything in the bedside locker.

Now for the bed! As my Mum knew only too well, Pete had an aversion to bed-making. Yeah, Mum, I just hate making my bed. Can't you get one of them to do it, my sisters, three of them? So that is the starting point, no experience and no interest. Two sheets (no fitted ones then), a blanket, a grey cover and one pillow. The mattress was about four inches (10 cm) thick, the bed was small and, as I quickly discovered, the fucking thing was fixed to the floor and was firmly up against the wall. Disgusted and depressed at this finding, I sat on the metal chair, which, until now, had not made its presence known.

Minutes later I gathered the strength to tackle this awesome task. I invented ways of fitting sheets that no person had ever tried before. When it was all finished, it looked like Mum had made it; maybe she was there somewhere. *Mum I'll need your help every day, please stick around.* I was horrified that this would be a daily occurrence.

*

Fast forward to 2019. I am sitting on the veranda at home writing this when my wife, Karen, who is doing some scrap booking, comes out with the last letter Mum had written to me and a newspaper report and photo of her car accident fifty-four years ago. How strange! How sad!

*

Everything done and with time to spare before 1730 parade, I wandered down the hut to meet some of the other victims of this venture. I was fortunate being the first to be issued with the gear, each one took some time and the guys at the end were just arriving back at the hut. My offers of assistance were eagerly accepted. There was raucous laughter as we joked about the Army gear and their way of doing things. 'In ya fucking pocket— should I put the fucking thing out first, Sarge? Bloody smart arse he was!' We had a great time and got to know each other a little bit better as 1730 parade drew closer.

I went outside a minute or so early to find Corporal K— "Kropper" we had decided to call him— waiting. He glanced at his watch and in his characteristic booming voice yelled, 'On parade, Hut One.' The guys moved out quickly. 'Collins, right marker, three ranks on him, move it, dinner is waiting. Before moving off I have some announcements and orders. Tomorrow morning, I want you on parade here in greens, boots, belt, gaiters and slouch hats at 0530. You have 'til Monday morning parade to turn those khaki gaiters and the belt into a nice shiny black. As well, your boots have to be spit-polished with a high shine. You have two pairs of boots, one pair are parade boots, the other fitted with studs are for fieldwork. Be sure to polish the correct pair. Squad, attention, left turn, quick march. Collins, take us to the mess.'

Dinner at the mess was a quiet affair with most of the guys in pairs talking quietly. I chose to eat alone and sat there thinking of home, family and friends. I was missing seeing Karen and wondered what she might be doing now. We had agreed to go our own ways, so to speak, as two years was a long time to keep a relationship alive when separated. It was my idea but that did not mean I was happy about it. I thought it unfair to expect Karen to stay home and wait.

I left the mess quietly and went to see if the canteen was open. The boozer next door was closed and would remain so to us for some weeks, but the canteen was open. I found some large tins of black Nugget shoe polish and some brushes and cloth which I took to the lady behind the counter.

'Ah ha,' she said, 'you have some new boots to polish.'

I said, 'And a belt and gaiters.'

This very helpful lady said, 'You will be needing some of this stuff, it blackens things, and you can then polish with the Nugget.'

'Is it okay with the corporals?' I asked.

She confirmed that everyone uses it, it is messy, but it works. She then warned me about using a special lacquer on the boots. 'Using that will buy you some trouble.' I thanked her for the help and advice and walked back to the hut. Payment at the canteen was effected by pay deduction each fortnight. I had given the lady my full name and service number.

It was reasonably early, so I began preparing for the early morning parade, the first in uniform. The greens needed ironing and probably washing as they were very stiff. The boots needed the laces fitted. How does the Army do it? I decided to use the football system so one cut up the centre would release the lace. I put the belt together next assuming the male part of the buckle to be on the right and the female on the left. Half a chance of being correct.

The slouch hat fortunately was a good fit. Many of the other guys were swapping to get a better fit. The Q store had not bothered with sizes, they just handed stuff out and left it up to us to sort it out.

I had to turn up the brim— simple enough— fit the Rising Sun badge and fit the chin strap. I had a mate, Bill, at high school who was an under officer in the school cadets. I remembered him telling me how many new cadets got the chin strap wrong. The correct fitting goes like this: with the hat on the head and in a position for a correct salute, the right arm horizontal and the tip of the third finger touching the brim, the chin strap adjustment buckle must be in line with the corner of the mouth on the left side. I passed on my knowledge to the other two blokes in my section and suggested they pass it on, which they did.

I suddenly felt very tired, dead on my feet. I grabbed a towel and headed for the shower block. Wow! This Army is in the modern era with "open plan" showers, about twenty places and not a wall in sight. The urinal was on the other side, but there were private toilets with half-size doors. So, they can see anyone hiding in there, no doubt. They think of everything, except how we feel. Shower, etcetera done, I returned and hit the bed. I didn't even notice the mattress or the pillow. I was to learn that sleeping comfort was a thing of the past.

Light streaming through an open window woke me early, about 0500. I decided to get up and get ready for the parade in half an hour. A few minutes later my missing roommate arrived loaded with all his new gear plus his personal stuff. He was very, very slightly-built and suffering somewhat under his load. He dropped onto the bed and sat for a bit.

'Hi there, mate. I'm Peter.'

He looked at me with tired eyes and a bit apprehensively, standing there in my greens, 'Yeah, hello. My name is Alan. So sorry I am late, had car trouble on the way from Mackay in Queensland.'

Not surprisingly he had trouble as he later revealed he was driving a Hillman Imp, a very tiny thing with a rear engine. He had finally got a lift with a truckie from near the New South Wales border to Singleton and a taxi to the camp.

'What's happening?' he asked.

'Mate, we have parade in five, dressed in greens, boots, gaiters and slouch hat.'

'Bloody hell, how the fuck am I going to make it, hey?' Poor bastard, he was stressed to the max.

'Hang on, Al,' I said.

I went out to find Kropper about to make his descent upon the hut. I said, 'Excuse me, Corporal. A quick word, if you would.'

'Certainly, Pete. What's up?' I told him Alan's dilemma. Kropper said, 'Let's go see him.'

Alan was told to come on parade as he was, 'After all, we are going for breakfast, we can't starve a little recruit like you.' Kropper turned on his heel, changed his personality, and bellowed in a threatening voice, 'On parade now, you mob of slack ex-civvies! Collins, right marker, three ranks on him, move it. Squad attention, left turn, by the left, quick march; right turn and double time. Private Collins, take a right turn onto the road.'

'Sa, yes sa!'

I could hear the mumbling going on behind me. 'Where the fuck are we going?'

'Yeah, mate, I'm bloody hungry, I want my coffee right now.'

'Stop the chatter you lot or I'll double the distance,' boomed Kropper.

Alan was behind me, 'Glad I've got runners and shorts on,' he puffed.

Someone replied, 'Somehow I don't think this will be the last run we ever do, these pricks are cruel bastards.'

Kropper again: 'Collins, take a right onto the dirt track coming up.'

'Sa, yes sa!'

Some wag at the back said, 'Bugger this shit, my new boots are getting dusty.'

'Too right, mate. I'm going home after breakfast.'

'Left, left, left-right-left,' Kropper started calling and told us to join in. 'Left, left, left-right-left,' we all yelled out. This somehow broke the monotony, changed the mood of the squad and it was almost fun; almost, I said. We came to a sharp rise in the road which caused a drop in the volume but at the top, we saw the mess hall not too far off.

Someone said 'There's the mess, thank fuck for small mercies. Bring on the coffee.'

A few more metres on, Kropper called us to quick march and halt, 'Parade outside the hut at 0800, dress inspection, squad left turn, fall out.'

THE PARADE GROUND AND MARCHING DRILL "ROT" SETS IN.

Almost 0800 and the gang had formed a loose three ranks on me as right marker. Why me all the time? Maybe Kropper can't be bothered finding out any other names.

'Squad attention! We are going to learn spacing. This is usually done after a sequence called sizing, but we will dispense with that today. The right marker will stand fast, and the ranks and personnel will form on him. Second rank marker, raise your left arm and touch the shoulder of the right marker, now move to that distance. Third rank marker, do the same action. Squad, eyes left, raise the left arm and shuffle sideways to a position just touching the next soldier's shoulder. Squad eyes front. Your left arm must snap to your side as your head snaps to the front. Have we all got it? Let us try. Squad eyes left, squad eyes front ... Okay for a first try.'

Kropper, in a series of snap movements, came to attention in front of me. Looking me up and down, he said, 'Are you happy in the service, Private Collins?'

'Indeed, I am, Corporal K,' I replied.

'Bullshit!' he said.

He moved on down the ranks, advising on errors made. Things like, 'Those gaiter buckles will rip your balls out, put them to the outside. You need to polish that brass, soldier. You have a setting sun, not a rising sun. Turn the badge over, dickhead.' There were a few, 'Head up, soldier. Be proud of yourself, stand up straight, and square those shoulders. Be proud of your uniform.'

Back out front, he said, 'A few stuff ups, but overall, not all that bad for a first dress inspection. Those boots need to be polished, and the belt and gaiters black and shiny by Monday morning parade. One more thing before we move off. Every chin strap was correct, how come?'

'Pete told me, and I passed it on.'

'Collins, was that you? Were you a cadet or something?'

'A friend who was an under officer at high school once told me how chin straps were always wrong,' I remembered.

'Good stuff, well done all of you.'

From in the back row a voice called out, 'So can we go home now?'

Kropper replied with, 'Squad left turn, quick march ... Squad halt!'

We are on the parade ground for the first of a million fucking times, to learn how to march correctly and the various other stuff involved in Army parade drill. The parade ground is sacred turf at any company or Battalion Headquarters' precinct. One does not "fuck up" on a parade ground or walk upon it without authority. I would learn this in the future much to my chagrin.

The first person I saw punished for a "fuck up"— he did the "fuck up" several times— was punished by being made to march from corner to corner of the parade ground for sixty minutes, halting (correctly), left turn (correctly), salute (correctly), right turn (correctly), quick march to the next corner and repeat the shit. Any incorrect drill and a further ten minutes were added. It paid dividends to pay attention while on the hallowed ground and respect its boundaries.

*

Fast forward my story to 6RAR in Townsville, Queensland, which is where I was posted in February 1968. On a Sunday morning, I was required at the Task Force dental clinic. My journey required me to pass or circle the 6RAR Battalion parade ground. At the last corner, I cut across about ten metres early, after all, it is Sunday morning. 'Get the fuck off my fucking parade ground, you fucking idiot!'

Stunned, I skipped sideways onto the concrete pathway. The voice had come from the top floor of Battalion Headquarters (BHQ) some two hundred metres away, from RSM WO1 Cruickshank. A slightly-built man, but what a voice he had. I stepped up my pace to disappear into the distance, somewhat glad to reach the dental clinic. Rather a dentist than the RSM to have me captive.

*

Hour upon hour was spent on that parade ground practising all the drill moves. Timing was the thing— one soldier a little slow and on we went, in step, get in step, stay in step, swing those arms, stay in time, form a fist and lead with the thumb, swing those arms to horizontal, stay in step, heads up, get those shoulders back. Getting better but stay in your ranks watch the soldier on your right and your left, stay in line.

Bloody hell, who invented this stuff? Is it only to piss us off or does it serve a purpose? Yes, it does, but we had not learned that yet. We would, and we would appreciate the reasoning. However, the worst was to come. The next step in parade drill was known as "rifle drill". Rifle drill means one needs a rifle; no, not so easy, cowboy. To be the custodian of your "own" weapon you must acquire a weapon licence. Your rifle is your friend and must be treated with the utmost respect. Regular maintenance and cleaning are the responsibility of the custodian and will be inspected on a very regular basis. Obtaining a weapon licence depends on a demonstrated ability in both operation and care of the weapon. While a reliable rifle, the SLR (Self-Loading Rifle) had a complicated gas reload system that needed specific care. We were required to be capable of stripping the rifle, reassembling it and demonstrating its correct operation. This required repetition of the task innumerable times. Once this was achieved in a set time (which I don't recall) the task had to be achieved at night. The final test was to do it successfully while blindfolded. The reasons for all this are obvious when a combat situation is considered.

The next step in qualification was on the firing range, which would follow on from the platoon efficiency at rifle drill. These drills involved new actions for us to master. Order arms, shoulder arms, present arms and stand at ease. Each drill required snap action with everyone in time, exactly in time. There were a few blokes in the platoon who hated marching, rifle drill and parade drill and did not pull their weight. The corporals would pull the repeat offenders out of the line, embarrass them and send them on a jog around the parade ground. Any lack of enthusiasm and around they went again and again. While one corporal watched the offenders, the other, usually Kropper, would tell us, 'Those slackies are costing you guys. We stay out here until you ALL get it right. You should speak to them, remind them they are in a team.' And that we did. It took some convincing of a couple, but they all agreed we needed to be a team, work together, support each other in all this Army bullshit. The team construction was aided by other difficult trials, obviously designed (now obvious) as team building by the Army experts.

4. ARE YOU FIT? ARE YOU READY, PETE?

The other trials were based on physical fitness and teamwork. The platoon of thirty-two men— a combination of Hut One and Hut Two— were required to run a four hundred metre oval in two minutes. Dress was sports gear. This meant everyone must finish in that time or the exercise was repeated over and over until that was achieved. On our second attempt, the fittest of us ran an extra lap to recover and encourage or carry the back markers over the line. The corporals applauded the teamwork.

The same requirement was attached to a longer run, dressed in greens, boots, gaiters, belt and slouch hat. This little gem of a test required the platoon to complete four laps of the oval and all finish within eight minutes. We achieved success on the first try due to excellent teamwork and a huge effort by a few blokes to literally carry stragglers over the line. It was interesting to see the "drill slackies" were involved in the rescue mission. Indeed, the Army teamwork training was working.

The most difficult physical trial was a five-mile, cross-country obstacle course. Two hours was the time allocated. Again, all thirty-two of us must finish on time. Having learned what obstacles were on the course, none of us wanted a repeat performance thrust upon us. The course consisted of several difficult obstacles, but while the course covered relatively flat ground, the finish was on the other side of a hill. We had to go *over* the bloody hill, not around the bastard. Typical Army— stick the boot in at the end.

The big problem was getting everyone across the line in the two-hour limit. The course consisted of rope climbs, traversing a creek on a rope, rope walls, wooden walls and narrow log crossings. There were sections of low barbed wire fifty metres across to crawl under and numerous creek or gully crossings. We had some training in rope climbing and traversing. Traversing could be either under or on top of the rope. On top is more difficult to master, but once achieved is much quicker and easier. Rope walls are an energy-sapping thing requiring coordination and strength.

The strategy to get everyone finished was discussed beforehand and we knew there was no chance to double back to pick-up stragglers, so some of us would wait at each obstacle to assist and ensure all were through. The fittest guys would attack the hill last and pick-up and assist any stragglers. It worked a treat, and the platoon qualified under the allotted time on our first attempt.

Rifle qualification was with the 7.62 mm SLR on a thirty-metre range. A qualifying score was required from twenty shots (one full magazine). I don't recall the required score, but it was high. Rifles were provided at the range and were supplied and maintained by the Armoury. One expected, therefore, that the rifles would be in good working order. But … just how good were they?

*

I had owned a single shot .22-inch rifle a year or two before being conscripted and I could hit any barn door around every time I took aim. My brother-in-law, Barry, had also taken me duck shooting early one Saturday. We were using double barrel over and under shotguns[4] on the unsuspecting ducks.

'Have you fired a shotgun before, Pete? They kick a bit,' said Bazz.

'I'll be right mate,' says me, 17-18-year-old guy, yeah!

Perched on top of a bank in between two dams we spied our duck dinner, swimming about unawares. Barry said, 'Get ready, Pete. I'll fire a .22 over their heads to make them fly. When in the air let

---

4   Shotguns with vertically, rather than horizontally, attached barrels.

them have it, both barrels.' Barry did not mean both barrels at once, I would later discover. Bang! The ducks took off. I fired, yeah both barrels at once, didn't hit a thing; not a duck anyway. Arse over tit I went, backward into the dam behind me. I surfaced to see Bazz pissing himself laughing and pointing at me in the damn dam.

Another shooting adventure was wild pig hunting— with a bow and arrow. Do you believe that? Many wouldn't, especially if you know anything about how ferocious a wild pig with big sharp tusks can be. The idea was to climb up a sturdy tree, because as we all know pigs can't fly and they can't climb trees. After finding a suitable sturdy tree, locate a pig and sting it with a rifle shot; the angry pig will charge while you retreat to your tree. When the pig is snorting angrily at you up that tree, you shoot it straight down the snout; result, dead pig. Stupid what?

*

Needless to say, back at the Army rifle qualifying I considered myself a fairly good shot and had no concern about qualifying on a 25–30 m range with fairly large targets. I was in the first group of five to shoot. After my twenty shots, I had not scored a hit. Kropper came over and said, 'Not bad, Pete. Not bad at all, you managed to miss with every shot. Here, try again. This time try aiming the bloody thing at the target and keep those eyes open.'

With another magazine loaded, I said, 'Thanks, Corporal. Be better this time.' But it wasn't! After three more attempts, Corporal Kropper said, 'Give me that fucking thing.' He fired three shots and missed with all three. The Armoury Sergeant was on the range. Kropper called out, 'Sarge, over here if you will.' Kropper told him I had fired one hundred rounds without hitting a fuckin' thing and he had also missed the target.

The sergeant took the rifle and shook the hell out of it. 'Ah ha,' he said, 'the bugger rattles.' Eventually, he said to me, 'I'm not surprised you had trouble,' as he showed me the front blade sight was very loose and would move with the recoil of the rifle. Given another rifle, I qualified easily in twenty shots.

'That's a record, Pete. One hundred and twenty rounds to qualify. Well done, mate.'

'Thanks, Kropper,' I said.

'What? What? What did you say?'

'Sorry, Corporal, I said thanks.'

'Yeah? Thanks what?'

'I said thanks, Kropper. Kropper is the name our squad has given you.'

'Spelled with a K?'

'Sure is!'

Before the Armalite M16 came into the Australian Army, soldiers who were forward scouts, sigs, officers and section commanders carried the F1 9mm submachine gun. The F1 was a light weapon designed to be used at close-range contact in the jungle. It fired a 9 mm short round from a thirty-four-round curved magazine that attached to the top of the gun. We were informed by the training staff that beyond twenty metres a wet blanket would be adequate protection against the F1. Good maybe for gangsters, but not for us. The M16 that I would eventually carry as a sig was a very different weapon. Light, but very powerful, 5.56 mm with a muzzle velocity of 950 m per second. Automatic, reliable, accurate and could destroy wet blankets.

For the moment, this was the end of weapons training. Later, in training, we would move on to the M60 7.62 mm machine gun, the Carl Gustav 84 mm antitank rocket launcher, and hand grenades (pineapples).

5. MEAN AND NASTY TRAINING TACTICS: TEACHING DISCIPLINE?

Kropper and the Hut Two corporal had designed punishments they imposed for small and insignificant blunders by us. Every one of us suffered these punishments and was committed to doing some worthless, unnecessary task. Here I will relate a few I suffered.

My first occurred quite early during a hut inspection. I had left my toothbrush on the bedside unit. My locker arrangement, bed-making and general tidiness passed with flying colours.

'What is this doing here, soldier?' asked the corporal.

'Absolutely nothing, sa!' I replied rather flippantly.

'You will report to me at the shower block at 1700 with this brush. Got it?'

'Yes, sa.'

The menace in his voice stunned me as it did others nearby. After inspection, some said to me, 'He didn't like your answer much, Pete.'

To which I replied, 'I told the truth, didn't I?' We all had a laugh at the pettiness.

Come 1700, I reported to the shower block. The corporal arrived promptly. 'Okay, you will clean and polish all the brass fittings on these urinals until I return.' I had noticed before how shiny this stuff was and now I knew why. I quickly went to the hut and got some polish, where the guys in my area asked, 'What's the go, Pete?' I told them and left. When the corporal came back in about thirty minutes there was me and six others busily polishing the pipes. 'Well done, fellas. Off you go,' he said. That was the time

5. Mean and nasty training tactics: Teaching discipline?

we named him "Kropper". And how good did it feel to be backed up by my mates? Bloody good.

You will remember I purchased stuff at the canteen and was told payment would be deducted from my pay. One day I received a message to attend the company orderly room to see the sergeant. Of course, I shit myself. This seemed serious. What had I done to upset the sergeant? At the first opportunity, I hurried to the orderly room.

'Private Collins, Sarge. You wanted to see me?' This big burly man stood and towered above me.

'Yes, I do.' All he wanted was for me to sign an authority for pay deductions to pay the canteen account. Then he said, 'I want you to come back and see me at 1700, okay?' I said yes and left in somewhat of a dither. What now?

Seventeen hundred rolled around and I was in the orderly room. 'Private Collins, thank you for being on time,' the sergeant said as he handed me a small pair of scissors. 'I love my grass outside this office, so I need you to trim it neatly.' I was thinking, *yeah, you love the grass, but why the fuck pick me to look after it? Haven't you heard of a lawn mower you big wanker?* So, there I was, on hands and knees cutting the grass with scissors, passers-by having a laugh. An officer approached and said, 'At ease, soldier,' as I was about to rise, 'Doing a good job I see. Keep it up.' It was almost 1800 hours when the sergeant came out.

'It is almost dinner time,' he said. 'I am going to the mess, you had better do the same.'

'Thank you, Sarge,' I said.

'In future, do not cut corners. It never pays. Follow the correct path and be safe. Do you understand me?'

'Yes, Sarge, I do,' I said.

Well fuck-me-rone, I remembered then. When I had come here previously, I had cut the corner of the path across the precious grass. That big wanker had obviously seen me. Lesson learned! And my sore fingers would remind me.

Parade ground misdemeanours would be punished in various ways. The most popular (with the corporals) was to make the victim rake and smooth the fine gravel on the surface of the whole parade ground, which was a bloody big thing. The frustrating bit was the worn-out, gappy rake you had to use— it ensured the punishment lasted at least two hours, usually much more unless a corporal showed some mercy. Big fucking chance of that happening too often, Dolly.

Repetition of drill errors was met with a unique punishment referred to by the corporals as "guarding my parade ground". The offender was required to take post at a corner of the parade ground, come to attention, present arms, come to attention, right turn, quick march to the next corner, halt, attention, present arms, attention, right turn and quick march to the next corner, and repeat the drill. Corner after corner, ten maybe fifteen or twenty circuits of the parade quadrangle depending solely on the corporal's wish. The secret was to be crisp and precise in the early phase with all drill actions, then you might get an early reprieve.

The two blokes on the other side of the corridor were made to clean their floor with a toothbrush. They had several black boot marks to remove before repolishing the floor. The corporals returned several times to check their progress and ensure the toothbrush was used. They received an inspection pass at 2100 hours, poor bastards! We figured those corporals must have been frustrated dentists, with toothbrush cleaning the only thing on their minds.

There were some punishments handed out to the entire hut population at times. A cigarette butt was found outside a window of our hut. The two blokes near the window copped a fair old bollocking, but without proof it was they who deposited this dreadful thing on the sacred ground, we all were subjected to their mean streak.

'Hut One, fall out immediately. Move it, you mob of slack untidy pricks.'

'Three ranks, hurry up, move it!'

'Squad, quick march, squad on the double.'

'Collins (once again right marker), onto the road and right at the dirt track.'

'Yes, sa!'

Before long, Kropper called a halt. 'Rear rank, stand fast, other ranks quick march, halt, second rank stand fast, front rank quick march, halt!' We were in a single line. 'Squad right turn.' Kropper stood out front in all his bossy glory.

There were mumblings from the line, 'What's got up his arse?'

'This squad is responsible for the cleanliness of this area. You have failed in that responsibility. You will now conduct an Emu Bob to clean up the whole area in front of you.' (An Emu Bob means the squad advances in a straight line and picks up any foreign objects seen.) 'If anything is missed by you, the Emu Bob will be repeated until I am satisfied. Squad advance!'

There was not very much to pick-up, but we bobbed along for fifteen minutes or so.

'Squad, halt! Squad, about turn! … I found this cigarette butt behind you, you slack mob of drongos, so we go again. Get it right this time or you will all be doubling around the track. Squad, advance!'

One of the blokes a couple to my left said, 'Hey, Pete. Did you see that? Kropper dropped the bloody butt behind us, the prick.' Other guys confirmed seeing the incident.

'All right, if he does it again, tell me and I will double back and pick it up,' I said. Sure enough, Kropper dropped something again.

'There ya go, Pete,' a few said.

I turned around and ran back to where Kropper was standing, I picked up a gum wrapper and said, 'We almost missed this bit, Corporal,' and I ran back to my position in the line.

'Squad, halt. Squad, dismiss,' chortled Kropper. One could detect laughter in his voice. Chalk one up for the boys, Darby.

The other really annoying thing these bloody corporals did was what was called "bumps". Bumps always happen in the early hours, 0130 to 0430. Designed to interrupt sleep patterns and really piss us off. Later in Army life, we saw it resembles being woken for picket duty, be it forward watch or machine gun. Clever bastards, these corporals! If one looks closely at each of these so-called dirty tricks, they all have a connection to Army survival and efficiency in operation. For example, the Emu Bob: look where you are going, check the ground every step for mines, pansy pits and other booby traps. While that may be so, when they pulled the "bumps" it was not good. This is how bumps worked. They, "the arseholes" (alternative spelling of corporal), would rock up at whatever hour and call 'Parade in five minutes dressed in boots, gaiters and great coats, move it, move it, move it.' Whatever "IT" is, you move "IT". Me, I am sleeping. But up we would get, dress accordingly and stagger outside, a head count conducted, and, "Dismiss". Back to bed. If it was early morning, 0130 hours or so, we would lie there waiting for a second attack, which did happen a few too many times. The whole idea of "bumps" made more sense when the dress was greens, boots, gaiters and rifle. One could imagine a sudden call to arms in a war situation.

One of the most difficult, arduous and painful exercises occurred one morning around 0330 hours. We were told we would be spending a night under the stars. At some time during the night, the order would be given to fall in and march off two minutes after the order. Anyone not in the line-up must stay until daybreak and make their way back to base. Apart from some undisclosed punishment, these people would be required to complete the exercise at a later time, with extra "incentives" added. Dress was boots, gaiters, greens and rifle. Any other items could be taken, but everything must march off with you. Two minutes is not long to wake up and get to parade— collecting stuff, and packing would take precious time. At this stage, we did not know what the exercise entailed, but you could bet it wouldn't be easy-peasy. Army shit never is! I decided to take the bare essentials. These were a backpack with a hutchie, a couple of chocolate bars and breakfast bars, and a canteen of water. Trucks were taking us to the overnight site before dinner; dinner would not be supplied.

5. Mean and nasty training tactics: Teaching discipline?

It was a dark and moonless night as we settled down to try to sleep. My hutchie provided good ground and body cover. I slept with my boots on (some didn't), so all I had to pack was my hutchie. Everything else was in the backpack. Eventually, I slept, then awoke to loud voices, many very loud voices. 'Get up, get up on your feet, we leave in two minutes,' over and over they yelled. A little dazed I got up and only then realised where I was and what was happening. I stuffed my hutchie into the backpack and moved to the only light visible. When we were about to step off, they told us we were going on an eight-mile forced march. A forced march is at a quicker pace step and there are no breaks. 'Fuck me,' said someone, 'I am flat out driving eight miles let alone marching eight of the bastards.' Another said, 'They are trying to kill us but very slowly and painfully.'

There were still some blokes not in formation. Caught out with their boots off and desperately trying to get them on in the pitch-black. Those bloody hob-nail boots are uncomfortable at the best of times, but to march eight miles in boots not fitted correctly is a recipe for disaster. 'Squad, by the left quick march!' I prayed for this to be over, two hours of torture coming my way. Goodie, goodie gumdrops. The pace increased with the corporals calling the time. At least those two bastards were also doing this thing, but they had the latest Australian Army General Purpose (GP)-style boots. The pain up the shins became almost unbearable, the muscle up the shin (whatever it is called) was screaming out, 'Stop, you are hurting me!' I tried everything to get relief; turning my feet out or in gave only momentary relief. Put it out of your mind and think of something pleasant. Anything compared to this shit would be pleasant.

Finally, the pace slowed and I could see the trucks up ahead. The cooks were there and ready to serve breakfast. Just let me sit down—anywhere. 'Well, that fucked me for good,' someone said.

'Too fucking right, me too,' replied several others. There was no rush to join the breakfast queue. That was by far the most difficult and demanding exercise I had encountered up to that stage of training. A year or so later in Vietnam our company received orders to move post haste to a location several kilometres north. This forced march was not on sealed roads but across rough country and jungle and in full battle gear. The training back in 3TB Singleton made sense at last.

The live firing range qualification was completed on a Friday and the weekend was leisure time we all spent in the continual task of boot, belt and gaiter polishing. Washing, ironing and bed sheet changes were part of the weekend chores. Thankfully sheets etcetera, were supplied. Come Monday morning it was back to the parade ground for more advanced drills including the "slow march".

Tuesday morning, I struggled out of bed for breakfast parade. Nothing at the mess interested me except the coffee. I had three large ones. First up for the day was some practice rifle drill. I noticed during breakfast that my right arm was stiff and becoming hard to bend properly. On the parade ground standing at ease (feet apart, rifle butt on the deck, and barrel extended forward) we received the command, 'Parade attention. Parade shoulder arms.' Rifle lifted to the waist. A loud crashing sound followed by a deathly silence. Someone, that would be me, had done the biggest NO! NO! in the Army and had dropped his weapon on the ground, the fucking parade ground.

The parade ground has a long history. After a battle, when retreat was sounded and the unit had reassembled to call the roll and count the dead, a hollow square was formed. The dead were placed within the square and no one used the square as a thoroughfare. Today, the parade ground represents this square and hence, the unit's dead. It is deemed to be hallowed ground, soaked with the blood of our fallen. The area is respected as such by all.

'Soldier! Drop to the ground and kiss that weapon,' which I was already in the process of doing. 'Twenty of the best (push-ups).' On the first push-up, my right arm collapsed and I grunted in pain as blood appeared on the ground. The soldier next to me (bless his butt) kneeled to help.

'Corporal, this bloke's elbow is a mess.'

Kropper came over to where I was now sitting. Looked at me and said, 'Fucking hell, you get him to the RAP (Regimental Aid Post) now.'

I spent the next five days in hospital with cellulitis of the right elbow. The injury had been caused on the rifle range when I was attempting to qualify. The constant abrasion of the elbow on the ground had caused cuts that eventually became infected. It was a pleasant rest and I emerged from hospital as fit as a fiddle and ready to rumble. Naturally, the hut had fun "taking the piss".

'Look, guys, the goose who can't hold onto his gun is back. He owes twenty of the best, come on Pete!'

'Sorry guys can't, doctor's orders.'

'The poor little soldier has a sore arm, so sad,' said Bean. 'Poor guy, he must be worn out from lying on his back for five days with bedside service.'

'And getting needles in my arse twice a day,' I said.

I didn't get needles but it sounded good and they accepted the hardship. I am allergic to penicillin, so was given Tetracycline tablets instead. My rifle was in my bed, barrel on the pillow and neatly tucked in. A note was attached that read, "Drop me again, ya bastard, and I will blow ya fucking brains out." I pissed myself laughing and they all joined in.

'Good to have you back, Pete!' they all said.

The slow march training was still happening. Some of the blokes were having trouble with timing. It might be slow, but it is very tiring requiring unnatural marching movements. Despite the difficulty, it provides a great display when a large contingent gets it right. We would be required to perform the slow march among other drills at the marching out parade before Christmas leave.

The thought of escaping from this prison camp was foremost in all our minds. Plans were being hatched even though Christmas was six weeks away. The bloody corporals, who never missed an opportunity,

Marching Out Parade, recruit training, Singleton, December 1967. That's me, third from the back in the first line facing

made regular threats of leave cancellation if performances were slack. Kropper was often heard saying, 'Private, you will be keeping me company for Christmas dinner unless you smarten up. Now get your arse into gear.'

Part of our responsibilities was to provide guards at the front gate to the base. Everyone, as part of a three-man team, was required to form a twenty-four-hour guard. Instructions were specific and were not to be compromised under any circumstance. The three guards worked on a system of two on duty, one resting. The mess cooks supplied meals, and coffee and tea-making facilities were provided. On a Saturday night at 2400 hours, a car approached with lights glaring. I was standing at the lowered boom gate watching it approach. Proper procedure rolled through my mind: Obtain ID; Refuse admission if ID not shown; Call MPs (Military Police) if warranted; Hold subject under guard until MPs arrive. Our rifles were loaded with live ammo.

The car rolled to a stop, the driver's window rolled down and a familiar voice said, 'Ah, good evening, Private Collins. How has your night been, mate?'

'It has been a quiet night with no incidents to report, Corporal,' I replied. The person driving the car was none other than Kropper!

'May I see your ID please, Corporal?' I said with authority.

He replied, 'Come on, mate, you know who I am. Just open the gate and let me in.'

'My instructions are clear: no ID, no admittance, end of story,' I said.

Kropper let out a long sigh. 'Listen, Pete, I left my ID in the barracks, so I can't produce it here, can I?'

I said, 'Corporal, I cannot authorise your entry. I will have to call the MPs.'

'Don't do that, mate. It would be embarrassing.'

I called to my fellow guard to wake the third guard and to take post at the gate. I said, 'Righto Corporal, get out of the car and you and I will march to your quarters and retrieve your ID.' I wanted desperately to add, 'Move your arse, Corporal!' but I just grinned to myself feeling this was all a nice little charade to test us.

'Go and get fucked, I am staying right here in my car.'

'Alan,' I said, 'call the MPs please, now, we have a problem on the main gate.'

'Got it, mate,' as he picked up the phone.

Kropper yelled, 'Okay, we will go get my ID,' and got out of the car and staggered a little.

'You out in front, Corporal, left, left, left-right-left,' I called from the rear. After one hundred metres Kropper raised his hand with his ID in clear view. Back at the guard house, we relaxed a bit, all three duty guards now wide awake. Kropper appeared and said, 'Very well done. I was impressed with the authority, professionalism and teamwork shown tonight.'

'Corporal,' I said as I raised the gate, 'you may proceed.'

That is a night I will not forget, ever.

6. LET THE GOOD TIMES ROLL

Our lives were not all doom and gloom. There were times we enjoyed ourselves immensely. For example, "Taking the Piss", a good old Aussie pastime. For the uninitiated, this involves having fun at another person's expense and was usually based on an unfortunate "stuff up" that resulted in some form of bizarre punishment. This form of entertainment occurred very, very often as someone was always in trouble. It involved good humour, no personal attacks, re-enactments of the "stuff up" taken over the top by one of the guys, and another issuing some ridiculous punishment. It is a shame mobile phones were not around then to record some of the acting. The victim was always very much involved and enjoyed the "play" as much as anybody. It served to bring us closer together as a team and to know each other better. As had happened when I was sentenced to pipe polishing earlier, the victim received support from the rest of us during their punishment.

The most daring (and the funniest) was when Bean (I don't remember his real name) copped the parade ground guard. After Bean had done about ten circuits, he looked a bit tired. His roommate dressed in his gear and snuck out to a position close to the parade ground. When Bean came to a stop his mate called out quietly, 'Hey, Bean. Fall out over here for a piss stop, mate.' The mate replaced him on the circuit, and being fresh and good at drill did it all correctly and smartly. Kropper appeared and called a halt. 'Good recovery, soldier. You should take a piss more often. Dismiss.' Kropper knew the ruse, but appreciated the support.

There was the "boozer" where we could drink some fine New

South Wales beers, a perfect choice for a mob of Queenslanders brought up on XXXX. But, alas, we were only twenty-years-old and the legal drinking age was twenty-one. It was okay for us to be in the bloody Army, copping all the shit in the world, but no drinkies allowed. Common sense did prevail for once, however, and we were allowed to drink on the Army base. Hoo-fucking-ray for the Army nobs. Even so, the occasional nights at the "boozer" were rather low-key. Darts and the pool table were popular and soon developed into a team challenge. There was always an early morning start after a night off and it was a favourite time for those two bloody corporals to call "bumps" just in case someone was absent and sleeping under a bush.

A boxing competition began which was a weekly knockout (pun intended) competition. The winner of Hut One would fight the Hut Two winner for the "championship". Reminded me of *Hogan's Heroes*, Stalag Thirteen: 'Today we will change underpants: Hut One you will change with Hut Two.' The bouts were over three, three-minute rounds. The corporals were the referees and judges. I had had three fights before this Army crap came along. Bob, a neighbour and a friend from the first day at school, and still a close friend sixty-plus years later, talked me into attending a boxing gym. The owner saw some potential and entered me into three local fights. Having acquired the name "Canvas Back" from Bob was indicative of my career. I won two— the first two. Number one was by forfeit by the opponent; number two I won by at least one hundred metres; and the last, well, I did feel the canvas on my back in the last round. I don't know how I got there. And no, despite my stellar boxing career, I didn't become the champ.

Playing cards was a very popular pastime. For the gambling types, those who had radios and followed the horses, poker was the choice. Of course, there is always someone ready, willing, and able to run a book on the horses, and poker was a way to recover lost funds. I learned Five Hundred from a good mate and fell in love with the game. I became involved in Team Five Hundred tournaments in Singleton and Townsville— what a relaxing pastime it was.

"Mail Call" was the highlight of the week. Letters from wives, girlfriends and family sent the hut into lockdown conditions, everyone (well almost everyone) totally engrossed in their news from home. The exceptions were cheers of joy and the opposite from the other end of the emotional scene. The occasional, rare thankfully, news of the death of a relative, friend or pet. The more frequent was the dreaded "Dear John" (DJ) letter. Unfortunately, our little group of thirty-two received too many. I didn't get a DJ, not then anyway (some more of that "love stuff" later in this story). Some men were very badly hurt by these letters and, in taking the time to offer support and advice, our "Band of Bros" became very adept at pulling the recipient of a DJ out of the bottom of the barrel.

To our great surprise, sometime near the end of November 1967, we were given a leave pass from 1700 hours Friday 'til 1700 hours Sunday. The deal was a courtesy bus would leave for the Cessnock Workers Club at 1800 hours on Friday and would depart the club at 2330 hours to return to 3TB. On Saturday, at the same time, the bus would travel to the Newcastle RSL returning to 3TB at midnight. Registration for each trip had to be made at the company's orderly room before midday Friday. Being a joyful person who likes the odd beer, I registered for both trips. Of course, the bus to Cessnock was full, full of excited young men released upon the world after eight weeks hard labour "behind bars". The dissenting factor to many was we were dressed in Army greens, so fucking unattractive to the local "chickie babes", we thought.

On arrival at the workers' club, we were welcomed with open arms by those in authority with open-your-pockets written all over their faces. We were the tenth National Service intake, and, from all accounts, the other nine intakes had also visited this club on their first leave. Someone in that club had marketing nous. There was a large crowd inside; some of our hopefuls thought the crowd was in response to our visit.

6. Let the good times roll

'Hang on a bit, mate. We're only Aussie Army privates, not American marines full of bravado and shit.'

'Yeah, Pete, but have a gawk at how many pretty chickie babes are waiting.'

'Ah get a grip, Bean. They haven't noticed us.'

'But they will,' said Bean as he took off into the fray.

Most of our crowd headed to the public bar where, to our great pleasure, they were serving the best beer in the world. Well, in the country at least: Queensland's XXXX. The camp boozer only had cans of New South Wales "piss", as it was called. How clever is this club management? The boss is no doubt a Queenslander. The meals were a splendid change from the mess cooking and the grog kept flowing and flowing. For a couple it flowed a bit too much, causing an induced sleep wherever.

Queensland did not have poker machines. The state government led by the controversial Premier Joh Bjelke-Peterson kept them at bay for many years. Sorry to say, after the political demise of Joh's government, the bloody machines crept across the border under darkness into our pubs and clubs. Like cane toads, they have spread and multiplied in their thousands at the expense of many who can't afford to lose. But lose they must, eventually. Cessnock Workers Club was my introduction to these "one-armed bandits". Unlike the current pokies that swallow fifty-dollar notes as quickly as one can feed it, the 1967 type operated by putting a coin of five, ten, or twenty cent denomination into the slot and pulling the arm (lever). It was a slow losing process that south of the border people were hooked on, permanently. That night I spent two dollars in five-cent pieces on the pokies and, to this day, two dollars is the total I have spent in that form of gambling.

The bus trip back began with a lot of, "I'll be back", "See ya, Darl", and "On ya, Fonda", cheers and yelling from the Cessnockians. It soon settled down to a dull roar, then a voice or so, and then a bloody lot of snoring. We were missing a couple of our number. They had better be back in camp by Sunday night. Me, I just crashed into bed and slept "undisturbed" for the first time in sixty days. Why don't we do that again sometime, like tonight?

Saturday provided an opportunity to do whatever needed to be done to make the following week as pleasant as possible. I did some gear cleaning, etcetera; lazed around in shorts and bare feet. Left foot said to his mate (the right foot, der!) this is nice to be outside those stinking boots. So sorry feet, it won't last but don't blame me. I wrote letters home to my dad, my sisters[5] and to Karen.

It is Saturday night, and a busload of refreshed, clean and tidy, eager young men are on their way to shake up Newcastle. Management and staff were expecting us and greeted us with, 'Come on in, fellas. The bar is this way, and the gaming room is over here.'

'They want our money,' one of our lot said.

'Right, then, let's get to the bar and give them some,' said Bean.

Some of the patrons at the bar were not so impressed with our arrival. The older blokes, World War II veterans, reckoned we were pretend soldiers and "short timers". I can remember the same thing happening at the RSL at home when I returned from Vietnam. 'Bloody Vietnam, that isn't a real war. We don't want your lot here,' was what the members had to say. I will have more to say about the treatment we received then. We didn't allow those people to upset our night out. We got pretty pissed, legless some of us, and had fun with the local girls. A few party animals decided to stay in Newcastle, saying they would hitch a ride back to Singo (Singleton) in the morning.

Sunday, bloody Sunday, blared into my life stabbing at my tired sore eyes with its bright sunshine and pounding on my head from the inside out. Bloody hell, did those "Newcs", as we called our hosts in Newcastle, poison me with their shitty beer? Breakfast at the mess with a few coffees helped in the recovery process. After walking back

---

5 Only recently my oldest sister, Sandra, said how much they enjoyed the letters and how much I had to say about my fabulous exciting new life.

to the barracks, I was feeling much better. Time now to write some letters home to Karen, tell her I will be home for Christmas and perhaps we could see each other; and also, alert Lindsay, her younger brother, who had joined the Navy when he turned fifteen years old. Lindsay and I were very, very good at leading each other astray and always consuming more XXXX beer than we should. I looked forward to linking up with my friend, both of us as servicemen, but with the realisation that Lindsay would really piss me off because he was in the "senior service" and would constantly remind me of that observation. Big fucking deal, mate. How hard is it to cruise upon the "ogon" (the ocean in Navy speak) all day? We would have some fun, no doubt, rubbishing shit out of each other while getting legless.

Monday morning began with, you guessed it, the fucking corporals trouncing into the hut with all the noise they could muster. It was 0530 hours. 'Get out of the fart sack now! Parade in fifteen! Move it, move it.' A good song title maybe *Move it, move it, Baby!* Thankfully we were all present, but not all were correct. The later arrivals back at the barracks were a bit worse for wear and a bit dishevelled. They would all be given some inane punishment by the corporals. A dry shave on parade was a favourite. 'Private Dickhead, on the double, get your razor and get back here.' I copped this once in Townsville in 6RAR. It is not a pleasant experience, especially with three-day's growth. And so, we were back in harness.

Around this time in our training the "powers that be" must have assessed our abilities, etcetera, as some of us were offered a test to assess suitability for Officer Training School at Point Cook Academy in Victoria. I sat the test. It was the usual IQ-type questions in favour at the time. I heard nothing more about this, nor did anyone else I knew involved. Guess we were all unsuitable dumdums, or too smart, to be an officer.

The other decision we were asked to make was which part, or corps, of the Army organisation we preferred to join for the remainder of the two-year commitment. Close to one hundred per

Me (right facing) with fellow recruits at 3TB Singleton, October 1967

cent of our group in Hut One was from a clerical background—banks, insurance companies, finance, organisations, etcetera. Some of us wondered if the "birthday ballot" was real or if we were selected on the basis of our civilian employment with the view to building up particular sections of the forces. As an example, to raise or rebuild an infantry battalion, soldiers are needed to form the foundation on which to build. Our group members applied for various corps—medical, transport, armour, service, artillery and so on. We all were sent to Infantry Corps, "crunchies, boot boys", the absolute foundation members of the fighting force. Other Army corps were in existence to support the Infantry Corps. During the Vietnam War, even the Navy and RAAF filled this support role.

There was a suspicion that the decision makers were perhaps afraid of upsetting the current regular soldiers by placing well-trained "civvies" in some areas. Some guys complained that having completed an apprenticeship as a mechanic would secure their choice of "transport", but it did not. The exception was an education as a dental technician. Anyway, I, with most of us, went to Infantry Corps just up the hill in Singo. I guess it could be possible for a government to target a specific demographic for a particular need.

Who knows?

So, it was business as usual in the run-up to Christmas leave and a much looked-forward-to break from this very intense life. I, for what it is worth, had now accepted the style of training adopted by Army personnel. Sure, they were tough, hard and plain bastards at times, but it all boiled down to one thing: discipline. I realised the importance of discipline in an Army unit, especially in a war environment where discipline would save lives.

7. HOW DO I GET "OUTA" THIS PLACE? CHRISTMAS LEAVE

Finally, the day has arrived. I am to be free for a couple of weeks. First, the Army crap has to be dealt with. We are subjected to injections of various types. The RAP staff have arranged a line of tables in the mess hall; we are to attend each table in order. The tables are arranged left then right (Army to a tee). First table, bang in the left arm, next bang in the right arm and on and on. I don't recall how many needles I got that day, but I was feeling a bit deflated. Then came the issue of a new "dress uniform" including nice leather shoes and a beret and Rising Sun badge to fit. This was nice clobber (for the Army). Finally, it was line-up in alphabetical order to be issued with the ultimate prize: a leave pass. This came with a short lecture by the WO1.

'Soldier, you are a valued member of the Australian Army, behave as such. You are to wear your uniform at all times. Carry this leave pass at all times, contact numbers are on the reverse. Be on Base prior to the expiry of your leave. Enjoy your leave, young man.'

I cannot remember how I got home that Christmas, but I did. Of course, the family were very happy to see me home in one big piece. The ole mates at the White Horse "Clinic" rubbished the fuck out of me and my uniform, 'Look at him, he is all green. When he falls off his legs in the grass we won't be able to find him'; 'Bloody good thing I reckon, looks like a gook'; 'Yeah, look at his stupid hair, or where his hair was once'; 'Lovely shiny shoes, spit-polished are they, soldier?'

Lindsay and I were out and about often in uniform. Lindsay wore what I think he called "the sixes": white shirt, short sleeves and white longs with bell bottoms, very noticeable, especially in a pub. We had many a good time with other patrons. Mostly the reception was pretty good, except for one occasion. I, and two of my number, were walking down the main street when three young untidy "punks" made a smart comment. The mate on my right called, 'Halt, about turn.' We faced the punks and me being the smallest of us said, 'Sir, do you have something to say to us?' The punks ducked and ran off up the street. Onlookers clapped.

During the Vietnam conflict, there was unrest building among the population. Part of this was a protest against conscription and part was against Australia's involvement in Vietnam. Both protests would grow and grow. We, as young soldiers, were shielded from these protests by lack of media access and so were unaware of the public sentiment. More of that issue later. That Christmas leave it was party, party and party and we did. Karen and I got together a few times and, from my faded memory, recalled some connection. Well, I went back to Army life hoping so.

Before Christmas leave, we had completed recruit training and were given our new postings. My new posting was to the School of Infantry which was also situated at Singleton. I decided to drive my "Little Beige Bomber", the Morris 1100 back to Singleton. This little beast could hold its own with the best the local Morris Cooper S crowd could muster. It had lowered suspension and all those good bits we youngsters used to fit to our cars back then. I had three passengers and with all the gear the Morrie was riding pretty low. From all accounts the roads were fairly good. Yeah, we will see!

We left home (Toowoomba) late in the day. I enjoyed night driving, and I thought the cooler night air would be good for the high-revving little engine up front. As for the road reports, before we reached Warwick we were sending showers of red sparks out the back. The exhaust pipe was constantly hitting the road surface, and the two guys in the back seat were enjoying the show. Me, no not so much, but push on we did without other drama until we reached a place called the Moonbi Hills, a couple of steep hills going straight up and straight down; should be fun methinks.

The Morris was built with a foot-operated high-beam switch. Thinking this was old-fashioned, I'd altered it to a steering column mounting. It had worked well for a thousand times this trip until these hills. On a high-speed bend, I lowered the beam, the lights went out and would not come back on. The front passenger screamed as I said, 'Shut the fuck up and look for somewhere to pull over!'

After a quick fix, we continued. The next drama followed a few minutes later on the descent side of the hills, a long straight bit of road, downhill rather steeply.

Someone in the back said, 'Pete, there is a fuckin' big truck trying to get in the boot.'

'Yeah, I can see his eyeballs staring at me.'

I was going pretty fast— 140 km/h— but this big rig was still there. I put my foot down to the floor, the little Morrie accelerated for a second or two, then coughed and spluttered. It was starving for fuel. We were now well over 160 km/h and the thing was still there. My 1100 had been timed on a flat track at 102.4 miles per hour (164.8 km/h). Suddenly the fuel supply returned, and we got away from the big bastard. Back at Singo, we were told by some regular Moonbi Hills travellers that trucks used "Angel" gear (neutral) to coast down the big hill, and most likely had little chance of stopping, with fifty tons pushing. Thankfully we arrived at Singleton in one piece, even little Morrie. Well done, little mate.

Somehow, we got through the guard post and were directed to the Infantry Corp temporary office where we received our barrack allocation. I parked the car where I was told, unloaded passengers (some asleep) and gear, and we trudged to our digs. Beds were ready, thankfully, and I collapsed quickly into a deep sleep that I had not had on leave.

8. INFANTRY CORPS

I immediately noticed a difference in our instructors at the beginning of Infantry training. We had completed recruit training and were now officially Army privates who were entering the corps that formed the basis of the Army's fighting capacity. A conflict is not won until you have secured the enemy position with ground troops, a.k.a. Infantry.

Briefings were conducted by our instructors, a mixture of sergeants and corporals who explained what we would be doing during training. They congratulated us for choosing Infantry: it is the toughest corps, but it is the best and is supported by all the other corps in the Australian Army. You guys have come to the right place to become an elite Aussie soldier. Don't know about it being our choice, though. This was a point I raised with a top sergeant I grew to respect and admire; a "reg" (regular, i.e., permanent) who had seen action everywhere in the world, including Vietnam. What he did not know about being a successful infantry member was not worth knowing. I broached the subject of the high percentage of our call-up being sent to infantry school.

'It is simple, Pete,' he said. 'The Army needs men, intelligent individuals who are fit and can be trained to do a job. There are insufficient regs to fill the growing need for good infantry soldiers.'

I asked, 'So anyone doing the recruit gig reasonably well got the infantry prize?'

He replied, 'Yeah mate, something like that.'

The instructors told us to dismiss any war movies we had seen on how the infantry operated. 'It is very different now. There are no trenches, except the ones you will dig yourselves, sometimes every night. The emphasis is now on a mobile force, constantly searching out the enemy. By necessity, our training concentrates on close-encounter jungle fighting, as in Vietnam. Also, more open area conflict will be included. You blokes will be busy as your training as an elite infantry soldier progresses.'

One could ponder— 'What is there to learn about this stuff?' A bloody lot as it turned out. Here is a list of all we learned in about six weeks.

- Use of equipment: backpacks, webbing, erection of a hutchie; packing a pack
- Weapons: M60 machine gun; stripping, loading, firing, firing pattern, aiming
- Number 2 machine gunner, responsibilities for the second barrel and fitting every 200 rounds
- M79 grenade launcher, aiming, firing, maintenance
- Hand grenades (pineapples): safety, priming (pulling the pin), throwing technique
- Claymore mines: use, setting, wiring, aiming, firing, safety precautions, e.g., facing the enemy
- Bushcraft: in jungle, open ground, rocky terrain
- Formations in the field: straight-line advance
- Movement: only on undisturbed ground, never on a road or path
- Personnel positions: forward scout, tail end Charlie (a.k.a. arse end Charlie)
- Communication: in silence using specific hand signals, e.g., enemy closed-fist thumb-down
- Contact action: Move quickly to cover, facing contact, weapon ready
- Ambush positioning
- Night movement

- Night defence: create individual shell-scrape, dig in as deep as possible
- Night "pickets" with machine gun manned at all times
- Stand to[6] at dawn
- Armoured personnel carrier (APC) and helicopter dismount procedure

We were taught the structure of an infantry battalion and the reporting mechanism. In a nutshell, a battalion is made up of four Companies named: A, B, C and D (Alpha, Bravo, Charlie and Delta). Staid old Army language. Could have been Happy, Sleepy, etcetera. But where would one find a happy company?

Plenty of sleepies, though. A variation was the three Anzac battalions (2RAR, 4RAR and 6RAR) who, in Vietnam, had one or two New Zealand Companies attached, nominated W and Z (*Whisky, mmm, and Zulu*). Each company commander was called Officer Commanding (OC) with the rank of Major and reported directly to the battalion Commanding Officer (CO) who held the rank of Lieutenant Colonel. Each infantry company structure was as follows:

- CHQ (Company Headquarters) personnel in operational mode
- OC (Commander) (Major)
- 2IC (2nd in Command) (Captain)
- WO2 (Warrant Officer Two)
- Supply (Staff Sergeant)
- Administration (Sergeant)
- Battalion Signalman (Lance Corporal)
- Company Signalman (Private) that would be me, me, me

---

6 "Stand to" is usually called when Army troops are occupying a position. This is usually at first or last light. Everyone will occupy a pit or position and face the perimeter. This will occur daily or if there is an attack about to occur. Once over, they will then be told to stand down. Gun pickets will then commence, followed by day or night routine. Depending on the threat, pits or positions may be at 50 per cent with one person facing out, the other digging or resting.

- Two Medics (Corporals)
- CHQ was also supported by a rifle section

After completing the majority of our basic infantry training, it was time to put it into practice to evaluate progress. Our own bush adventure! The Company and support units headed to the mountain ranges near Kyogle in northern New South Wales. Anyone who has driven through these particular forests (think jungle) will know the terrain is very steep and rocky. After being there for three weeks or so, I can attest to the fact that there is not a flat and level square metre to be found anywhere. I was supposed to raise my hutchie and eat, sleep and shave. Yes, they did inspect our faces every day. A clean and tidy soldier is an alert and reliable soldier. Besides, it is a personal discipline, is it not?

The other pain in the arse thing about this place was it was wet, always bloody wet, and everything became wet and muddy. There were constant whinges coming from the guys, 'Fuck me dead, mate. When do we get out of this shit hole and back to my lumpy mattress at Singo?'

I had my share of "hissy spits" when trying to find a couple of nearby trees suitable for stringing up my hutchie. There were lots of trees, big ones, small ones and some as big as your "imagination", but too close or too far apart or another bastard was in the middle. Finally finding a suitable pair, I'd pull the anchor ties tight and one of the rotten rotting trees would fall over. Fuck this, I'd sleep with the hutchie as a blanket.

Hang on, did I say "sleep"? Fat chance of that! Lying there in the dark, dark jungle I prayed for the sun to come up so I could get out from under my hutchie and off the ground sheet that was now below mud. I was afraid to move for fear of making the situation worse. Worse? How could this be any worse? A huge downpour is how, it just rained, and fucking rained.

I had to wonder what Kyogle meant other than my interpretation of it, i.e., "shit hole". There would be worse places as it turns out. As a brutal learning experience, the exercise did, apart from piss us off, show how important the Army teaching was in making us aware of hardship and how to cope with uncomfortable situations. In the debrief, the staff told us as infantry soldiers we would not always have a comfortable night's sleep and a fine meal in our tum-tum. How true that was!

At one point during this outdoor adventure, the Company driver was ordered to go to Kyogle township on a special mission. For reasons unknown to me I was assigned to accompany him. Now the driver, let me call him Bernie, was a product of a very successful cattle property in central Queensland. He cared little for the discipline of the Army but was an accomplished driver. Bernie would, in his future Army career, be charged with being absent without leave (AWOL) on many occasions. I had no idea why we were going into the township and Bernie said nothing. I was happy to get out of the bloody muddy camp for a few hours.

At about 0800 hours we headed off to town. Bernie looked pretty clean and tidy compared to my exceptionally grubby and probably smelly appearance. I had not showered for about two weeks, but I was clean-shaven— should be a plus! Bernie, on the other hand, had had the luxury of sheltering in his nice dry Land Rover; some bludgers (a.k.a. Company drivers) got it good. Bernie parked the vehicle in the main street. We got out and walked towards some shops. There were a lot of people in town.

'Hey Bernie, looks like we are expected,' I said.

'We do have a known appointment down here a bit,' said Bernie. Then Bernie turned into a shop.

'Bernie, no way am I going into a chemist! They'll smell me and toss me out.'

'Pete, it's okay, they know we're coming.'

'So, they expect something from the "Black Lagoon" do they?' I was soooo embarrassed. Everyone was looking at us, me, with a scowl on their faces. I looked back behind me and could see my muddy footprints. 'Come on Bernie, let's get the fuck out of here.' He was at the prescription counter and collecting the medication the RAP required.

'Come on. Pete, we're going to the pub.'

'Great, I need a drink after that experience. Do I smell bad, Bernie?'

'Ah, mate, I've smelled cattle worse than you. Come on— let's have a beer.'

The pub experience was only marginally better. Plenty of pointing, sniggers and grins. The barmaid was very friendly.

'G'day, diggers, how ya goin' terday? Looks like you need a drink among other things.'

I burst out laughing and replied, 'You mean like I need a bath?'

'Yeah, digger, but not to worry. What's yous havin' ter drink?'

'A big beer and a big rum and Coke,' said Bernie.

When she returned with our drinks she said, 'No charge, the blokes up the end shouted!'

We showed our appreciation, and I said to the lady, 'Just as well. I have no money.'

'Thought so. If you go again, it will be on the house, okay?'

We left after two drinks with a donated packet of spearmint chewing gum. What a great experience. People can be really kind if they have a mind to be. But bugger, it was back to the muddy smelly jungle, but at least I fit in there.

On the following couple of nights, they put us through some night exercises. Obviously, they had calculated the Moon's positioning as the nights were as dark as they possibly could be. This is a very unnerving situation and somewhat scary when you can't see the bloke in front of you. The only help was pieces of rotting wood off the ground which glowed brightly placed on everyone's backs (a function of bioluminescence known as "foxfire"). This same idea was used on exercises at Mt Spec in North Queensland and in Vietnam. We woke a day later to the news we were going back to Singleton. What a fucking relief.

On arrival at Singleton 3TB, we were briefed before leaving the trucks. The quartermaster appeared peering over the tailgate and issued orders in a rapid fashion. 'I bear good news and bad news,' he said grinning. 'As of now, you have three days on-the-base leave. When I let you off this truck, you will follow directions given to the letter, got that?' Oh yeah, we've got it. 'Upon disembarking you will be told to strip naked, to dump clothing in the bins, carry your boots with you and proceed in single file to the shower tents. Rifles and packs etcetera will be identified to be retrieved later. At the other end pick-up new greens, socks and underwear at the Q store tent. Have you got that you pack of smelly, disgusting bastards? Now get off my truck, left rear first. Have a nice weekend, fellas.'

This was a de-lousing of sorts as the shower in each shower tent was different, the first nice clean warm water, then two with differing chemical smells followed by warm soapy stuff and finishing with a blast of cold, invigorating water that caused screams of delight. Well, maybe not all was delight. The experience was a great start to three days' rest and recreation (R&R), even if it was on-the-base restriction. Climbing into new greens was a pleasure, but the shirts and trousers felt like cardboard; my first job would be to wash and iron them, after donning shorts and t-shirt. Even that hard lumpy bed was inviting.

Yet again the Army had taught us a very good lesson on how to cope with adversity that at times threatened your very existence, requiring one to withstand extreme personal discomfort that required a strong self-discipline to survive the moment. The Army training personnel had perfected this procedure of teaching discipline without saying a word about discipline. It was a slow but sure self-realisation of the requirement of discipline.

I spent the three days' leave resting, writing to all and sundry at home, cleaning my gear, especially the boots I had worn at Kyogle.

What a mess. I ran the four hundred metre track every day and the cross-country circuit once. I felt rested and fit by Monday morning.

Next came speciality weapons training. First on the training agenda was "the art of throwing hand grenades". It is an art, in a way, as some of the blokes would prove later in training. But first, we had lectures on safety of the grenade itself and, secondly, safety on the practice throwing range.

'These things are dangerous, fucking dangerous, to me and to you guys,' said the range sergeant. 'We will talk about safety here in this room and again in the "bunker". The bunker, as you will see tomorrow, is a substantial structure with solid thick concrete walls and divisions. There have been accidents when a first-time soldier has pulled the pin, panicked and dropped the bastard of a thing inside the bunker. Please, you guys, don't do that as I will be there beside you to "hopefully clean up". On one occasion it was necessary to throw the soldier over the wall and follow him myself. If you feel stressed when you enter the front of the bunker, for fuck sake tell me.'

'The weapon is very powerful and fires shrapnel in all directions when it explodes. It is particularly deadly in confined spaces. While the "pin" is in place it is entirely safe. The pin holds the firing handle in place. Only when the handle is released will the grenade be armed and capable of exploding. To throw the thing, you hold the bastard in your throwing hand and with the other pull the pin out. It is still safe. In an overhead extended arm action, you launch the little bastard at your target at the same time yelling loudly, "Grenade!". It will explode three seconds after the handle is released, so duck behind the wall immediately. If any of you drop it, I will retrieve it and "try" to remove it over the wall. If not, I have three seconds to get both you and me over that wall.'

We had many practice throws with unarmed grenades as a qualification for the live range the next day.

'How do you feel, soldier?' the range sergeant asked.

'I am nervous but confident I won't blow us up,' I replied.

'Good stuff, mate. Here, hold this.' My first time holding a small but dangerous killer in my right hand.

'Okay, let's see a dummy, er, practice throw ... Good. Next time is for real.'

I had a look over the wall and selected a target as the Sarge had asked: a tree 15 m out and slightly right, and informed the Sarge.

'Righto, son, whenever you are ready, throw that little bastard over the wall!'

I saw it heading in the right direction as I ducked behind the wall, then the loud crack as it exploded. The Sergeant and I rose to see the bloody tree was gone.

'Well, I'll be fooked,' he said. 'Good stuff, well, do it again next time.'

We all had three throws that day, but while I threw correctly, I could not repeat the first-up fluke.

The M60 machine gun is an impressive weapon. It fires the same 7.62 mm projectile as the SLR rifle. The ammo is contained in two hundred-round belts that are carried by both the gunner and his number two. The number two also carries a spare gun barrel, used to change the barrel of the gun every two hundred rounds if possible. The change procedure is very quick and is designed to protect the integrity of the gun accuracy that is affected by heat generation. Unlike earlier machine guns (e.g., the Thompson) that fired in a direct pattern, the M60 formed a cone-shaped pattern in the target area. It was a highly effective weapon in the Vietnam jungle terrain. The M60 in the hands of a well-trained and strong gunner provided magnificent support for advancing infantry troops, as well as static support in firebases, etcetera. Stripping, reassembly, reloading, and refilling an ammunition belt together with firing in a prone position with bipod in place formed our comprehensive training. Quick change of the barrel was a major focus along with the reloading procedure. An infantry section is vulnerable without the M60 operational.

We were introduced to the M79 grenade launcher, a 40 mm

light weapon that "lobs" a grenade in an arching manner and is quite accurate when aimed correctly. In Vietnam, I used the M79 to great effect in an operation on the beach dunes close to the Long Hai Hills. Our orders were to ensure no boat traffic travelled to the base of the Long Hais. Perched atop a ten-metre steel sandbagged tower, D Company HQ members, with the support section, watched with binoculars and star scope (at night) for any movement offshore. Any craft in the restricted area was met with a warning grenade from the M79 that exploded on impact with the water. Failure to turn back met with certain destruction. From this tower, we also monitored any movement in the caves of the Long Hai, a stronghold of the Viet Cong. Below the tower, the engineers had built an underground (think sand) command post using heavy timber and corrugated iron and protected with sandbags. Within this command post were my VHF (very high frequency) and HF (high frequency) radios that were constantly manned. Hopefully, I will return to this operation later in my story, as some very interesting "stuff" happened there.

The other very interesting weapon we studied was the 84 mm Carl Gustav antitank rocket launcher. We never got to fire or use it in action as it was Swedish built and the Swedes, who did not support the Vietnam War, would not allow it to be used in combat.

Things changed considerably after transferring to the Infantry Corps. The emphasis was on instilling the skills an infantry soldier needed to be effective and protect his mates and himself. The inspections, as they were in recruit training, all but ceased. There were far fewer parade drill and dress inspections, but they tossed in a hut inspection occasionally to keep us on our toes. During one of these inspections, the sergeant ran his white-gloved finger across the top of my locker.

'Look at this dust up here, soldier. What do you have to say, hey?'

'Sergeant, that is a very high place, is it not?'

'Bullshit, mate, you can reach it easily.'

'But Sarge, you know the Bible, from dust to dust is our life.'

'Bullshit. What has that got to do with anything?'

'Well, sergeant, if you are familiar with the Bible, our lives are from dust to dust. That dust might be a relative or good friend visiting me!'

'For fuck's sake, just clean it will ya.' The Sergeant left the hut laughing and saying, 'You fucking Nashos will be the end of me.' Did I say that? A bloody good excuse though, don't you think?

After Kyogle there were several lecture sessions on what we had, or should have, learned so far. We did various "duties" within the base. Mess duty remains in my memory. I was assigned to mess duty. I reported to the head cook (a.k.a. "head tucker fucker") and was assigned to potatoes. Oh no! Peeling bloody potatoes. I had visions of World War II movies. The head tucker fucker showed me a big barrel-type machine and said, 'This sucker will peel the potatoes, you just operate it, got it, mate? The operating instructions are here on the wall, those are the potatoes there.' A veritable fucking pile of potatoes I could not jump over even if I had a mind to. I read the instructions and fired up this monster. It began to spin like mad. A bit like a cement mixer out of control. I threw in a few very big potatoes. The very big potatoes after a minute or so were little potatoes, a mere shadow of their former selves. It was no wonder the pile was so big; half had gone down the drain.

Of course, there was the task of "dixie bashing". Cleaning up the pots, pans and other sundry items the tucker fuckers had managed to burn so badly the dishwashers could not cope with the task. There was a suspicion among us that they burned these on purpose. The chef waddled, his fat body jiggling as he laughed out loud. 'You're a bloody wanker, Sarge,' I remarked (but not too loud); strategic defence you know.

A few days later the same sergeant served me scrambled eggs in the breakfast queue. When he saw me, he said, 'So didn't you like my little joke?'

'As I said, Sarge, you are a wanker.'

He laughed and gave me an extra helping of bacon.

Scrambled eggs are a favourite of mine, but when they are of a consistency that they are poured onto the plate, I become confused. Everyone can make edible scrambled eggs, even young brides. These cooks? They are trained to prepare meals for hundreds each meal; why are eggs so difficult for some of them? In Vietnam, we were at times served powdered eggs. The cooks tried in vain to make scrambled eggs out of this powder. It became a white runny yuk that everybody refused. Other eggs, some said, were etherised, they were a "knockout". No, they were not, but I couldn't resist the pun. These eggs smelled crook and tasted bloody awful. There were some "good eggs" in the Army though, especially later in Lavarack, Townsville.

Guard duty and some cleaning duties were included but, in general, life in the Infantry Corps was far more pleasant than the first three months. We were treated like we mattered. I do not recall ever hearing any regular soldier or officer denigrating us as Nashos. This acceptance would continue into our battalion postings not too far in the future. In fact, there was very little complaint from anyone as we steadily slipped into Army routine. To many, having one's current and future life mapped out by others was totally acceptable.

9. MOVING ON: THE REAL DEAL

In early February 1968, we left Singleton for a further training excursion somewhere. I do not remember much about the exercise except there was lots of tall grass and scratchy bush growing on rocky terrain. There was no resort, no beach and no surfie girls. Nothing. Boring and more boring as we tried to dig weapon pits. It was bad enough to be "out of the comfort zone", but this shithole was the pits. One quickly realises that the Army barracks, although not up to home standards of comfort, are a bloody lot better than "in the bush". One can only ponder how those men in Gallipoli and France survived those trench conditions for so long. Makes us look soft.

All we were told was that our fun little exercise in this place was to last something like twenty-one days. So help me God! As it turns out it seems, He did help. After about seven days (I was not counting, much) the word arrived that we were going back to the base as our full contingent had been posted to the 6RAR at Lavarack Barracks, Townsville North Queensland.

The regular Army guys were able to tell us that it was 6RAR, D Company that was involved in a huge battle in South Vietnam that was now known as The Battle of Long Tan. One hundred and five soldiers of Delta Company and three New Zealanders from New Zealand's 161 Field Battery had encountered a combined force of North Vietnam Army (NVA) and Viet Cong (VC) numbering an estimated two to two and a half thousand. The Australians, supported by artillery fire from Nui Dat (an Australian task force base), forced the withdrawal of the enemy, inflicting heavy casualties. Australia lost eighteen men, seventeen killed in action, one of the twenty-five wounded in action later dying of wounds. Soon I would be a part of this famous Delta Company.

Orders stated I was to report to the guard house at 6RAR prior to 1800 hours on 20th February 1968. The current date was 10th February. Although Townsville was at least thirty hours nonstop driving from Singleton, the Army had given me ample time to get there by car. As my home city, Toowoomba, was on the route, this meant I would be able to spend time there. What a BUZZ! February 16th was my birthday, and my twenty-first to boot. Look out Toowoomba, here I come!

Turned out it was not such a fun trip.

Leave commenced at 0600 hours. I drove out at 0601. I had two passengers, both from Toowoomba: Mick (remember Mick from the first day in Brisbane fetching chairs?) and Paul. For once in his life Mick was on time after a threat of being left behind even if a minute late. All three of us were over the Moon to be going home for a few days. It was an unexpected reprieve from an intense training schedule.

'Go faster, Pete! Yeah, get up it!' my passengers yelled.

'See ya, Singo, you shithole, you won't see us again.'

I did move the little Morrie along as quickly as I dared. With three adults and all their gear, every spare bit of space was filled with whatever would fit. The poor little bastard was overloaded to the max and beyond. I hoped, even prayed, Morrie would make it home under his own steam. The Moonbi Hills were on the way forward; would this little 1500cc engine in the Morris make it over them? It was a slow drag up and over "them thar hills" but we all made it to the other side!

'Thank God for that!' said Paul. His brother was a Christian Brother, so it was a genuine thanks.

'No fuel pump problems,' said Mick.

'No, mate, I checked that out. Just a bit of shit on the terminals was all,' I replied.

Amazingly, the British Motor Corporation, the manufacturer

who built my Morris, put the electric fuel pump under the fuel tank exposed to anything sprayed up by the car or any other vehicle on the road. Showing masterful engineering skills, they placed all the engine electrics, distributor, coil, and spark plug leads directly behind the grill (in front of the radiator). So, all the electrics were exposed to the elements. They managed, in a whole range of cars, including the famous Mini, to fuck up the fuel system and the electric system. How many of these cars ever ran properly in the UK has "got me wet".

On we travelled, Mick and Paul singing (?) songs (?) and laughing at their own poor jokes. Here are a couple to ponder: Mick on his wife Judy: 'Ya know, Paul, since the snow came, all my wife could do was look through the window. If it gets any worse, I'll have to let her in.'

Paul in reply: 'After years of research, scientists have discovered what makes women happy: nothing!'

I laughed so hard that tears ran down my leg.

At Glen Innes, Mick needed to stop the tears running down his leg. I grabbed some fuel and a sanger and off we went again. We passed Tenterfield and could now smell the sweet smell of Queensland. I could feel something not quite right with Morrie. I didn't say anything to the others, but it felt like the clutch was slipping when under acceleration. I kept going hoping all would be well. But all was not well. Somewhere south of Stanthorpe the little engine shuddered violently and stopped. Engine temperature was through the roof and steam poured from the engine bay.

'Guys, this is terminal. Sorry, but we are fucked.' We climbed out and all kicked a wheel.

'You bastard of a car,' said Mick.

'Well,' I said, 'what do we do now? Any ideas?'

'We will have to hitch a ride to Stanthorpe and get a bus,' was Paul's idea. He stood on the roadside with his thumb stuck out.

The very first car, a 1964 Holden EH ute, came to a dusty halt in front of us. It was one of our guys, from Hut Two. His name was Jim. We had met in the car park on the base when I was looking at the fuel pump problem. He was impressed with the Morris. Jim came up to me, 'Hi, Pete. Bit of trouble? What's the prob? Any clues?'

'Buggered engine, dead as a maggot,' I replied.

He then made an amazing suggestion, 'Pete, I can tow you as far as Warwick. From there you could get a truck to carry the car home. Mick and Paul could catch a bus to Toowoomba. Buses run quite often and they don't want arms and legs for the ride. What ya reckon, mate? I have a good rope in the ute.'

This was a very considerate offer. Jim and I had only met the once in the last five months, yet here he was offering help to a fellow digger who was stranded in the middle of nowhere. It genuinely struck me as a fine gesture of mateship the Army had tried to instil in us from day one.

'Jim, thank you from the bottom of my boots.'

'Mine too,' said Mick.

'And mine,' said Paul.

We got the show on the road pretty quickly after hitching the rope. Both cars would operate hazard lights. The headlights on in my car would indicate slow down and, flashing headlights, an emergency stop. I warned Jim my brakes would be less efficient without the engine running. Paul would travel with Jim to watch for any signals or problems. So less than thirty minutes after stopping, off we trundled. Towing is a difficult thing at the best of times and with the distance we had to cover I prayed for our safe arrival in Warwick. I had asked Jim to stop at a servo so I could ring Dad and have him meet us.

We all cheered and waved our arms out the windows and blew the horn when we crossed the border into Queensland at Wallangarra. 'Not all that far to Stanthorpe and then about an hour to Warwick,' I said to Mick who was sitting beside me in a state of shock. At times our speed exceeded 120 km/h. I could see it frightened him. Mick had never been a car enthusiast, unlike most young guys. Just short of Stanthorpe, Jim stopped, I made the phone call, and we all took a well-earned breather.

Dad had said he would leave immediately, and I arranged to meet him at a servo on the approach to Warwick. He said the road from Stanthorpe to Warwick is total shit so be careful. Dad was right, as usual. It was a narrow, rough, undulating, twisty bit of shit with some steep hills. To describe it as "shit" was to be kind, very kind.

The trip was going quite well except for a couple of scary moments with the tow rope becoming too slack. My rear brakes would be worn out with the constant use of the handbrake to correct the tension. We crawled through Warwick and arrived at the servo just as Dad did. 'Let me out of this fucking car,' said Mick, as he had a big "laugh at the ground".

Paul, in his inimitable way, said, 'Carrnn, Mick, get over it or you will make us all spew.'

'Thanks a lot,' I said to Jim. 'Everything will be okay now, mate. I owe you. See you in Townsville.'

Dad chipped in and complimented Jim on his effort, then said, 'I couldn't locate a tow rope. Where in Warwick could I buy one?'

'Keep mine. Pete can bring it to Townsville.'

Dad replied, 'The Army has gained some fine men I can see!'

Dad had been alone for nearly three years and had been told by all and sundry, including professionals, that he should get on with his life. He had an attractive woman with him. Her name was Nada. She was a vivacious person and easy to like. She certainly liked me, maybe too much, sufficient for me to mention it later to Dad. Also, Dad had sold our old circa 1900 Queenslander and purchased a new brick home on the range escarpment in Toowoomba. I would only discover this on arrival at the new address.

In Toowoomba Dad towed the Morris directly to Howard Motors, the local BMC dealer where he was friends with the workshop foreman,

Eddie, who said he would check it out and give an assessment in the morning.

MY TWENTY-FIRST BIRTHDAY: AT HOME

Friends, family and lover could not believe my luck in getting home for my twenty-first birthday. Remember readers, this is 1968, one became "an adult" at twenty-one, not eighteen as it is now. In 1968 we could drive at seventeen, but not vote or drink legally until twenty-one. Somehow, though, nineteen was old enough to be forced into the Army with the prospect of going off to war. Go figure! This anomaly was ended by prime minister Gough Whitlam in 1972. One of the many great ideas that man had!

I had, as is obvious in the early part of my story, frequented hotels on a regular basis albeit underage. On my first day home (within the first hour), I contacted Karen. I had not told anyone I was coming home. I wanted to surprise them. Imagine arriving at number eighty-three to find it deserted. That would blow my surprise out of the water. Karen was excited and I arranged to pick her up at work at 1700 hours. 'I finish at 5 pm, Peter, not 1700 o'clock or whatever you said.' Karen worked for the local Ford dealer, Falconer Motors, and would eventually be the PA (personal assistant) to the boss man, Edsel Falconer. The name coincidence to Ford Motor Co. was amazing.

Karen must have called home to tell her brother Lindsay I was home. The phone rang. 'G'day, ya slack arse Army dickhead, it's the senior service here.' Lindsay, now approaching nineteen, had joined the Royal Australian Navy (RAN) at the age of fifteen. He had already travelled the world. 'See you at "the Cri" in ten,' he said and hung up! "The Cri" was a little pub, The Criterion, in the CBD.

Lindsay and I had become very good friends, reinforced by my now "service career". Constantly he reminded me he was in the "senior service" and I was a, 'What do they call you? Private? What the fuck is that for a rank? At the fuckin' bottom where you belong.'

Lindsay's grandfather fought in France in 1915 and was wounded in action. And his father served in both the RAN and the Army. He was a clearance diver for the Navy in World War II and an instructor in the Army during the first Australian National Service call-up in the 1950s. To this day, Lindsay proudly wears his own medals as well as his father's and grandfather's. I have five service medals to wear on Anzac Day. Lindsay is decked out with about forty. Nevertheless, my two years' service and his twenty-year service are never questioned. A mutual respect exists.

I arrived at "the Cri". Lindsay was already there with a pot waiting. 'About time ya slack bastard, you are ninety seconds late.' I was in civvies, but he was in the Navy white bell bottom uniform, the name of which I don't recall. We settled in for a bit of a session. After about thirty minutes two coppers walked into the bar. They immediately approached me and asked for ID, which I produced proudly.

'So, you are twenty-one today. Congrats. Have a nice day,' they said, and left.

It was as if Lindsay was not there. I felt like calling out, 'Hey, this wanker is only eighteen!' But I didn't.

Lindsay said, 'They respect servicemen. Wear your uniform and experience the public respect.' That was the one and only time I was questioned about age in a pub, ever. On my twenty-first birthday. So be it. We had several beers and lots of laughs with each other and with other patrons. Many beers were shouted for, especially when Lindsay told everyone I was in the Army. Near to 5 o'clock, 1700 hours, or two bells, I left to pick-up Karen. I borrowed Dad's blue Valiant for the day; he had a Morris Cowley ute he drove to work.

I parked outside Falconer Motors' front door and waited for Karen to appear. Ah! There she is looking perplexed and confused. She was looking for the Morris and would not recognise the Valiant. I sat there for a moment admiring this stunning girlfriend of mine. Way out of my class, I thought. I jumped out of the car and called her. She ran to me, and we embraced on the footpath. Man, oh man, did it feel good to be back home.

Karen had no arrangements for the afternoon, so I said, 'Dad has bought a new house in Fairholme Street, how about I show it to you? And also,' cheekily, 'my new bedroom?'

Dad arrived home and was happy to see Karen. He asked her to stay for dinner and said, 'How about staying over? You can help me arrange a twenty-first for Peter tomorrow downstairs.'

I drove Karen home to change and collect a few necessary bits and say hello to her mum, Elsie. We invited Lindsay and Elsie to the party. Karen also asked Lindsay to invite all the gang of thieves and cut-throats he hangs out with to the party. 'Bring some grog too,' I added, 'could be a long one.'

After dinner, a few drinks and some laughs I was bushed and went to bed. What about Karen? Go figure! I woke early, extricated myself from the bed and found Dad making coffee. Big, black and two, please. We sat on the deck and enjoyed the sunrise in silence. The house was on the edge of the Great Dividing Range and offered uninterrupted views of the valley below.

Quietly Dad said, 'Good to have you home, Son.'

'Good to be home, Dad, and thanks heaps for your help yesterday.'

I did a quick check on Karen, still asleep and looking quite pleased with the world. Dad and I headed off to see Eddie at Howard's about the car. It was Saturday, but Eddie had come to work to assess the damage.

'Pete,' said Eddie, 'it's not good mate. You did a bit of a job on it that's for sure!'

'Tell us the bad news, Eddie,' said Dad.

Eddie's report went like this: The engine is cactus, kaput. The slipping clutch seems to have become extremely hot. The heat travelled to the first crankshaft journal and bang! The crankshaft broke in two. It was only held together by the bearing collars. Consequently, the crankshaft is buggered as is the engine block. A new or replacement engine is the only fix.

'So sorry, Pete. It is a lovely little car. Such a pity. Gordon, it can stay here until you decide on the next move.' We thanked Eddie who, by the way, charged nothing, and went on our way.

We stopped outside Austral Motors, the Chrysler Valiant dealer. I asked Dad what he was doing. He looked at me and said, 'Driving about 2000 km to Townsville in a small car worries me. You need something bigger, safer; we are going to talk to the boss here.'

The boss, Len (a.k.a. "High Pockets"), who I would have much to do with in my future career in finance, was a little Italian but was feared by many businesspeople. His nickname was because he wore his trousers high above the waist, hence the high pockets. He did, however, present a smart business look. He was tough to deal with where money was involved.

Dad said, 'He owes me. Let's go see the little Italian bastard.'

I thought, *What could this top, tough businessman owe Dad?* Must ask later.

Len was in the showroom inspecting the display cars.

'G'day, Len, do you have a minute or two to make a dollar?'

'Gordon, ya bastard. What the fuck do you want ya tight arse?'

'It's up to you, Len. Give me a good deal and we buy. I want a good, reliable, big car for my boy to drive to Townsville this week.'

I almost burst out laughing at the first sight of this man. Small in stature, rotund, slicked back Brylcreemed hair, immaculately groomed but, yes, those pockets sitting high above his non-existent waist. Suffers from small man syndrome no doubt. I instantly liked him and despite the bravado, I suspected Dad did too.

'Len P, meet my son, Peter. He is six months into National Service and has been posted to 6RAR in Townsville.'

Len was gracious and congratulated me on my commitment to the country. Dad's voice changed, and he said, 'A white Valiant SV1 auto has been in your yard for a bit because the price is too high. I'll pay you $X cash now.'

'You can go and get fucked at that price,' said Len.

'Okay,' said Dad, turning and walking away.

'Hey, where are you going?'

Dad replied, 'Going to get fucked by the Ford dealer!'

Len was known for his colourful language. He told a long-winded story about being woken up by a Cucking-fuckin-burra on the clothes-fuckin-line! We bought the SV1 Valiant at Dad's price, the deal was done, and I drove my new car home. 'Dad, you amaze me,' I said. The Valiant was a white auto sedan with a push-button radio. It felt big and powerful after the little Morris. On the long hike to Townsville, it would be the "duck's nuts".

*

So, what did Len owe Dad? Interestingly it had to do with the Valiant SV1 exhaust manifold. It had a habit of cracking and causing an awful noise and drop in performance. Dad was able to weld these and provide a guarantee they would not crack again in the same place. As it turns out the Chrysler dealers had a substantial number in stock. As word spread about the "fix", more were being repaired than new ones sold. Old High Pockets got upset and complained bitterly to Dad.

'Listen, Len, my price of repair is way below your replacement price.'

'Well raise your fucking price, Gordon.'

'No way, Len. Drop your price or we continue as we are.'

Eventually, Len did drop his price, but this, in the wash-up, gave Dad more work until Chrysler fixed the problem with the new model. Little-big man versus little-little man.

*

I arrived home, drove up the steep driveway in a cloud of tyre smoke to the cheers and jeers of several mates and friends milling around, most with grog in their mitts. When I climbed out of the car there was a raucous cheer of, 'You fuckin' wanker, Pete.' I thought *This is going to be some party today, tonight and tomorrow.*

Karen had absconded, gone home to sort out her dress and stuff for the party. Heaps of mates were there. Karen had started a phone tree and it worked a dream. Lindsay had organised a five-gallon keg with a pump and heaps of ice. This thing, the keg, was a novel idea in 1968, something rarely seen at a private party. Later on, Lindsay and I had fun with it, in our hungover state. The new house had a downstairs rumpus room which opened onto the front lawn before a steep grassy slope onto the stone fence. Many a drunk slipped down the slippery slope during the party. No one suffered, drunks never do!

Karen arrived dressed in a long figure-hugging dress I still adore. We danced, laughed, drank, ate and talked until the next day arrived. I almost forgot I had to soon leave to resume my Army life in Townsville. I had a wonderful night dancing and smooching Karen. It was going to be hard, bloody hard, to leave her in a day or so.

The next morning, rather late, Lindsay and I returned the almost empty beer keg to the White Horse Hotel in the CBD. I was carrying the thing under my arm and pumping the pump (what else do you do with a pump?) while Lindsay carried the gun in his hand. He offered a beer to every passer-by: 'Ere, have a beer. It's free, it's cold but a little flat. Here ya go parking meter, have a beer.' It was a hoot, and everyone seemed to get the joke. Imagine doing that now; get to the slammer, you fool.

Too soon, though, the party was over, and it was time to head north to Townsville. Paul and Mick contacted me and inquired about a ride to Townsville. I was pleased to have company on the long trip, eighteen to twenty hours by road which, from all accounts, was pretty ordinary. The 240 km stretch from Rockhampton to Mackay was known as the "Crystal Highway" due to the number of broken windscreens along the way. Sounds like a fun drive, not!

I decided to have a low-key departure, only informing family and

Karen. I intended driving straight through, stopping only for fuel and a regular food break. My plan was to travel the inland route to Rockhampton: west to Dalby and Miles and north to Wandoan, Theodore, and Biloela, and join the Bruce Highway at Rocky. An estimated eight-hour drive. However, my passengers disagreed and wanted to go via the coast road through Brisbane and north on the Bruce Highway. I eventually agreed by telling them they were paying for the fuel and that the coast drive would cost more. They both agreed, so via Brissy it was to be. We would leave early morning, one day from now.

My new car was about five years old, so I did not anticipate any dramas or mechanical failures. Dad had insisted on good tyres in the purchase deal, so all was go for a fun trip over new territory. Down the "Range", a single lane (in 1968) steep and twisty road. I and many, many others had raced each other in our Mini Minors, etcetera down this road. Today I was coasting in gear, occasionally touching the brakes and concentrating on the foggy road. Suddenly out of the bushes appeared a uniformed police officer.

'Sir,' he said, which Mick immediately corrected.

'He's a Private, mate. Can you see any shit on his shoulders, apart from his head?'

Ignoring the smart-arse comment amid our laughter the copper said, 'The speed limit here is sixty. Our radar clocked you at seventy.'

Big deal. If I concentrated on the speedo instead of the road, would that be safer in these conditions? I didn't ask, but I should have.

'Here's a ticket and three demerit points on your licence. Have a nice day.' In that era, a driver was given nine points and, if nine or more were lost, had to "show cause" why the licence should not be suspended.

Before long, this drama faded and our trip continued with music and humour to the max. We all had a store of jokes in our heads, especially about the traffic police. Brisbane traffic was not heavy, but the drivers did not have any consideration for visitors. Still the same fifty years on. After a few wrong turns and unknown one-way streets, Brisbane was behind us, and we headed towards and past the Sunshine Coast. Nooo! Not past the coast, but through it from Caloundra to Noosa. I was outvoted by my two insistent passengers. Finally, I agreed, but said there would be no stops, just a look around. This was a major hold-up, which added heaps of time to our trip. 'Next time you arseholes will be signing a contract,' I said.

Somewhere outside Maryborough, where we would stop for fuel and eats, the Valiant was coasting down a long sloping road, my foot was off the go pedal. Suddenly a copper ran out of the bushes waving his arms like a clown. He reckoned I ran their radar off the scale. Enough of the compliments, just give me the ticket. At the servo in Maryborough, the attendant filling up the car told us the police always had their radar either south or north of the town so we should be safe from further police problems. 'Yeah, thanks mate, see you round,' and off we trundled.

The scenery just outside Maryborough was all new to Mick and Paul. Sugar cane fields right up to the road and acres of pineapples on the hillsides. I was familiar with the area having holidayed with the family at Hervey Bay from 1960 to 1963. The road ahead was like a tunnel through cane fields with an occasional area of bush that travellers were able to use as a rest stop. I was cognisant of my speed, but this car, with an automatic transmission, did not seem to slow down on a downhill run with the no-go pedal. It was the "perfect storm": a downhill run, a patch of bush, and out came another cop waving his arms like a clown.

'Fuck me,' said Paul, 'do these bloody coppers live in the bush?'

Unbelievable— three, fucking three, speeding fines in a day, in ten hours, and we still had a long way to go. While the nice policeman was booking me, Mick wound down the window and said in an educated voice, 'Officer, do you live in the bush?'

The officer must have heard Mick, but he just said, 'On your way guys, thanks for stopping by!'

The servo guy got a mention or two. Mick reckoned he was an off-duty cop.

Thankfully, that was the end of speeding fines, for this trip anyway, and despite the shithouse roads further north, we arrived in Townsville at a time I do not recall, but the pubs were open. 'Look there's a pub selling Cairns Draught beer. S'posed to be bloody good shit'; we all agreed. After three pots we decided it was time to report in at Lavarack. The way to the barracks was well signed; there would be no problem finding our way there. As I reversed out of the parking area, a taxi ran into my car. The little Italian cabbie leaped out and said a million times, 'So sorry, my fault.' There was no damage to my car, but the taxi looked like it had had many altercations with other objects.

10. LAVARACK BARRACKS

AT 6TH BATTALION, ROYAL AUSTRALIAN REGIMENT (6RAR)

This was a daunting experience. The first-time reporting to our posting in the Australian Army. My mind was in turmoil as I drove. I still have eighteen or so months of this commitment to go, this next bit will make it or break it, I thought. The main entrance was signed to guide us to 6RAR reporting. This is it fellas, probably locked in for whatever time takes their fancy.

An armed soldier directed us to a building nearby. 'Park there and report to Captain X who will direct you to your quarters. Welcome to 6RAR.' Captain X was a true gentleman. He requested our transfer papers and then gave each of us directions to our new digs. I was in Delta Company, situated on the front row of the buildings. When we were all processed, the Captain said, 'Okay men, see you on Monday parade 0800. Civvies only outside the base.'

As we drove up the road to the barracks everyone was silent, until Mick said, 'Well I'll beef hooked, what a turnaround.'

'For the better, hey guys,' said Paul.

We all agreed that life in a battalion might just be bearable. There was just one problem. It was so fucking hot, and the humidity combined with the heat made life very uncomfortable. Having lived in Toowoomba for twenty years where the temperatures and humidity were sensible, physical exercise in Army greens here in the tropics would be shithouse, to say the least. It teemed with rain every day at the same time as if someone turned on a tap. Nobody worried, they just got wet and carried on regardless. Besides, in no time you were dry and once again sweating like a piggy.

The accommodation was brand-new. Lavarack was set up as a task-force-sized base, comprising three infantry battalions with all the other supporting services: artillery, armour, transport, medical, etcetera, etcetera. It was a huge organisation. The 6th Battalion was in a rebuilding stage after returning from a twelve-month tour of South Vietnam in 1966. Delta Company of the 6th, of which I was now a member, had earned high praise for winning the now famous Battle of Long Tan, fought in a rubber plantation in torrential rain not far from the Australian base, Nui Dat. It was close enough that the music and singing of Little Pattie could be heard. The Company was awarded the US Presidential Unit Citation for bravery. I proudly wore the award affectionately known as "The Swimming Pool", due to the rectangular shape and the bright blue colour. A significant battalion parade was held for the presentation by the US Ambassador to Australia. I will speak more of this later. Do not miss that enthralling episode!

The 6th Battalion base seemed deserted. Our group of the tenth intake of National Service, circa one hundred, was the basis for rebuilding the battalion. Our members were sprinkled throughout the four companies Alpha (A), Bravo (B), Charlie (C), and Delta (D) which had little impact on the almost deserted scene. Mick and Paul were sent to other companies, so I was to have little contact with them after this weekend. This meant meeting new and interesting friends.

I did not realise it then but the next few months working and playing in the battalion environment would be the basis for the formation of lifelong friendships. The armed forces speak of mateship as being a special bond among its members. Whether this emotional attachment between men and women of the forces (only men in my era) is peculiar to the armed forces is perhaps debatable. Sporting teams develop a certain attachment that looks towards a team's success, but do they form a connection with others that still exists in the same intensity as fifty years ago? Yes, perhaps one or two of the team may for special reasons, but not the full team. I believe the Army does form such a unique bond among its members. The difference from other groups is formed in the situations encountered, both in training and in combat. In every situation, the support of a mate "watching your back" is why the Australian Army is so very successful in all its attempts. The success is based on mateship and discipline.

*

Fast forward to 2017 when a reunion of the tenth National Service call-up was arranged to celebrate fifty years. The attendance was simply amazing as was the recognition and renewal of now old friendships. To see someone fifty years down the track and feel as if you have never been apart is just so special. Laughter, fun and tears filled the caravan park in Sawtell, New South Wales, for a full week. Recollection of good and bad times often shocked the wives and partners.

Several years earlier in 2005, at a similar reunion, my first, I met up with my other sigs[7] of D Company: Frank, Trevor, and Geoff: call signs Forty-one, Forty-two and Forty-three respectively. My call sign was simply Four. We were a very close-knit little bunch, having trained together in radio operation, voice procedure (never say "repeat" unless you are talking to artillery), VHF and HF radio communication, as well as Morse Code. I will tell a story of the Morse Code training exercise if you stick around a while.

When a company of infantry is widespread across the area, the only communication is by radio. Sometimes in Code, if location position is involved. It is the sig's job to encode and decode messages,

---

7   For the un-initiated, a "sig" is a signalman, radio operator within an Infantry unit. Each platoon (four) of a Company has one sig who reports to a sig in Company HQ. Sigs are responsible for all communication within the unit whilst the Company is involved in operational duty. Always travelling in close proximity of the Officer Commanding, the sig is a vital part of the unit and integral to success in a war environment.

often on the move and a very difficult task. Carrying this bloody radio on the back was difficult enough without recording and decoding a message on your field message notebook while staggering through jungle or avoiding being snared by thorny bamboo bushes. These radio sets were not light, in fact, they were fucking heavy bastards.

Plus, we carried a spare battery the size and weight of a house brick. It was fitted with a one metre aerial, but in poor communication areas, a six-metre aerial was fitted. This was usually in the jungle where the fucking aerial would catch onto every vine, branch or twig and attempt to pull your arms off. My backpack during operations in Vietnam was so heavy, that if I landed on my back, I was stranded like a turtle until I could roll over and struggle to my feet. In addition to the radio, rations and personal camp stuff, I was loaded with one hundred and twenty rounds of ammunition for my M16 rifle, four water bottles, a couple of grenades, compass and maps and two spare legs [8].

Did I mention the pick-and-shovel combo used to dig a hole to keep one safe at night? It was strapped to the back of the pack. A necessary bit of kit but a real pain in the arse.

When four men suffer the same shit every day, day after day, an appreciation of each other's position develops into a strong, unbreakable bond. Such was the case with myself, Frank, Trevor and Geoff. When one is gone, it is devastating. Such was the case when we lost Trevor, call sign "Forty-two". Trev travelled around Australia, mostly on his own, in a small camper van. In 2009, he was found dead in the back of his van beside the road somewhere in southern Victoria. A bit more about Trevor.

Trevor's home base was the Gold Coast, specifically Surfers Paradise or, as we always referred to it in Trev's presence, "Slurpers Parasite". Trevor loved a drink, as we all did or do, especially his

---

[8] This, of course, is a joke. There were no "spare legs". Such poor humour was part of the language used to lighten the moment. The rest is real and is what I carried on my belt around my waist whenever on an operation. There was nothing light about that load!

favourite: port. He had gained the knowledge on making port and arrived at the 2005 reunion with a twenty-litre bottle with a tap on the bottom. As a port (or as we must now call it, a "tawny") lover, Trev's brew I thought was pretty good stuff.

L-R: Trevor Harrison, Geoff Dartnell, Frank Douglas and myself at the 2005 reunion of D Company 6RAR Sigs, Vietnam 1969

Many of our tenth intake survivors attended Trevor's funeral service in Surfers Paradise. The local RSL hosted drinks, food and tears at the club in the middle of the city. I had been a member of the Toowoomba RSL Sub-Branch Management Committee for some time and had formed a group of veterans who made up a "funeral team". This team conducted the traditional "Poppy" service— a moving, very respectful occasion to honour a passed comrade— at any Defence Force funeral when requested. I had the honour of conducting a Poppy service at Trevor's funeral. Not having my regular team to assist, I asked Frank to hand out the poppies to be laid on the coffin, and to assist me in removing and folding the Australian flag from the coffin. Frank willingly accepted the tasks and spent the rest of the service in tears. Frank was not alone. The RSL tribute service was very emotional and many, if not all, were in tears.

Trevor Harrison's funeral service in Surfers Paradise, February 2009

At the later celebration of Trevor's life, the remaining sigs from D Company got together to remember our time as a team. Frank, the ever-joking Frank, reminded us of the "rap over the knuckles" I received for incorrect voice procedure on one too many occasions. It was general practice to conduct a radio check at stand to at dawn and sunset. It was my responsibility to conduct the check. In operational status in Vietnam, the procedure went like this, or it was meant to go like this:

'Forty-one, this is Four radio check.'

'Forty-one receiving, out.'

'Forty-two, this is Four radio check.'

'Forty-two receiving, out.' And so on for all operators in our net.

My friend and Five Hundred (card game) partner, Frank Douglas, and myself celebrating Trevor Harrison's life at Surfers Paradise RSL, on ironically, our joint birthday in 2009

The ever-joking Frank, as Forty-one, organised a different response from all operators including the support section as call sign "Forty-four".

'Forty-one, this is Four radio check.' What came back was funny and happened intermittently on too many occasions, resulting in a stern rebuke by the Battalion.

'Forty-one, oh what a beautiful morning.'

'Forty-two, oh what a beautiful day.'

'Forty-three, I have a wonderful feeling.'

'Forty-four, everything's going our way.'

'Out. This is Four, you idiots. Radio check complete, out.'

The response from Battalion direct to the OC of D Company via my radio was relayed to me by Major "Jock" in a pleasant manner, as was Jock's manner always. 'Pete,' he said, 'it seems something rather amusing occurred on our radio communication with the platoons. The Colonel was amused, said "the singing needs work, and if he hears it again, he will conduct singing lessons back in Nui Dat."' I sent a coded message telling the guys to cease and desist immediately at the Colonel's request.

The Battalion CO was aware the sigs involved were tenth intake National Service men. He had respect for the attitude and commitment of this group of his men. They had been the core of his training battalion as it had tackled challenges of Canungra, Mt Spec (near Innisfail), High Range and Shoalwater Bay (near Rockhampton). The 6th excelled in all these training areas. It was considered the best battalion to complete the Canungra Jungle Training Centre series of challenges which was somewhat of a benchmark gauge of performance.

In addition, the CO was a rugby (Union, of course) supporter and encouraged a rugby team to join the Townsville competition. The majority of the winning teams of 1968 were tenth intake men. A few of our radio crew were in that team, and the CO knew who they were. We wondered later what the singing lessons would entail, but thankfully the guys behaved themselves, so we never found out what the boss intended.

Apart from the tenth intake blokes, I made a very special friendship with a reg (regular three-year soldier) who was also known as "Jock".

*

ROBERT ("JOCK") BUCHAN: MY FRIEND ALWAYS!

About a week after I settled into the D Company 6RAR barracks in Townsville, my life was destined to be changed forever. On a bright and sunny Monday morning, I woke at six, sat up and looked across the room. *Fucking hell,* I remember saying to myself, or maybe it was out loud. No matter, it reflects what I saw. Last night over "there" was a neat and tidy space, nicely made bed and nothing out of place. The other two residents and I had prepared for an inspection early on this Monday morning.

The "over there" space was a disaster. Clothes, gear, boots, shoes, bags, whatever were strewn across the room. On the bed lay this hairy-backed, hairy-headed "thing" on its stomach and snoring and twitching with every breath. It was big and looked pretty tough.

I got out of bed and did whatever I needed to do to prepare for the inspection. You readers don't need to know those details of when I shave, shit or shampoo. On return "it" was still there snoring and twitching. After organising my own bed, dressing, and preparing for inspection I started to clean up a bit around "its" bed. All I was doing was picking up stuff, folding it and making some semblance of order.

Suddenly it said, 'Hey, cunt, what the fuck are ya doing with my stuff?'

The thing was awake and looking menacingly at me. I can't write broad genuine Scottish speak, but that was what it was. I said, 'Mate, I am just trying to help you and me and the others in this room. We have a room inspection coming up and we will all suffer.'

'Ya just fuck off. Let me sleep,' he said.

'I will fuck off, but breakfast is in five minutes and the inspection in sixty. So, I will fuck off to have breakfast, if you miss out too bad. As I said, there is a room inspection at 0800, so I suggest you get tidied up before then for all our sakes. See ya in thirty, mate.'

When I got back from breakfast, "it" was up and dressed in rather rumpled greens, something I would become accustomed to as did the NCOs, etcetera. This was Jock. He was a tough, strong, practical soldier who did not give a shit about the spit-and-polish routine. I came to assist him in as many ways as I could. I often ironed his greens when there was a special parade or straightened his bed to pass inspections.

'Sorry about earlier. Thanks for your concern. I hope we will be mates.'

And we were. From that moment on Jock and I were together in most everything we did. One day Jock said, 'Pete, I want to say something to you that is important to me.' Jock was not one for too many words, more often just a grunt (with a smile of sorts). One had to know him to understand him. I understood him and I grew over time to love him and enjoy his company. Jock is ironically evoked in the title of this book once I began writing about our friendship. Spit, polish and discipline was what it was all about. Jock did not "fit the bill" in spit and polish, but was a good, disciplined soldier in the combat field.

'Pete,' Jock said in own inimitable Scottish accent, 'yoo n I have been good mates noo for a few months. I want our relationship to continue after all this fookin' war crap is over and we agree to get-together back in Aussie land.'

'My fur coat we will, mate, by hook or by crook!' I replied.

'Yoo fookin Aussies, you are all full of shit.'

That was our pledge and we exchanged our Aussie home contact details. I was later transferred to Company HQ at Lavarack but remained in my same digs. This meant I saw less of Jock during training exercises. But we played up like crazy when we had time off.

11. LIFE IN THE TROPICS: PARTYING

It was a short boat trip from Lang's Wharf to Magnetic Island where soldiers from Lavarack often went to relax, and drinking on board was tolerated. We had quite a few trips to "Mags", but it wasn't until my last weekend leave visit there in early 1969 that I set a record. Put a group of stupid male soldiers together and there will be some absurd challenge or competition devised. On a visit to Mags the challenge was to drink as many seven-ounce beers without going to the toilet, relieving oneself, pointing Percy at the porcelain, or having a piss! I had a couple of pots (ten-ounce beers) on the boat but the ten or so piss-heads with me convinced me to take on this challenge.

It was recorded at the bar by an independent, not-so-pissed person. It was, it seemed in those days, that anyone on Mags was pissed. My apologies to the locals. Anyway, to cut a long afternoon short, I set a new benchmark of twenty-seven— yeah twenty-seven— seven-ounce beers. Number twenty-seven was consumed while hurriedly heading for the pisserie, very quickly! I was a legend (in my own dream time).

Life in the barracks was damn good. We were all the same ilk (i.e., National Service tenth intake) mixed in with a few regular soldiers. All the NCOs and officers were regs, but they respected the soldier for what he was, a member of a team. I never saw or experienced any animosity towards us by regular soldiers. In fact, it was quite the opposite. Our acceptance into the ranks without difficulty was often commented on by the CO, Lieutenant Colonel Butler (Butler 2021). On more than a few occasions I was told by sergeants and corporals how they felt about having a group of fit, intelligent, young men of the same age to train. They were of the belief that the standard of a fully trained soldier had risen.

The accommodation, although basic, was new and served its purpose well. Other facilities provided were excellent. Jock and I spent many hours in the "Other Ranks Club" (ranks below sergeant) drinking gallons of Cairn's Draught, a bloody good drop and the choice of most beer drinkers. We must have thrown thousands of darts. I had played A Grade competition darts for the White Horse and the Post Office Hotel teams. Jock was a purely social player. In the beginning, I beat the shit out of him on many occasions. Jock being a competitive bastard with British darts heritage began to come good at the game. Eventually, he was hard to beat, but when we were challenged by other teams, Jock was amazing. His back-room commentary, while the opposition player was trying to concentrate, was something to behold. His Scottish drawl, prevalent after a few beers, and his quick wit caused havoc with the opposition. Jock would simply say, 'I wasn't talkin' to you, mate,' if they complained. There was never anything more than a round of beers at stake, about a buck or less, so no one ever got upset.

The "Club" served hot takeaway food all day and its retail shop sold everything a soldier needed for personal use and Army requirements. It had a tempting display of electrical goodies. No, not digital shit, real "plug it in" stuff, like radios, reel-to-reel tape recorders, gramophones— okay, record players, the vinyl seventy-eight, forty-five and thirty-three-speed type. We could buy anything on what is now called lay-by, but it had to be paid for before leaving the base.

The café provided a menu of good takeaway-type food. I would often partake of a couple of big six-inch sausage rolls and a litre of Coke for morning smoko when the Company was doing on-the-base training stuff. This, combined with three regular meals in the mess, raised my weight to an all-time high. All my life I had been ten to eleven stone (64-70 kg). The physical exercise involved in training, and the demand for food to fuel it, raised my weight to thirteen-and-a-half stone (85.7 kg) on departure to Vietnam. I would return at about nine-and-a-half stone (60.3 kg). More of that later. The three meals a day in the mess hall were of a high standard. Good wholesome food designed for a highly active, physical group of young men. The cooks were generous with their portions as we filed past each day. They were a "dry" bunch of guys, thoroughly versed in the usual smart-arse comments about their food. 'Yeah, cookie, pour some scrambled eggs on, some burned bacon, and some of that ??? stuff.' They gave back as much as they copped, all in good humour. The sergeant cookie was different, he was the "chef"— fat, loud and obnoxious. He didn't like the banter, poor, sad man. When on kitchen duty one was advised to be respectful to his "highness" or suffer days of cleaning the discarded burned pots, pans, etcetera.

One weekend Jock and I went offshore fishing (in a boat) and we each bought home a largeish Red Emperor, a prized eating fish. Jock said, 'Pete, what the fuck are you going to do with these fish things?'

'Jock, my son, I have a plan. Come with me and bring those things with you.'

It was late afternoon on a Sunday and the cookies would be preparing dinner in the kitchen. Sunday was an easy day for them, and their mood was always good. A cook I grew to know, a corporal, was usually on duty on Sunday and, as it happened, he was.

'Corporal Ben, my friend Jock, of Scottish origin, thinks our Queensland seafood is shithouse. We have two fine Reds caught today. To prove this Scottish bastard wrong, could you, would you cook them for our breakfast tomorrow?'

'As it happens, I am on duty in the morning. No promises, but I'll see what I can do.'

'On ya, Ben,' said Jock.

Jock was late getting out of bed the next morning. It required the usual, 'Get up you hairy, dopey Scottish bastard!' bellowed into his ear. To which he would come up fighting. One needed to stand back a safe distance until the red haze settled.

'What the fook! (the usual first words of Jock's day). 'Oh, you again mate. What da ya want wit mee?'

'We have fish waiting,' I said.

'I'm sleeping, not fishing, so fook orf.'

'At the mess, fool.'

He looked at me like he didn't have a clue what I was talking about. Usually, I was saying, 'Parade in thirty minutes,' every morning. 'We have fish waiting,' didn't compute.

'Do you remember yesterday?' I asked.

'Of course, I remember yesterday. We went on a boat and got pissed, we must do that again, mate.' Jock did get pretty pissed, as per usual, on the boat. But he was a "good" drunk, full of fun and laughter.

'You caught something, remember?'

Perplexed, Jock replied in all sincerity, 'Not VD again?'

'No, dickhead, fish. We caught fish. Ben at the mess is cooking them for our brekkie, so get your arse out of bed.'

Eventually, we turned up at the mess. Ben spotted us, gave us two large oval plates and said, 'Back in a flash!' Ben dumped a whole fish on each plate (cleaned of course) and said, 'Eat that if you can.' The bloody things were huge, one eye staring up at me, and covered the plate.

'Fookin hell, would ya loook at that! Come on, Pete, let's eat the buggers.'

Fifty-six years later I remember the experience, the taste, the reaction of the other blokes as I ate with glee. Jock didn't come up for breath until he finished the first side. He just belched, smiled broadly and went on eating. Corporal Ben, bless him, had cooked the Reds in a steam oven. Thanks, mate, if you read this book you might see how our appreciation on the day fell so short. Jock ate the whole fucking thing without a word. I left most of the second side to be consumed by several eager onlookers. Yes! Jock changed his mind on Queensland seafood.

Food is a large part of a soldier's wellbeing. The Aussie Army cooking staff are well-trained on what is required in a concentrated training environment like the tropical north of Australia. They provided an excellent diet to hundreds of hungry men three times a day. Sometimes under a barrage of tongue-in-cheek complaints about their ability as "tucker fuckers". Their efforts in organisation and logistics in providing substantial hot meals to troops in the field when on training exercises in places like Shoalwater Bay and the High Range were so much appreciated by infantry soldiers. Meeting their mobile kitchens at the end of a long hard day dragging oneself through the bush was like heaven sent.

As I said earlier when I went to Vietnam, extremely fit and healthy, after months of training, exercises, and physical tests I was thirteen-and-a-half stone (85.7 kgs). The Army machine had turned a disparate group of men into a disciplined and very capable fighting force. How did they do that in less than a year?

12. TRAINING AN ARMY BATTALION

My experience says to me there are three key requirements or elements needed to produce a reliable soldier, particularly an infantry soldier. These elements are endurance, capability and discipline.

As one of my readers, you will recall me bleeping on about what shitheads the corporals were during recruit training. It makes sense now why they acted like arseholes. They knew the three elements required. They set out to instil these as quickly as possible. Their task was to take nineteen-and-twenty-year-old civilians with attitudes that did not encompass endurance, capability and discipline, at least not all three, and change them. I saw a video once, *You're in the Army Now*, which proposed the possibility a person could suffer Post-Traumatic Stress Disorder (PTSD) as a result of intense training and intense discipline. I am not sure if the Army were aware of this impact, most probably not, as PTSD was to be recognised much later as an injury to soldiers who served in war zones. Include me in that recognition.

How did the Australian Army prepare us for a war in a country with a variety of terrain, vegetation and climate? The Australian Army boffins realised the necessity of exposing the troops to conditions expected in South Vietnam, or at least close to those conditions. The selection of Townsville in Far North Queensland as the training venue fitted the bill in many ways. Townsville itself was hot and humid much of the time and often experienced regular heavy rain downpours that passed quickly to be replaced by hot and humid torture. It was not unusual to see a vapour rising from rain-soaked clothing when the sun came out again.

12. Training an Army battalion

Within a reasonable distance from Lavarack Barracks (the Townsville Task Force base), the Army had access to several training areas, each of which provided conditions similar to those required. Mount Spec, near Innisfail north of Townsville, was a rugged jungle with heavy undergrowth and a thick canopy. Mt Spec was very much like the jungle of Vietnam.

The High Range Training Facility northwest of Townsville, an open tree-covered area, was used for tactical movement training by various groups: sections, platoons and full companies. Included was the development of cooperation with the Armoured Corps which included the use of APCs. A significant amount of weapons training with live ammunition was conducted at High Range. Later, I will tell a story of building a "sandbag bunker" we used for hand grenade (pineapple) throwing practice. Shoalwater Bay near Gladstone, about 600 km south of Townsville, is a major training area. It was used to assess the capabilities and capacity of a battalion as a complete unit. Each and every component of the battalion was tested and assessed from the basic unit, an infantry section of ten men up to BHQ. The 6th Battalion RAR excelled.

Before leaving for overseas service, every Australian Army unit was subjected to the rigours of the Canungra Jungle Training Centre. Feared by most because of the tough conditions and difficult individual tasks, we arrived in late 1968 in anticipation of a difficult couple of weeks. The staff were spit-polished arseholes full of shit and bravado, loud and obnoxious. For the 6th, Canungra was a cakewalk. Some of us so enjoyed the terrifying leap off the high tower into crappy water, we asked if another go was possible.

'No, you f'ing wanker, get goin' or I'll have ya!'

'Yes, sa!' Sergeant, you dick-wit!

We had to crawl under barbed wire (400 mm off the ground) while a Thompson machine gun fired live ammo above. The Thompson machine gun was used as it fired in a direct pattern, whereas the M60, you will recall, fired in a cone-shaped pattern. Safety first training, eh wot! Daytime and night ambushes were set in the jungle by each platoon. The enemy soldiers were the training staff, who failed on every occasion to detect the ambush site.

Our battalion left Canungra Jungle Training Centre after two weeks with the reputation as the best-ever performing battalion to visit the centre. The reason of course was the training we had undertaken in much more formidable conditions than the trampled-down jungle presented at Canungra. There was even an occasion when six or so left the "secure" establishment for a night with friends in Brisbane, totally unknown to the expert trainers.

Our CO received a report on his battalion's performance at Canungra which finished with the comment, 'The 6th was the best-ever unit to complete the (Jungle Training Centre) course.' At the parade, called on return to Townsville, the CO thanked the men for their commitment to the heavy training regime that contributed to this excellent result. He made mention of the National Service men within the unit, 'These young men are now indistinct among the regular soldiers. Their commitment is appreciated by all concerned.'

Apart from the diverse training we undertook, there was another difference in how training was conducted that contributed to the battalion's success. Our instructors, the officers and NCOs, were part of the exercise and "copped as much of the shit" as we did. For the most part, respect for these men grew as a trusting relationship developed in both directions. Corporal, sergeant and sir references faded as time went by, replaced with a less formal manner of order and reply. In other words, this is when the, "I've got your back, mate," mentality of the armed forces is born. The DISCIPLINE component of preparation has been achieved.

Capability is very much a personal task. Like a civilian professional, one learns, practises and performs. Sports people, doctors, dentists, builders, on and on, achieve efficiency in their own fields. The Army unit is the same. Recognise a certain ability in a man and build on that ability with training and exposure to the tasks involved. A person doing what they enjoy will learn quickly.

However, each and every member of a fighting infantry unit must be fully aware of the weapons involved and be capable of operating each and every item, when and where necessary. Training on each weapon was undertaken by everyone and from the results, such as speed in stripping and rebuilding an M60 machine gun, specialists were selected. This was followed up with specialist training in that aspect of weaponry.

As for me, I was left with the task of becoming a rifleman carrying the 7.62 mm SLR rifle. It was a clever devil, very accurate over long distances (six hundred metres) and it packed a mighty punch. It used the same ammo as the M60 machine gun. Very clever, hey wot! Not as clever as the enemy i.e., the North Vietnamese Army though. They used a Russian-made rifle: the Kalashnikov AK-47. This rifle was similar to our SLR, but with one important difference. The calibre of the AK-47 was slightly larger than the SLR which meant the AK-47 could use our SLR ammo, but we could not use their AK-47 stuff. Clever little buggers.

To become a rifleman, one was required to take an accuracy test on the firing range over fifty, one hundred, three hundred and six hundred metres. Failure of this test could end any hope of an infantry frontline position. Now, as you may recall, I ended up in hospital after trying to qualify on a twenty-five-metre rifle range in recruit training. Trying to qualify up to six hundred metres seemed a daunting task.

The fifty-metre shoot was standing, one hundred metres kneeling and three hundred and six hundred metres lying prone with sandbag support. One advantage was my SLR was brand spanking new. This time, unlike the trauma of Singleton recruit training, I would have a fair chance of qualifying. And I did, easily. Not only did I qualify, I topped the score for the platoon on the six hundred metre range. These days I can just make out a Mack truck at six hundred metres.

The platoon commander, Lieutenant V ("Stumpy") said, 'That's a turn-up, Collins. You will have my back in 'Nam.'

'That, sir, will be my target,' I said.

'Carry on, private,' he said with a smirk.

So, there I was, a fully qualified infantry rifleman; "fuckin' big whoop" you might say. As the lieutenant walked away, he was pointing at his back. I laughed out loud until the tears ran down my leg.

HIGH RANGE TRAINING: THE BUNKER!

Late in April 1968 a small contingent of Delta Company was sent to the High Range training area with the task of building a sandbag bunker to be used for live grenade-throwing practice by the battalion. It would also be used for practice and firing of the M79 grenade launcher. This very light weapon fired a forty by forty-six-millimetre grenade (shell). It could be an accurate and effective close-range weapon in practised hands.

The bunker was to be three-sided; three metres long with two-metre sides and approximately one and half metres tall. I was part of the group along with the Company driver, Bernie, with his Land Rover and trailer, one of the platoon machine gunners, Roger (may he rest in peace), who was a professional woodchopping champion from Texas, Queensland and two others whose names I don't recall at the moment.

It was a huge task. A suitable location had to be found that provided a plentiful supply of sand and also be suitable for a company-size campsite. The bunker should have clear flat ground out the front. Bernie's family ran a large Santa Gertrudis cattle property in central Queensland, so he chose our sand site nearby to the chosen bunker site. Bernie's experience was to prove valuable in the following days.

After setting up our own hutchies, etcetera, and preparing a cooking fire we made a brew (coffee) and laid out our attack plan.

We would fill sandbags (they needed to be large and consistent in size), load them into the trailer and dump them at the prepared bunker site. Pretty simple, two filling bags and two laying them. Soon we realised how slow filling the bags with sand was. Bernie, the bushman, unhooked the trailer from his Land Rover. 'Carry on chaps, I'll be back,' and off went Bernie in a cloud of dust. The rest of us carried on slowly filling sandbags.

About an hour later the Land Rover appeared in the distance. Roger said, 'Bernie must have had a cattle sale to go to nearby.'

'Yeah!' we said in unison. 'Would not surprise.'

'Ah! So sorry, Bernie,' we all said when he stopped, and we saw what he had. For sure he had a cold carton of XXXX, but also two plastic buckets. In his bushie wisdom, he recalled filling bags at home. It is common knowledge that it takes two people to fill a sandbag, one to hold it open, the other to spoon in the sand. Not with Bernie's idea. Cut the bum out of the bucket, insert it into the bag, fill the bucket, lift the bucket and bag and do the same again. It is fuckin' brilliant. Works like a dream.

With the bag filling sped up, our plan started to work, and the bunker began to take shape. A long way to go though and there was a big gum tree directly in front, thirty metres out. It had to go somehow.

We are five soldiers, we are all armed with SLR rifles, and the Armoury has supplied a full box of ammunition, enough to win a war. Roger the woodchopping boffin didn't bring his axe. Otherwise, as Roger said, 'It would be gone in a few flashes of my trusty blade.'

Someone said, 'Let's shoot the bastard,' and so we did. The bastard was about eight inches (20 cm) across. A target was placed a metre up and all five of us emptied a twenty-round magazine into the bastard. It just stood there looking at us. Fall down, ya bastard. Maybe all one hundred rounds did not find the target. We decided to shoot the bastard at sunrise, midday and sunset each day until it fell over.

Filling sandbags is a very dusty, dirty pastime. The only water we had was in jerry cans to be used for cooking, drinking, etcetera. We all needed a bath badly. Bernie suggested we do a "recce" (reconnaissance) of the area. There must be a creek or dam we could use. So off we went one morning, fully armed, trailer in tow, in search of water. The herds of brumbies were a lot of fun as they charged away from rifle fire, not aimed at them but in the air. Bernie showed his driving skills as we followed behind on foot.

Up on the rocky outcrops were wild goats, standing looking at us as if to say, 'Fuck off.' Five SLRs opened up; the goats just stood there. 'No wonder the tree is still standing— you blokes can't hit a thing.' We did hit one goat but that was from a ricochet. Good shooting, guys!

Eventually, our bushie driver found a dam with plenty of water. 'Follow the green line, below the hills— all that sort of thing,' said Bernie. The dam had gently sloping banks. Being people who expect convenience we decided, in a fit of wisdom, to reverse the trailer into the dam, fill it with water and use it as a bathtub. And it worked a treat. As we headed back to camp, Roger and I continued our luxurious bath.

On ya, Bernie!!!!

A bright spark among us said, 'Now that we are all sparkling clean, let's go to the pub for a counter tea.' Up jumped the troopers, one, two, three. My "fur coat" (rude word), come on we are going to the local boozer. It wasn't very far, a couple of miles down the highway. I have no recollection of the pub's name, but I recall the welcome perfectly

On arrival, we were cheered by the local "bar flies" like we were heroes. They shouted us beer after beer, we hardly spent a cent. The fact all of us were Nashos improved our standing even further. They asked a million questions about how we felt about our call-up. Many were surprised to hear our answers. Answers like, 'At first it was hard to take in, and recruit training was a fucking bitch. The corporals

12. Training an Army battalion

Our innovative bush bathtub, High Range training area, April 1968

made it as tough as they could, but further down the track, you get to realise what that was all about.'

'And what was it all about?' asked the barmaid.

'In the end, it is all about discipline. The Army cannot exist without discipline! It means we all work together and protect each other without needing to think about how to react.'

When it came time to leave the locals broke into song: 'For they are jolly good ... ' as we left their pub with food and beer handed to us by the patrons and staff. There was silence on the trip home, each one lost in his own thoughts. At the campsite, Bernie said, 'That was a fucking fabulous night.' And it was!

The tree was still standing, obstinate bloody gum tree, it had to

*Bernie and I washing off the sandbag dust,
High Range training area, April 1968*

go soon, even if the Land Rover was to push the bugger over. The bunker— Roger named it "Sandy Castle"— was looking great. Nice and square and consistent. It was about three-quarters done.

We had another go at the tree, all firing twenty rounds in quick time, all at once. Roger said, 'You lot are bloody poor shots, I suspect. I bet half the bullets are missing.' I looked at my rifle and could see I had one round left. I had loaded a twenty-round mag with one up the spout, hence twenty-one shots available.

'Hang on, guys, I have one left.' I took aim and fired my one shot. Nothing.

'Missed it,' said Roger.

12. Training an Army battalion

A couple of seconds later that bloody tree gave in, and gently fell over. 'May it rest in pieces and provide many travellers with firewood,' pronounced Roger. Ah! Roger, you big sook. 'I could have felled that tree in fifteen seconds if I'd had my trusty axe,' said Roger.

Bernie unhitched the trailer and took off somewhere in the Land Rover. He filled as many bags as the rest of us, but always had something in mind. He was back before the trailer was full, proudly waving a young 'roo he had caught and killed.

'Dinner,' he said. Kangaroo stew with added vegetables from the pub.

Later on, he hung the body in a tree and bled it out. Before proceeding any further, he cut the hock open and was pleased with what he didn't see. 'That,' he said, 'is how you check for worms.' Skinning and dismembering took little time and it was soon in a pot on the fire to cook slowly. I can tell you, that was the first bush-cooked food I had ever eaten, and it was just bloody fantastic. On ya!

Two days later, in the early hours, the OC D Company arrived with the Company Sergeant Major (CSM). We were up and about, having shit, shaved and staggered to the sand pit. The major and the WO2 were impressed to see us at work, as we weren't told of their visit. A surprise visit, go figure!

After inspecting "Sandy Castle", the boss expressed his thanks (as only a senior officer can) and trundled off to Townsville. He made a couple of requests (read: orders) and said after that we could return to Townsville. When we did get back, we were given three days leave. Good stuff, boss man.

All five of the "Sandy Castle" operation thought that should have earned us some significant brownie points. If not, we had a bloody good time, and our three days leave was no different. Jock had been stuck at the base and was totally pissed off. He said, 'The only fuckun thing we have done for three weeks is parade drill and bloody marching. I could have marched home to bloody Scotland by now.' He stalked about the room for a bit.

The Sandy Castle bunker, High Range training area, April 1968

'And what pissy little job have you been doin'? Fuck all, I s'pose.'

'Filling sandbags, hundreds of the bastards, to build a sandbag bunker so you dickheads can learn to throw a grenade without killing the wrong people.'

'Yeah, I bet it is some fart-arse thing I could kick over.'

'Jock, me old ever-cranky Scottish friend, you are on, and soon you will get that chance.'

At the parade ground drill, all Jock was bitching about is the subject of my next chapter. To me, a thoroughly enjoyable period in the Army.

13. ON THE BATTALION PARADE GROUND

The 6th Battalion RAR was formed on 6 June 1965 at Enoggera in Brisbane. The battalion had toured Vietnam in 1966–1967 and was due to do a second tour beginning May 1969. It was now May 1968, and the battalion was to be presented with its inaugural Queen's and Regimental Colours, a significant event in a regiment's history.

This major ceremony requires a lot of parade work by every unit of the battalion. Under the instruction of the RSM, the senior NCO (non-commissioned officer), the troops and their officers would learn the parade procedure. The RSM was a detail, detail, detail, soldier who would settle for nothing less than perfect. Repeat after repeat was the order of the day, every day, which became too many every fuckin' day.

'Will this shit ever end?' Jock complained constantly. Jock was a great soldier, but not on the parade ground. I often said, 'Jock, you have two left feet.' Remember all drill orders are called on the left foot striking the ground. The order is executed on the following step.

Performed with precision there is not a better sight than 1200 soldiers aligned and moving in unison. The sound, the crunch of the boots on the specially prepared surface, amid the surrounding silence, is amazing.

This very special parade, never witnessed in Townsville before, would be attended by most of the Townsville residents, who had come to have a very healthy respect for the Army. There was an extensive list of invitees from the Army hierarchy and the political sphere, both state and federal. Each battalion member (digger) was allowed to invite three guests. The only person in my family in a position to attend was my dad. He was very excited about visiting me in the Army, as I was to also see him. The downside for him was he was about to take his first aeroplane flight. Probably not all that unusual in 1968 for a forty-eight-year-old to be doing so, but he was apprehensive, to say the least. He made it safely to Townsville a little shaken and stirred.

The Queen's and Regimental Colours would be presented to the battalion by His Excellency, General the Honourable Lord Casey, PC, GCMG, CH, DSO, MC, K St J, Governor-General of Australia.

The parade involved considerable rifle drill in the form of fixed bayonets, shoulder arms and present arms as well as the usual stand at ease and attention. Every movement had to be spot-on timing, even down to the second "click" as the bayonet was fixed. The click of hundreds of bayonets is an awesome sound. We marched at quick time and slow time, executed every drill in the RSM's book, quick march, halt, left turn, right turn and quick march.

Each unit of the battalion would slow march past the Colours, breaking automatically into quick march. The huge crowd was enthralled. Dad said he had never seen anything so precise and impressive. 'And you, my son, Private Peter T. Collins, never faltered,' he said with a tear in his eye.

The final act was a slow march past the Governor-General as he took the salute, each unit passing with eyes right, then quick marching off the hallowed ground (remember— the parade ground was originally a place where dead soldiers were brought back during a battle) and out of sight. We all fell down exhausted. What a day it was. The battalion was given ten days' leave after our excellent parade performance, compliments of the CO. 'What a nice bloke,' said Dad.

AN UNEXPECTED TRIP HOME

I decided to drive home with Dad to Toowoomba that afternoon. Dad was quite happy to avoid a second plane ride. It is a considerable distance, about eighteen hundred kilometres, to Toowoomba, a long haul of about eighteen hours nonstop, but I was keen to get home. As usual, Mick and Paul were with us. The trip was going well until the middle of the night when some arsehole in a passing car threw a small Coke bottle at us. The bottle hit the windscreen of my Valiant leaving an unmistakable shape. The windscreen glass shattered into a million fragments. After knocking all the glass out, our journey continued into the night.

'It's fuckin' freezing my arse off back here,' said Mick or Paul from the back seat. This was late May, almost winter, and any cold weather down south blew up the Bowen Basin of central Queensland. It was indeed fuckin' freezing.

We raided my travel bag and before long Dad was sitting beside me with my undies on his head and whatever else he could find wrapped around him. I had two pairs of socks on my hands. The freezing wind was coming in the big hole and returning for a second bite at our feet from under the seats. Efforts to block it were mostly unsuccessful and opening the rear windows brought a howl of protest from the back seat.

Our survival was helped by a few rays of sunlight from the east shortly before arriving at Nanango. An early opening servo, lights still blazing, came into view. It sold bacon and egg burgers and coffee. But the best bit was a large mirror outside reflecting sunlight. The three of us huddled in front of it eating our "B & Es" and enjoying the warmth.

While he was filling the car with fuel, the servo guy noticed the windscreen, or lack thereof, and without saying anything contacted a local business handling broken windscreens. What service! We left soon after with new glass and the heater on full bore. Sometimes good to have your dad tag along when his pockets are not too deep.[9] Look out Toowoomba, the Army is coming.

This was an unexpected visit home, so it was fun to walk into the pub, the White Horse of course, in my uniform, slouch hat and all. They didn't recognise me until I ordered a beer from Anne behind the bar, 'Well, fuck me! Look who it is. Welcome home, Pete, the beer is on Ron.'

The mates, playing darts as usual, heard Anne's shriek and took some notice. Then the "shit" set in. One by one they had their bit to say, all the time laughing and joking (at my expense) while slapping me on the back.

Ron, the owner, came in response to the noise. 'Hey, Pete, welcome home! I had better get more XXXX in today. Anne, Pete's beers are on the house, and a round for this mob of nice young blokes on the house. See you later, how long are you home, mate?'

'About a week Ron, will see you often no doubt!'

The following morning, I visited the ANZ branch to say a quick hello. The quick bit took two hours. I was even ushered into the manager's office. Graham, the boss, wanted to know what I had been doing. He was amazed at how much I had learned and made particular mention of how he was impressed by the mateship and discipline aspects of my training. 'How about a beer next door? Ted, come on,' he said, inviting the office manager to join us.

The rest of the week played out the same way. I did see Karen on the nights I wasn't legless or three sheets to the wind. My sisters made a fuss and made me many meals. They seemed to think I needed fattening up. I don't think they realised how fit and healthy I was.

Soon it was time to head back to Townsville, again with Mick and Paul tagging along. No arguments this time, we are going the back way which will meet the coast highway at Rockhampton, about six

---

9 An old saying about how someone with deep pockets never pays, as they can't reach their money. Dad was not a "deep pocket" man.

hundred and fifty kilometres north. It was a quiet, uneventful trip, thankfully both passengers slept most of the time. I was content concentrating on driving; long distances no longer worried me. If distance worried me, I would not have made it home for the whole two years I spent in the Army.

14. BACK TO TRAINING: SERIOUS STUFF & GOOD STUFF

FIRST THE GOOD STUFF!

As I have mentioned, at Lavarack I was trained in receiving and sending Morse Code. This old-world communication medium has the advantages of longer distance and being transmitted on HF as opposed to VHF; it suffers less interference. It is not easy to master, especially receiving.

Initial training took place in a classroom. First up was learning the code itself. Everyone knows SOS (save our souls, send help quickly), but could everyone recognise *** --- *** on a headset? There are twenty-six combinations of dots (*) and dashes (-), one for each letter of the alphabet. One needs to not only learn the whole Morse Code alphabet, but also recognise the sound instantly. Not such an easy task.

After a few weeks of listening to dit, dah, dit, dit dah fuckin' dit, I could hear the shit in my head constantly. Frank, who was a roommate, was also on the course. We confused our other two residents by communicating in Morse, by voice that is. Frank would send me a message by saying, out loud, 'dit, dit, dah, dah' or whatever. It confused everyone. Small minds are amused it seems.

Eventually, we headed out to the bush at High Range. Several two-man communication posts were established. The only means of contact with the command post at Lavarack was by Morse Code. Teams were tested by command, and we practised "talking" to the other outposts.

On day one the Company driver (ole mate Bernie) dropped us in a predesignated spot. Our radio, a week's rations and our usual gear were delivered. 'See you blokes in a week,' and off went Bernie in a shower of shit and stuff. The field exercise was to last for three weeks.

'Fuck me,' said Frank, 'we have to live here for twenty-one eff'ing days? Give me a break.'

Guess what? We had a ball! Our camp was on the side of a grassy hill, lots of trees and a pleasant outlook. Frank found two smallish trees a suitable distance apart and erected his hutchie. My hutchie extended from one of Frank's trees to form a nice V. After securing personal stuff and with bedding prepared, we moved on to set up the radio. The HF 510 radio requires an extensive T-shaped aerial to send and receive transmissions. Erecting this thing was the next task. It has to be high, straight, taut, and, from our briefing, face north.

'So, where's north, Pete?' Got me wet Frank! But I can work it out methinks.

'I was told by a wily old sergeant how to do it. In the afternoon, point the twelve on your watch at the sun, north will be midway between twelve-and the-hour hand. So, my friend, north is that way,' I said.

As I said, there were a lot of trees we could use to erect the aerial. Being clever little privates, we selected a tree as one anchor point with the thought of then swinging the aerial to face north and select the other tree anchor. The aerial is only a T-shaped wire. It should be erected at least thirty metres up in the air between two trees some thirty metres apart.

'Here, Frank, tie this around your neck and climb up that tree!'

'Go bite ya arse,' said Frank.

Despite Frank's self-preserving attitude, we managed to erect the aerial in the correct position. It wasn't a "lay down misère", as Frank loved to play in our hundreds of games of Five Hundred as my partner.

Our relationship later developed somewhat beyond the Army vogue. At the celebration following the tenth intake sig Trevor's funeral in Surfers Paradise, Frank and I discovered, now about forty years on, that we had the same birthday, 16th February 1947. Is it any wonder we are still committed mates fifty-plus years on?

Now the radio was operational we set about making our campsite as livable as possible. The hutchies were up but the radio sat on the ground and the Morse key was difficult to use sitting on one's arse. What do Infantry soldiers do? Seek out comfort as much as possible? Comfort is not familiar to Infantry in the bush. There were a lot of trees nearby, small ones but tall and straight and about 50 mm in diameter. We fashioned a table frame lashed together with twine and tape and made a stool to match. The table and seat tops were smaller 20 mm tree bits lashed together.[10] It worked!

The other necessity in the bush is a latrine (a.k.a. shit box). A deep hole in the ground is sufficient but very uncomfortable. Being a clever dick (pun intended), I dug the required hole in a desirable location with a great view of the landscape. A two-man ration pack is two cartons held together by a strong cardboard open-ended wrap. With this outer wrap, I stood up over the hole. Two neat pieces of tree formed the seat. Quite comfortable it was and very effective.

In later years, dear Frank thinks he was the inventor of the shit box. He also thinks he was the best Five Hundred player in our platoon. Frank was, however, the best Morse Code operator. I was okay at sending as I knew the code well, but receiving is more difficult to master. Efficiency relates to the recognition of the sound of a letter in code, not to hearing individual dots and dashes and then processing through the memory. That is just too slow. Thanks to Frank for his help and expertise. But, I built a good "crapper"!

The boffins were pleased with the outcome of the exercise, and we received a 'Well done, chaps,' recognition. Looking back on that time, I think it clearly shows the commitment and the discipline we had gained from the training. The other aspect was the cooperation shown among the several two-man stations. It was a considerable amount of time for two young men to put commitment first. The

---

10 You can see a photo of this engineering masterpiece on the front cover.

14. Back to training: Serious stuff & good stuff

The ration box toilet, High Range training area, late 1968

best outcome, of course, is that Frank is a most highly respected mate, fifty-six years later. That, my dear reader, is the Army.

It was good to get back to the barracks, the mess hall, the bed, the crapper and the showers. Oh, the shower was nice. In the bush, we relied on a daily heavy rain shower at midday followed by bright, hot sunshine. It was laundry and body-cleansing-in-one. Very refreshing and dry in no time. The Australian-designed ration packs are not too bad, especially in a "dug-in" location. However, we always appreciated the endeavours of our own "tucker fuckers" (cooks). There was never a problem with the food, or the amount of food, served to me by the Catering Corps during my seven hundred and thirty days and "awakie"[11].

What happened next, or rather how it happened, to shape the direction of my Army career is a bit of a dilemma. I cannot remember how it occurred, but while undertaking the radio communication course, I was posted to a position at BHQ where I assisted the pay clerk. Payday was a big deal with hundreds of men arriving in unit categories and, of course, A to Z order. The order never changed no matter what the parade was, be it breakfast, lunch, dinner, needles, other health-related issues or leave passes. A friend of mine with a "U" name said he and others at the end of the line formed a lasting relationship based on their extended wait, always! My time in BHQ led to a further training adventure involving a two-week course in Brisbane.

BRISBANE: TYPING COURSE

'Fook me,' said Jock, 'You get to go to Brisbane for two weeks to learn what? How to type? What the fook is this Army doing mate? You are a fooking good soldier, me best mate. What the fook has typing got to do with anythin'?'

'Beats me, Jock. We will have to wait and see, but two weeks in Bris Vegas sounds good, hey!'

And so, it came to pass. I would learn to type on the machine of the day. No computers in 1968, no electronics, no electric typewriters, only the totally manual thing. "Imperial" was its name, a small compact bit of mechanical genius with keys that constantly stuck together where they were meant to strike the messy black tape that printed on the paper previously inserted onto the roller. Hit more than one of the small closely mounted keys at the same moment and they raced each other to a spot made for only one. Jammed, pull

---

11 "Awakie" is the last day, the day you wake up to go home.

them apart, don't touch the paper or anything else with those black fingers.

The teachers told us we were to learn "touch typing"! We were all males, no one had ever used a typewriter before. One inquisitive soul said, 'Teach', what the fig is touch typing?'

'The Army has requested us to teach you guys to type without looking at the keys and eventually achieve a standard of forty-five words per minute,' replied the boss lady. 'That will be a difficult task in just two weeks. It will require a commitment from you to achieve that goal.'

'And from you ladies, I think,' came from the back of the class.

'Yeah, you got that right,' said a pretty young thing in my row.

The desks were in rows of four and there were five rows. Each row of four was attended by a teacher. All female and all attractive in their own way. These girls demonstrated the mechanical operation of the thing, er, typewriter. Often there was a loud voice saying, 'My thing is stuck,' or whatever.

Having learned how to drive this contraption the real task began. If you have been unfortunate or fortunate enough to be a typist, you will remember this phrase: "the quick brown fox jumped over the lazy dog" then add capitals: "The Quick Brown Fox Jumped Over the Lazy Dog". Practise, Practise, Practise. Fuck the fox.

Now children, cover the keys with a sheet of paper, type the quick fuckin' fox three times and count the errors. Counting the correct bits might have been easier. Ten days of frustrating finger-poking exercises on this little machine that I hated. Finally, the test day cometh. We all passed; we all achieved forty-five words per minute; we all cheated.

On the bus, back to Townsville! This is a long trip of twenty-four hours, plus a bit for hold-ups. A stop here, a stop there, sleep a bit, sing a bit, eat a bit. The bus stopped at a café in Maryborough for lunch. The "gubberment" (a.k.a. Army) had made arrangements for payment. However, directly across the street was a large and inviting red and yellow sign: XXXX. 'Fuck the café, I'm off to the pub for a couple or three of XXXX nectar of the gods,' said Warren. I and one other of similar ilk joined Warren. The bus driver said with a threatening tone, 'I leave in sixty-five minutes, on or not. Got it, you blokes?'

He must have had an experience or two with us Army ratbags. This was Redline Coaches that ran a regular route to Townsville. The coachline became known as "Deadline" after an accident involving several 6RAR soldiers returning from a corporal training course at Canungra resulted in the death of one (Lance Corporal Michael Connors) and injury to others.

So, into the pub, we went!

'Three of your best XXXX pots please, luv, and keep 'em comin', said Warren. We demolished those in double-quick time just as the second one arrived on the bar. The bar attendant, Shirl I think, took the empties and returned with refills just in time.

'Thirsty are you, fellas?' she said with a smirk.

The pace slowed for the next round when Shirl said her boss wanted to buy us a beer.

'Thank you, Maryborough,' we said as the seventh beer disappeared down the hatch.

'I had better go "drain the cane", guys,' I said as they followed. After washing our hands like good little soldiers, we headed outside to the bus.

'Where's the fucking bus gone?' We said, or screamed, in unison.

Shirl appeared and said the driver had looked in, saw no one in the bar and left. 'I thought you three were on the bus,' she said.

'We were all in the pisser,' one of us said loudly.

The hotel boss man appeared and was obviously aware of the problem, 'My cabby mate is on his way. He'll catch-up to the bus. You'll be right, guys!'

'Jeez, what a fuck up,' said Warren.

The beat-up Holden cab arrived. There was nary a panel undamaged, and none of them matched in colour. What a shit heap!

The driver was a little Italian guy. He spoke English in a fashion and was eager to go as he knew what he had to do. Off we trundled in a cloud of smoke. No, not tyre smoke, but dense white exhaust smoke.

'Geez,' said Warren, 'this shit box couldn't catch a cold let alone a bus!'

Jackie, our driver, was like a man possessed, thrashing the old cab to within an inch of its life, and our lives too. Straight through intersections, over railway lines six feet in the air, passing everything on the road, on the left and on the right, who cares? Finally, after we had all shit ourselves, the Bruce Highway appeared. Jackie gave the Holden the full boot, another belch of grey and black smoke out the back.

'Now we'll get that fuckin' bus,' Jackie squawked as he passed a truck.

'If you do catch him, Jackie, how will you stop him?' I asked.

'Don't you worry, he will stop.'

This crazy little Italian did catch-up to the bus a couple of miles later.

'Ah,' said Jackie, 'we got 'im. Now stop the bugger!'

He passed the bus, pulled over in front of it and hauled on the brakes!

'When he come to abuse me, you guys get on the bus bloody quick.'

Sure enough, out came the bus driver waving his arms and shouting. I doubt he even saw us. We, all three, jumped into the bus to a rousing cheer, 'You fuckin' beauty, good job!'

Eventually, the cranky bastard came back, sat in his seat, started the bus and drove on towards Townsville. If you're thinking that was the end of that, you don't know the humour-shit-stirring ability of forty or so young male soldiers, especially trained typists!

We did eventually get to Lavarack safely although a little weary and hungry. It was a memorable trip, even more so for the bus driver I suspect. When we boarded the bus in Brisbane, we were greeted with a resounding chorus of, 'For they are jolly good typists,' etcetera,

etcetera. The other blokes showed their mateship concerns when the bus left Maryborough without us three. The driver "copped it" until the taxi appeared. Then a song began: 'Pull over driver, pull over driver, stop the fuckin' bus, driver.' It went on and on until he had to stop. Poor bastard! One needs to understand the cobber connection.

The rest of the Company had been doing courses and specialist training in the disciplines each individual had been selected to follow. Ol' mate Jock was now a number one machine gunner after topping the course in every aspect of the tests. These tests were substantial and difficult: stripping the gun and reassembling it in a set time; stripping the gun and reassembling it while blindfolded; test firing with live ammo each time; accuracy, of course; loading and reloading; fixing a jammed gun; loading a belt from loose ammo; firing with the bipod and without; and Jock's favourite, firing from the hip while on the move.

The M60 machine gun is a heavy beast and when spitting out the 7.62 ammo gives a decent kick backward and wants to climb up to the left. Only a good strong gunner can control the thing satisfactorily. Jock was the best. The number one gunner is always supported by a number two who carries extra ammunition (usually a two hundred-round belt), but just as important is the spare barrel for the gun. It is his job to stay with his number one and assist in changing the barrel when it overheats and assist in reloading. The number one also carries a two hundred-round belt on the gun and a further two hundred-round belt over the shoulder. It is, of course, the most important weapon in an infantry section.

The typing course led to some interesting experiences. I was requested (read: ordered) to report to the clerk at BHQ for duty. Jock said, 'Don't be playing silly buggers with the big guys or they will lock you up.'

My new job at BHQ was typing charges ("fizzers") brought against soldiers for breaking whatever rule or convention. These bloody things had to be typed without error using a sort of wax impression paper combination. These could then be copied on a Roneo machine. It is the 1960s, remember. For a hopeless typist, the job was a nightmare on wheels. The relief from this solitary confinement occurred when I was given the duty of "parading the guilty bastards before the CO". This was especially fun when I knew the soldier, or soldiers, involved. I appeared perfectly dressed, called the "guilty" to attention and marched them into the CO's office, where I read the charges.

I marched in three mates, all three had been here before, all three were excellent soldiers.

'Colonel, sir, all three have been here before, they are charged as being AWOL last Sunday night. They were on the football field in an intoxicated state. Sir, all three are soldiers of trust.'

'Thank you, orderly. I know these men apart from their past appearances before me.' The Colonel stood and faced the "guilty bastards" eye to eye. 'Come before me again before Christmas and you will spend your leave in the slammer.' He returned to his desk and sat down. 'Today you will report to the RSM and volunteer to clean his already immaculate parade ground. Orderly, march out please.'

That was it for these three, they would spend the next few hours raking and sweeping the hallowed ground under the very watchful eye and extremely loud orders of the RSM, a person one did not mess with.

This experience in BHQ gave me a different perspective on the hierarchy and their relationship with the men they commanded. The CO could have made life difficult for my three mates, especially as recidivists, but chose otherwise. Time in the slammer was one thing, but loss of leave was another thing entirely.

As our training regime ramped up the instilled self-discipline became more obvious. There were fewer and fewer charges for me to slave over and the daily routine became second nature. The officers and NCOs were not so "in ya face"; they were part of the team.

I did have a little run-in with the D Company WO2 on a regular

Monday 0800 parade though. This parade was basically a head count to establish who was not back from leave. I had had a bad start and was running late but I did get to parade on time; just. Like a red flag to a bull, the WO2 zeroed in for a close look. My dress was okay, but oops! 'Private Collins, double off parade and get your razor and get back here fast.'

Off I went across the parade ground, up three flights of stairs, found my razor and while desperately searching for a new blade all I could hear was, 'Collins, get here now!' So off I toddled down the stairs onto the parade ground and back into line.

Not a very pleasant experience I can tell you, known as a "dry shave", even though at that time I did not have a very heavy daily growth. Jock was beside me (he has heavy body hair all over him) and said, 'Better you than me, mate.' Others around me were making scraping sounds with, 'Ouch, fuck, ouch!' mixed in.

SPECIALIST TRAINING AND BATTLE EFFICIENCY TESTS (BETS)

Specialist training involved map reading. Infantry sigs are required to advise other units of a particular position by providing a map grid reference. A more important situation, requiring accurate map referencing, is calling-in and directing artillery support by radio communication using a grid reference. Standard operation procedures (SOPs) require this information be sent by the "code of the day".

Map reading exercises were conducted at the rear of Lavarack in the shade of the imposing Mount Stewart. These exercises were always at night when there was no Moon. The Army dudes never give you a free pass. It was all about reading a map, finding a direction and following the compass. Not an easy task in pitch-black bush grass and other unpleasant stuff up to the eyebrows. Tree roots and vines skulking on the ground waiting to grab feet or legs and throw your arse up into the scrub, causing loss of compass and torch, or both. One night I remember was frustrating and uncomfortable. My partner and myself completed the demanding course before dawn. To our joy, we passed with a wet sail and did not have to repeat.

Some time was spent on coding and decoding map grid references. The importance of the accuracy of these transmissions is self-evident. Disaster might occur if an artillery battery received an incorrect grid reference. Another safety precaution in communication with artillery is especially the use of the word "repeat". This word is only used when asking artillery, mortars or aircraft to fire again. All other communication uses the words "say again", never "repeat". The instruction is obviously to avoid a miscommunication caused by radio interference or network problems. The possibility is a bit remote but does ensure a barrage of 105 mm high explosive does not land on your head.

The importance of correct, calm, brief and to-the-point voice procedure was rammed home to all sigs in the battalion. 'You guys are the eyes and ears of your various units. Officers and NCOs rely on your accuracy in communication.' The infantry sig's role in the unit was important and very much so in any contact with enemy forces. In this aspect instructions in contact with Air Force jets, both Aussie and American, were provided. Contact with our fabulous helicopter force both in attack and in medivac support, a.k.a. "dust off", was vital. The wonderful role of the Iroquois UH-1 helicopter (Huey choppy) in Vietnam is prominent in Australian defence records.

With the signals training complete, the next stage was BETs. It was necessary that each infantry soldier was familiar with every weapon used in the unit. This involved efficiency in the use of the SLR rifle, the M60 machine gun, the M79 grenade launcher and the latest version of the 5.56 mm Armalite rifle, a high-powered, fully automatic weapon that was very light. In Vietnam, it was carried by officers, forward scouts and sigs. In addition, I carried a 32-calibre Browning pistol for close-quarters combat. After weapon qualification (our prior training was so thorough, every man qualified with ease), the emphasis shifted to gruelling physical tests.

D Company support group, Townsville, early 1969. That's me, far right and my fellow sig, Trevor Harrison, 4th from the right

Apart from obstacle courses that are difficult but never boring— that included log crossings, rope climbs, rope under and over crossings and walls, etcetera— the Army challenges invariably included running in various modes. BET included two such bloody awful challenges. Both were an absolute fuckin' nightmare, dreaded by everyone facing up to them. Remember, reader, the month is February, and the place is Townsville in the far north of Queensland. It is the middle of summer, thirty-five plus degrees and as humid as it can get without the sky falling in. Perfect for a gentle jog in runners and shorts. Did the Army people have other ideas? Of course, they did!

'Gentlemen of the famous 6RAR Infantry Battalion, Delta Company, today is a day of change, a change of underpants, D Company will change with B Company!' No! Wrong story.

'You will have two hours to complete.' Grumble, grumble fuck, fuck, fuck. Who does he think we are all, Superman in disguise?

'The dress of the day is long greens, boots, belt with water bottles, and rifle with full magazine. The CO knows this is a tough task, he believes you will "shit it in" as you men have always done. The Colonel will flag you off at 0800 tomorrow. Have fun, guys. You may stand down until 0600 tomorrow.'

Back in the barracks, Jock says, 'Pete, we are going to the club to play darts and drink as much piss as we can.'

'Righto, mate, I'm with you. Just wait for me to rinse out new socks for tomorrow.'

After a beer or two, Jock asked how I was feeling about the run tomorrow. 'Jock, mate, I am confident I can make it on time. It'll be fuckin' hard work— stinking hot and humid and the track is all bitumen surface.' The course we would run would take us past the James Cook University and back again to Lavarack.

'Yeah, gud on ya, little mate. I'll be with yuu all the way. We will show these sick bastards what we are made of.'

'Jock, me mate, I will be proud to run beside you until the end of whatever. Now I need a double thirteen to win again, for the third time, so you had better buy the beers yet again.'

'Okay,' said Jock, 'but it will be the last time, mate. I have been letting you win 'til now.'

'Bullshit! You tight-arse Scottish don't give anything away for nothing.'

The beer and darts continued until it was time to go to the mess for lunch after which Jock had to have his afternoon nap. I wrote a few letters knowing Jock would be zonked for hours. Five hours, in fact, I had to wake him for dinner. I stood close to him and yelled, 'Where is that fuckin' machine gun?' He erupted off the bed only to fall back in a fit of laughter mixed with abuse. After dinner and a couple of quiet beers, we both went to bed. Separate beds of course! At 0500 the corporal in charge of the barracks would gently wake us. Pig's arse it was gentle.

'Get those arses out of the fart sack NOW! NOW!' Up and down the balcony he strode with a sick smirk on his face. 'Today you wankers will be running nine miles. Be on parade in greens, boots, water bottles (full if you are not stupid) and loaded weapons. Got it? Move it! You have fifteen minutes!'

'Ah! Tell him to go fuck himself, Pete. Tell him I am too tired, thanks, but no thanks.'

'Just get out of bed, Jock. Here's your rifle,' as I dumped it on his chest. 'See you on parade, mate.'

Jock turned up on parade just in time. Belt undone, water bottles hanging low, shirt out and dragging his rifle by the barrel.

'Smarten up, private, get yourself into gear.'

'Yeah, Jock, you slack arse!' yelled the guys.

'Ah go an get yourselves well and truly fucked.'

With that fine remark, we marched to the front gates of the battalion. As we came to an undisciplined halt the Lieutenant Colonel, our Battalion CO appeared in his immaculate uniform.

'Good morning, chaps! This exercise is part of your BETs, and it is a test, a difficult one. You face a nine-mile run to be completed in two hours. The course is all bitumen surface, and it will be hot and humid as usual. Support each other, as in the past tests. I know you will all qualify, as you are D Company 6RAR, the best in the business. Good luck.'

The RSM stepped up to take control, 'D Company, atennnshun! The CO and I would like to do the run with you, but the pressure of organising our departure means we can't.'

The RSM WO1 Cruickshank was not a funny man at all, small in stature and feared by all, but this comment drew a loud burst of laughter mixed with cries of, 'Bullshit.'

With a huge grin on his face he continued, 'The CO has granted D Company three days leave plus the weekend to recover commencing at the end of this test. For those who qualify, that is. Good luck.'

We were a fit bunch of chaps, but this was a daunting task. The section commanders moved among us asking for support of anyone in trouble, 'I don't want any records broken, just a hundred per cent finish in two hours. At four-and-a-half miles per hour, you could probably walk. Keep a steady pace and look out for your mate.' There were cheers as each section prepared.

Although fairly early in the day, Townsville's summer weather didn't care about us running nine miles. It was hot already, especially in boots (albeit the latest GP Boots) and greens and the weight of water and the rifle, combined with the hot black tarmac underfoot.

'I am not a 'appy chappie, Pete,' said Jock.

'No one is, mate. At least they haven't made you carry the M60 and ammo.'

'Yeah! Considerate mob they are, hey!' said Jock.

Suddenly it was on! The RSM with a voice to break windows at fifty paces announced, 'You will begin the test when I call "one". Three, two, one!' And so it goes.

The section commanders (corporals) had been moving among us giving us rev ups. 'You have two hours to complete nine miles on foot. Four-and-a-half miles an hour; you could walk that fast. Keep a steady jogging pace, no heroics, no racing and we will all win. The company can only qualify if everybody finishes on time. Crawl across the finish line or carry your mate, just finish the fuckin' thing on time.'

'Remember you are infantry soldiers of D Company 6RAR, the most respected group of soldiers in the Australian Army. An Infantry soldier watches his mate's back. Support each other on this test, watch the man beside and in front and encourage him. Support of each other is paramount.'

The officers (lazy buggers) were stationed along the route about half-a-mile apart. They were on radios and were reporting progress to the boffins sitting on their arses with a nice cup of tea and a bickie. Each station had a supply of water bottles and a lackey private to hand it out if needed. On ya, officer! They were also in constant contact with the mobile medics cruising up and down the road. The runners were told to keep to the left giving the Land Rover ambulances easy access to any suffering digger.

'Nice of them to care hey, Pete?' said Jock.

'They need us now, mate. We are a valued commodity.'

Mile after fuckin' mile all the time getting hotter and more humid, sweat was running, I mean running, off everyone in buckets. 'Will the torture ever end? My feet are burning, my boots will catch fire soon.'

At about halfway our platoon commander, Lieutenant "Shorty" joined in for a mile or so. He moved steadily through the twelfth group speaking with everyone.

'Well, I'll be fooked,' said Jock, 'look at him.'

Shorty came in between Jock and me.

'You two seem to be travelling pretty well. I should have made you carry the gun and the radio,' he said.

Jock replied, 'Pig's fuckin' arse, sir.'

Shorty laughed and said, 'On a serious note, privates X and Y are struggling at the rear. Would you two keep an eye on them, they will need help by the end.'

And off he went, spit-polished boots flashing in the sunlight.

We reach James Cook University on our right. The Uni is at the six-mile mark, this nightmare is two-thirds over. Jock and I dropped slightly in pace allowing the rear to close in. Sure enough both X and Y were suffering. Jock and I took up positions with the two between us.

'Okay, guys. Pete and I will be with you to the end, only three miles to go. Good job so far,' said Jock.

We had them take off their belts with water bottles and ammunition pouches and threw them over our shoulders. They grunted something in response and showed an improvement. At the seven-mile mark, we removed their slouch hats and poured a full water canteen over their head. They revived a bit.

'Not fookin' far now,' said Jock.

Both X and Y laughed out loud at Jock's accent.

We are going to make it with time to spare. Not much but ...", I said.

By the one mile to go marker our "patients" were bad news. Jock and I took their rifles. Maybe a no-no, but it helped.

Jock said, 'Listen, guys, close to the end we will stop briefly so you can take your weapons and belts back, give a tough-as-nuts impression at the finish line.'

'Thanks, Jock. Thanks, Pete. Yeah, thanks, mates.'

We four crossed the finish line, side by side at a double-quick march, and in step, with Jock calling 'left, right, left and quick march, then halt.'

I called, 'Squad, attenshun. Shoulder arms, dismiss and well done.'

Shorty came over and thanked X and Y for their effort. He shook Jock's hand and mine with the comment, 'Thank you and well done.'

Delta Company had qualified one hundred per cent in the test. The CO stated, '6RAR has done it again, the battalion has passed this difficult test. I am proud of the men of the 6th.' He then said, 'There is one more BET to go before the battalion takes twenty-one days leave prior to embarking to Vietnam. That test will take place early Tuesday morning. You are on leave until 1800 Monday. Thanks, men.'

'Hey, Jock, that means five days leave. What shall we do?'

'Drink, my friend, we shall drink!'

And drink we did, gallons of the stuff. We were careful not to allow food consumption to get in the way too much. Two days were spent on Magnetic Island. In those days there was a pub and not much else. It was not our intention to stay overnight; we missed the last boat back to Townsville. Beer and rum were to blame.

Sunday afternoon we toddled back to Lavarack, went to the canteen for a few more refreshing ales and played some darts. Both of us enjoyed the game, had become quite good and very competitive. Competition was in good humour, mostly, apart from Jock's amusing distraction tactics. The Scot in him, I would think! After a decent dinner in the mess, we retired for a well-earned night's sleep, apart from the operatic snoring from my friend. Monday was a quiet day, no drinking, a few games of darts and three good meals at the mess. The cooks at Lavarack were good and generous. Most of the day was spent in preparation for the final battle efficiency test.

The final test was, as usual, a company versus company contest[12] amounting to a semiformal qualification for overseas service in South Vietnam. It involved each man running one mile (four circuits) in eight minutes wearing full battle greens, water canteens (two), ammunition pouches (sixty rounds), and an SLR rifle. In the 1950s some fit blokes ran a mile in just under four minutes, carrying nothing. It was not easy!

Twelfth platoon D Company would be the first to go! Lieutenant Shorty was quick to get involved, 'I want the fittest of you to complete the run, then follow up anyone struggling and bring them home!'

Darby, our twelfth platoon section leader said in his booming voice, 'Jock, Pete, Roger, Billy and anyone else, let's go.' He took off at a pace. 'This will hurt, but it is worth it. Drop back if you want,' he said. No one did.

By the end of the fourth lap, the boffins registered our completion of the test and we re-joined to "pick-up the strays". Darby in the lead said, 'Jock, this one is yours.' And so it went until every man was supported by at least one other.

Our twelfth platoon qualified, and Lieutenant Shorty was overjoyed at the effort shown, saying, 'Now that is what an infantry Army is all about. Well done. Your twenty-one days leave starts now. Your leave passes are at the main gate. See you in three weeks, when the serious stuff starts. Thanks, men.'

With all my stuff already stowed in the car and fuelled to the max, I was at the main gate faster than a speeding bullet (poetry). This trip would be on my own and would take at least 18 hours nonstop driving to reach Toowoomba. Provided, of course there were no mishaps similar to those I had encountered in the past. Off we go; next stop, The White Horse clinic in Toowoomba.

---

12 We ran as platoon groups, four platoons in a company 10,11,12, CHQ support section etcetera; four Companies in a battalion A B C D. Which Company qualified the quickest won the unofficial competition.

15. HOME AGAIN: ANOTHER LONG TRIP

I had done the Townsville/Toowoomba trip a few times. Most of them were straight forward: a broken windscreen, no surprise there; run short of fuel at 0300, wake some poor old grumpy servo guy at Gin Gin to get fuel; or, use one's brain, carry a jerry can (I called mine a "Tom can") of fuel. But, be aware of where the filler nozzle is on the car; a funnel might be needed. Of course, this had happened in the dead of night near Kilkivan. If you live in Queensland outside the stuffy old south-east corner, you will be aware of the hundreds of beer bottles twenty kilometres or so outside these small towns beside the road. Using the whole brain capacity, I found a couple of "tallies" and attempted to break the bottom off to make a funnel. It worked a bit, at least some fuel got in the tank. It was enough. However, before I talk about my final trip before heading off to Vietnam, I must tell the whole story of the events of a terrible trip my fellow sig, Geoff, and I endured during one particular drive home from Townsville.

*

After completing a few duties, goodbyes, packing and tidying the digs, we left the barracks and picked up leave passes at the main gate guard house. It felt bloody good to be going home for an extended leave. It was two pm as we met the highway. First stop Mackay, about four hours. We had a drink and a pie and refuelled the old Valiant. Darkness was descending quickly as we left Mackay behind.

As they say, "shit happens", and half an hour later, shit happened.

A giant red kangaroo charged out of the roadside bush in front of the car. I almost avoided him, but he struck the car low down on the left corner. I continued on, hoping there was only body damage. No such effing luck. The car made weird sounds in protest and began to overheat.

'Geoff, I think the radiator is buggered, mate,' as I switched off and coasted to a stop.

Sure enough, the fan had buried itself in the radiator, steam and water everywhere. On further inspection, the 'roo had pushed the radiator and mounts back some four inches (10cm).

'How the fuck do we fix that?' Geoff mumbled.

In a moment of utter dismay, I replied, 'With the Solvol, Geoffrey, with the Solvol,' a reference to a TV ad about soap.

'Get fucked, you idiot.'

After sitting in silence for ten minutes, I had a second look at the damage.

'Know what, mate? I could fix this if we had a replacement radiator. There's a good tool kit in the back.'

'What if I hitched back to Mackay and got one?' said Geoff.

That became the plan. I would dismantle and Geoff would go to Mackay. Hopefully sometime next morning the car might be fixed.

Geoff picked up a lift to Mackay almost immediately. Everything would be closed, but he might be back early morning. I had a small work light that lasted long enough to get the fan out of the way and the various hoses disconnected. Getting the old, buggered bits out was going to be difficult. Somehow, I had to straighten the mounting points.

There is a Moon, but the light is not sufficient to work by. I retired to the back seat where I lay there thinking of my problem and what of Geoff? Where will the poor bugger sleep, eat and so on? No "wuckin forries", he is Infantry. I felt cold, so I went to the boot to get a coat. I wandered here and there and over to a barbed wire fence. Leaning against a post was a star picket not connected to anything.

I picked it up and took it to the car, not really knowing how I could use it. I lay in the car thinking I should be near home by now. I fell asleep, I guess, and woke at first light.

My dad is an inventive, clever man. I wished he could help me now. I remember once I broke a cylinder head stud in my Morrie. I freaked out, throwing the end somewhere in the garage. 'Hey, take it easy,' Dad said. I told him what happened. All he said was stop and think about it. Somehow, he removed the broken stud in thirty minutes. Yeah, Dad, think about it! I turned around and tripped over the star picket. I swore and threw it aside. Think about it, think! Hanging my head over the engine I thought, *the radiator has to be pulled forward. The star picket! Anchor it in the ground and pull the other end forward.* I was not strong enough to move it.

Help me, Dad, I need your help. Physics popped into my head, then equal and opposite force blah, blah. That means use the power and weight of the car to assist. It was involved but the star picket and reversing the car eventually worked and the mangled radiator was out. It was as far away as I could throw the bitch. I tinkered around preparing for Geoff to return, all looked good to go.

Then a downer. Did Geoff know this was an automatic? The radiators in an auto had an inlet and outlet to cool the transmission fluid. Can only hope! Just have to wait.

Geoff arrived next morning, about 1100, in an Austral Motors spare parts ute, full of beans and bad humour as is Geoff most of the time. The driver carried a sparkling new automatic radiator over to me and shook my hand. 'There ya go, digger. Good luck fellas. I had better get back to work.'

Here is Geoff's story. A funny and very likeable man. Still is, fifty years later. As I said earlier, he hitched a ride back up the highway to Mackay. The first lift was with a truckie in a big semi about one hundred metres up the road.

'Hi, matey, where ya headin'?'

'Thanks for stopping, I need to get to Mackay.'

'Climb up. That's where I'm going. You from that car back there?'

'I am. Pete hit a big red and busted the radiator. I hope to get a new one.'

They talked about where we were headed and why. The Vietnam thing came up and the truckie seemed to change attitude.

'Fuck me, matey, good on ya. I respect you Army guys and what you do, bloody oath I do!'

On the outskirts of Mackay, the truckie (Wally) pulled over to the roadside.

'Mate, I can't go into town with this load, but hang about a bit.'

Wally got on the CB Radio and called for anyone in the area heading into the city to call. He pulled out some cold Coke cans and passed one to Geoff. Several calls came in. Wally said, 'I have an Army guy wanting to go to the Valiant dealer, can you help me?' Within minutes a small delivery van pulled up. Wally and Geoff climbed down to the little truck.

'G'day matey, good on ya. Geoff here is on Army leave, goes to Vietnam in a few months, had a coming together with a big red, needs a radiator for his mate's car.'

'Gotcha. Not a problem. Let's go, hey!' People in north Queensland would often finish a sentence with "hey". Quirky, what!

Geoff had a problem. He had five, six, seven or so hours before the dealership opened. The van driver offered to let him sleep in the back of the van at his depot.

'I start work at 6:00 am when I will drop you at Austral Motors, hey.'

And so it came to pass. Geoff went to sleep in the dealership doorway and was woken by an employee at 0900 hours, got a 'Feelin' a bit weary are we, mate?'

'Been up all night. You work here?' said Geoffrey

'Yep, I'm a counter hopper in spare parts.'

'Just the guy I need. You got a radiator for a Valiant?'

They went inside and the guy went to check his stock books.

'Manual or auto?'

'Ya got me wet,' says Geoff.

'Where is the car?'

'On the side of the road a couple of hours south. We hit a 'roo last night. My mate is working on it. I hitched back here during the night.'

'I suggest the auto type. It will be okay in a manual,' said the bloke behind the counter. 'Where were you headed?'

'I live in northern New South Wales, Pete lives in Toowoomba. We came from Townsville.'

'Army are ya?'

'Starting a few days leave before more training for Vietnam.'

'Ah, you poor bastards, what a shit hole that must be.' The guy said, 'I do have what you need and I will do it at cost price to help a bit.' Then he asked how Geoff was getting back to the car with a bulky load?

Geoff, in his inimitable way, replied, 'I'm Infantry, I'll carry the bastard.'

The man asked Geoff to hang a minute, he came back and said, 'Let's go, mate,' and opened the door for Geoff.

'What's the go?' said Geoff.

The response stunned Geoff. He'd told his boss the story and the boss said, 'Take a ute and drive him back. Just be back here as soon as you can. Give him back his money. Chrysler can afford an extra warranty claim.'

'Fucking unbelievable,' Geoff said.

Can you believe that story? Many would not. Maybe support by people for the Army diggers, in spades!

THE REPAIR JOB

I had done all I could think of to facilitate the fitting of the new radiator. Will it fit? Geoff, a dyed-in-the-wool horse racing man, gave it five to one against. He was on a good thing. The left front of the car was a bit out of shape, mangled by the big 'roo. He won the bet.

I bashed, crashed, hammered and swore; it still wouldn't clear the fan. Finally, I said to Geoff, 'I'm not a fan of fans so this bastard is coming out of there.' Getting that all done, 1960s technology, ya know, took a while.

Finally, I fired up the old girl, no leaks, no fan, let's go to Brissy, mate. Rockhampton was the next stop, two to three hours away, Marlborough (off the highway) about an hour out of Rocky. Ole Val purred along, temperature normal for two hours. Geoff had retired to the back seat comfort, snoring and telling stories in his sleep.

It was dark and twenty-four hours after the big red kangaroo incident. I was scanning the road for any sign of wildlife shining eyes in the dark. Came around a bend in the road and a huge bull charged out from the left. I swerved right, hit the brakes, but bang, it hit the left front, spun around and clouted the side of the car beside Geoff's head. It caved the side of the car in, leaving a 300 mm high peak in the roof. Needless to say, the new radiator was fucked and so were we.

GETTING HOME—HOW THE ... ???

Geoff woke in a flurry. I looked back— he was covered in cow shit. I guess if I was hit by a car at 100 km/h I might shit myself. I was told later this often occurred when a heavy beast is hit by a car— hit twice that is, not crap in the window, I mean.

'What the?' came from the back seat, 'Did we get another 'roo?'

'No mate, I did the business this time. Hit a bloody big bull.'

We both climbed out the right side. The bull had hit the front corner, spun around and clouted the B pillar (between the doors) and caved in the whole left side. We agreed we were going nowhere in the Valiant.

In the middle of nowhere, there was no other option, but to walk or hitch a ride or two, three or many to Brisbane. I thought, *Staying with the car was the best option.*

The first car past was a beaten-up Land Cruiser ute.

15. Home again: Another long trip

'What's 'appened 'ere then?' asked the driver.

'Hit a big bull we did,' said Geoff.

In a cloud of black smoke, the ute drove off.

'I would bet my arse it was his bull, hey Pete?'

The next car stopped, the latest Ford Falcon sedan, the driver opened the front left door.

'How can I assist you guys? You obviously need a ride!'

Geoff in his jovial manner replied, 'My fur coat we need a ride to Bris Vegas badly!'

He laughed and asked us to toss the bags in the back. You, my reader, have most likely heard stories of good Samaritans. Well, here is my recollection of my experience with such a person. To this day I do not know his name or anything at all about him, but I thank him.

I sat beside the driver, Geoff was in the back. Between driver and I, on the bench seat, was a large round plastic water bottle. Nestled in between his legs was a large bottle of Johnnie Walker Red Label scotch whisky. I thought, *What have we got here, he does not seem drunk or anything?*

'You guys Army?'

'We are. Driving home on leave, or were, for a few days before more training in Townsville prior to Vietnam deployment.'

'I heard about you in Mackay, something about a buggered radiator.'

'Yes, that was twenty-four hours ago. We drove for a couple of hours before hitting a big bull where you found us!'

'What about the car?'

'I'll leave it there until I get home and advise the insurance crowd.'

'It'll be stripped bare by then. We'll go into Marlborough, find a towie and get it moved. Okay with you?'

'Sure thing, sir. Thank you.'

So, we did. He knew the towie and made the arrangements and handed me a receipt for the car.

'Bob will bill your insurance company. Just quote the receipt details in your claim,' said he.

After a swig of scotch and a guzzle of water, we set off for Rockhampton. He offered me, but I declined. After a couple more swigs and guzzles we reached Rockhampton for a much-needed fuel stop for both car and passengers. This guy drove fast but was very competent and knew the road and its condition. I became relaxed with his driving.

After a bacon and egg sandwich, I was happy to join him in a swig of scotch. Rocky to Brisbane is a seven-to eight-hour journey, so, there were several swigs and guzzles. Eventually, we ran out of scotch.

'Damn it,' he said. 'It is way before opening.'

'Pull over,' I said. He did without question. I went to my bag in the boot and back to my seat. I handed him a bottle of Johnnie Walker Black Label.

'Well, we are in good hands with the Aussie Army. Good stuff, mate. And Black too.' He had a swig and a big drink of water and off we went.

'I'll stop at a good servo soon. Tubby (water bottle) needs a refill, as does the car; fifteen minutes, okay?'

Geoff, the sleeping champion, woke occasionally to complain his shoulder hurt.

When Brisbane came into view the driver said, 'Where you headed from Brisbane?'

'Catch a McCafferty's bus to Toowoomba,' I said.

'What about sleeping beauty?'

'I planned to drop him off close to the CBD. He had some arrangement, I guess.'

He eventually stopped near Central Station, where we unloaded Geoff. As I was about to get out he said, 'Hang about, I'll drop you at your bus station. It's nearby I think.'

He was an amazingly considerate person. He wished me well for the rest of my Army career. I have often thought of that man and wondered if he respected Geoff and I for what we were doing and the personal discipline we showed. Maybe he will recognise this story.

*

HOME PRIOR TO VIETNAM

This particular trip home— April 1969, my final leave before heading to Vietnam— went pretty well, no dramas, no incidents. I had received notice from the insurance company that the Valiant had been repaired at its location in Rockhampton after the 'roo and bull incident and that I could take delivery when convenient. I flew to Rockhampton on the start of my leave and drove to Toowoomba. At around 2100 hours, I pulled up outside the White Horse Hotel. My family would all be in bed. Dad was early to bed and early to rise. Usually, off to work by 0500, so I will see them in the morning. Meanwhile, there are mates to catch-up with and beer to drink. It was Friday night, a big one in Toowoomba, and the Horse was a big part of the scene. The cabaret out the back would be packed and bopping.

I walked into the public bar, stood in the corner and waited for service. Ron, the owner, walked up. I said, 'A pot please, Ron.' He turned away to get my pot then said, 'Fuck me, it's Pete!' as he turned around. In a loud and commanding voice, he called attention and announced, 'We have an important visitor. Pete, my friend and mate, is back where he belongs, in the White Horse. The next drink for everyone is on the house.'

Mates, friends and acquaintances came from all directions. I did indeed feel important for a moment. Then I thought, *They are all looking for a free drink*, a rare thing, Ron shouting the bar. They hit me on the back of the head, spilled my beer on my clothes, hugged me and kissed me, male and female both. Ron asked how long I was home on leave.

'Twenty-one wonderful days, then I go to Vietnam early next month,' I said.

The bar was full as usual for Friday night. Ron called for silence and said to all and sundry, 'In three weeks, our friend and mate is going to Vietnam. Look after him, I do not want to see him pay for a drink in my pub. Look after him!'

In the darts corner the singing began: 'He is off to see the wizard'; 'He's in the Army now'; 'For he's a jolly good fucker'; 'The Navy gets the gravy, and the Army gets Pete'. Ha, ha, ha, fuck'in ha.

What a fantastic reception it was. There were businessmen and women I did not know (before then) wishing me well. 'A terrible war. Why are our men involved?'; 'How do you feel about it?'; 'Are you concerned, scared?'; 'Are you one of those conscripted?'; 'May I pray for your safe return?'; 'What will you be doing over there?'. 'Do you like Army life?'; 'What part of the forces are you in?' The questions went on and on. I attempted to answer in a proper manner while constantly drinking. And Ron got his wish, not once did I put my hand in my pocket to pay. They bought drinks, food and cigarettes. I thought, *Australian people are strongly behind the defence forces; it gives me confidence in what I am doing for my country.*

Early morning (1 am) Ron said I was falling asleep at the bar. He gave me a key to a room upstairs, 'See you later in the day, little mate.' Little? To a guy two metres tall, maybe. I slept like a log and woke at about ten am. Saturday; the pub was open and the darts flying when I went downstairs. I resisted the temptation to have a drink, found my car, and drove to Dad's shop nearby. I knew he would be working; he always worked.

MY INVENTIVE FATHER

When I walked into the workshop the noise of machines was horrendous. Both big lathes were being used by Graham and Kev. Dad was arc welding. The big machine that surfaced cylinder heads, etcetera, was on an automatic cycle. No wonder Dad was hard of hearing. I walked over close to him and said, 'G'Day.'

He broke the arc and looked up at me beside him; with tears in his eyes he said, 'My son.'

Graham and Kev yelled out in unison, 'Hey, Pete, welcome home, mate!'

We tried to talk over the noise when Dad said we should go to the Canberra for a beer and lunch. I started the Valiant. Dad said, 'Shut it off. It has a cracked exhaust manifold.' While this was part of the damage from the coming together with the big red 'roo and the big bull earlier in the year, the insurance company had not fixed it under my policy.

Dad took the key, went into the shed and instructed Graham and Kev to remove the manifold for welding repair later. Off to the pub we went in his slow Morris Cowley ute: beige, three-speed, column gear change and the most uninspiring thing on the road. 'It's reliable,' said Dad.

*

My first car was a hand-me-down work ute from Dad. A Morris 8 ute with a wooden tray, rag top and little everything. I drove it to high school in my senior year. When I started work two weeks after finishing school, at the ANZ Bank, Dad helped me buy a 1953 FJ Holden. Sometime later, I tipped it on its roof chasing hares around a big paddock at night. My mates put it back on its feet and I drove it home, covered in dents. My uncle Charlie was a panel beater and painter, so Dad had him do the repair. I had it painted post-box red. It wasn't a red flag to a bull, but it was to the coppers, bless their hearts. When I was transferred to Brisbane, we thought the FJ was not up to the regular trip: Brisbane to Toowoomba return. I acquired a 1964 Morris 1100, with Dad's help, of course. This was the era of the Mini 850, Mini Cooper and Mini Cooper S. As all boy petrol heads do, I "hotted" up the Morrie with bits from Peter Manton in Sydney, a well-known Mini motor racing driver. I scared the Cooper S drivers. The old FJ just sat in the backyard.

As life goes, my dad also loved cars. He became the head "machinery inspector" at the Toowoomba Speedway. Speed cars in the 1950s and 1960s raced without any protection of the driver's head and neck. Dad was responsible for introducing "roll bars" to these cars. Some resisted change, but they were simply not allowed to race until their race car complied. Many deaths and injuries must have been avoided.

Speedway became very popular, and cars became a bit more modern than the 1937 Fords and Buicks. The Holden FX and later, the FJ became the cars of choice.

One day Dad said, 'How about using that "red thing" at Speedway? You drive and my business will sponsor you.' And so we did that. I had a "car nut" friend, Dennis, whom I asked to be pit crew. We eagerly stripped the old thing down to basics, had a roll bar fitted (by Dad), and a mechanic friend of Dad's, Jim, worked over the engine, etcetera. Jim was a wily mechanic. He knew his trade well. He wore the oldest, greasiest hat I have ever seen, and I never saw him without it on his head. The wheels were made by Dad in his shop by joining the inside of a Ford wheel to the outside of the Holden wheel. The result was a wider wheel and a wider track. Fucking brilliant, and, with only one join, legal on the open road.

At the end of the first competitive meeting on the four hundred metre oval track, I said to Dad, 'This is a bash fest. If I win a race, the car will be a wreck.'

The local auto club had opened a half-mile dirt track, a proper racetrack with left and right corners and straights. They combined a racing competition with a hill-climb. I raced there many times and I let Dennis do the hill-climb. I never lost a race. After I went into the Army, Dad sold the FJ for ninety-nine cents to Russ, who would drive it to a Queensland Speedway championship. A nice ending for the dear old girl.

15. Home again: Another long trip

*

Dad and I walked into the pub, known then as the "wet" Canberra. There was another unlicensed hotel in town with the same name, the "dry" Canberra. These days the "wet" Canberra is called the Irish Club Hotel. The public bar is called the "Michael Collins" bar after my son. Not really. That Michael was a famous Irish activist. The "big man" behind the bar, the owner, said, 'Hi Gordon, two beers?' Dad nodded, and we sat down at the bar.

'Why are you home, Pete? You weren't expected yet.'

'Pre-embarkation leave. I go to Vietnam in three weeks!'

Dad's eyes filled with tears as he shook his head slowly. We embraced as he whispered, 'Take care, my boy. I can't afford to lose another.'

The big man came back with the beers. 'Is all okay, Gordon?'

'My son here goes to fucking Vietnam in three weeks.'

The "big man", a fine person, informed the crowded bar. He bought our lunch and for an hour the other people shouted us drinks. Dad said he would go back to the shop and get the manifold fixed, 'Come when you're ready, Pete.' It was an easy pleasant walk, past Karen's house, to the shop. *I will see her soon I hope*, I thought.

Every man in the bar wanted to talk. They all had questions I tried to answer. The young guys wanted to know about Army life. 'Pretty easy going,' one youngster commented, 'is what I hear.'

I replied with the memory of battle efficiency training in mind, 'If you call running a mile in eight minutes in the heat and humidity of North Queensland in battle dress, carrying a rifle, two water bottles and sixty rounds of ammo easy, yeah, it's a cruisy life. Or if you prefer nine miles in two hours in the same clobber. But to a point you are right. In the Army, we all face the same challenges, but we do it together, support each other and rely on each other. In the examples I gave if one person fails, we all fail and we do it again. Outside the intensive training and discipline, including personal discipline, we've learned to take care of each other in a way I never thought possible. Why? Because our lives depend on it!'

A next generation "well-to-do" gentleman said, 'How do you feel about the fact you've been conscripted, forced into the Army under the threat of jail?'

'I, with my family, thought about that when I got my call-up. My father said he could try to get me an exemption as my mother had died in a car accident recently. Eventually, I said to him, "Dad, if I don't go, what will I think of myself later in life?" I was then, and still am, unaware of the implications of the Vietnam War. We, as Infantry, are trained specifically for that war, but the politics we don't know. Australia called and I responded as best I could.'

A loud cheer went up. 'On ya, Pete,' they said.

A veteran of World War II, with a stick and a craggy face, came to me and shook my hand and thanked me for my contribution to the country and wished me luck. He said, 'When you return, I will buy you a beer here in this establishment, young fella!'

I felt pretty damn good about myself and about the people. I was aware not all Australians supported the government's commitment to support the United States by sending troops to Vietnam. Especially if those men were conscripted. I had not been subjected to any of the political argy-bargy, of which I knew very little, in either Townsville or at home in Toowoomba. Also, I am unaware of any dissent among the ranks in 1968. I cannot recall ever hearing a negative politically based comment about what our government required of us. They had trained our mind, body and soul to believe in what was expected. Yes, we bitched about training, about the hours, about the conditions, about the heat, the wet, the cold and the discomfort. This training will save your life and your mate's life, so suck it up! And so, we did!

I left the pub and strolled back to the shop to get the car. It wasn't finished, so Dad said to take his ute home and he would bring the Valiant after work. Driving the old Morrie with a sloppy three-speed column gear change was a chore of sorts, especially through the CBD. Frustrating?

You better believe it. I had a cramp in my right foot from pushing the bloody accelerator pedal through the floor. The three "sugly isters from the Rindercilla" story were still at the "blancy fall" where "Rindercella had slopped her dripper" and the "pransome hince was looking for Rindercella at nidmight"[13], but my three not-so-ugly sisters were all at home.

Things had changed in the family since I'd been called up. Jill had married John and they'd had a daughter Leisa. Sandra and Barry had had another child, Toby, now six months old. Wendy, at fifteen years old, was now the only sister living at home. But while I'd been at the pub, Dad had called them all to say I had arrived home unexpectedly and could they all be at the house to surprise me when I got home? Though short notice, happily they'd all obliged, no questions asked.

I drove the ute up the long driveway and parked where it parked every night. Sandra spotted me first, getting out of the Morrie, and screamed something— an excited female squeal one might say. All three met me halfway to the house. Jill and little Wendy were dancing about, *Like fools*, I thought, very excited.

The questions flew in all directions, 'What are you doing here?'

'I live here, woman.'

'Where's Dad? Why isn't he with you?'

'Why are you back home?'

'What's happening?'

'Okay, let's go inside and I'll answer everything.'

I went to the fridge hoping Dad might have a stubby of XXXX in there. There was!

I said, 'Shall we sit out on the balcony? I'll answer all your silly bloody questions.' I told them of the day and that Dad would be home soon with my car when it was fixed. I had another XXXX, all was relaxed, my nieces and new little nephew playing happily,

---

13 Through the use of spoonerisms, this is a reference to a play on the words of the Cinderella story popularised by British comedian Ronnie Barker in the 1970s.

when Li'l Wendy said, 'Pete, how come you are home this time?' I had to tell them.

Tears, hugs and all that mushy stuff from sisters who love their brother. 'You can't go to that awful place. We'll hide you here.' The possibility of me going to Vietnam had not entered their thoughts it seems but they were aware of the violent protest marches in the big cities. They were aware of the mistreatment of returning soldiers, but of the war itself, they had seen absolutely nothing.

*

Many years later Li'l Wendy told me of some trouble she had at high school, the same one I attended. One day in the tuck shop line-up another girl said that all soldiers in Vietnam were murderers. Wendy created something of a ruckus, a brawl of sorts by attacking this girl. Wendy was, of course, to blame but was defending her big bro. Called up before the principal, Paddy (who was also there in my time), Wendy was asked to explain. She told "the boss", as she referred to him, about her brother being in Vietnam at the moment and she was upset to hear her brother called a murderer. The boss, Paddy, said he knew her brother Peter, did not know I was in Vietnam and said to Li'l Wendy, 'I completely understand your actions. Keep up your support of our men over there, no matter what. I respect your attitude, young woman.'

The next morning a general assembly was called by the principal. The only agenda item was the Vietnam War and its implications for the students. After an explanation of what the Vietnam War was about and what "conscription" was, he asked Wendy to join him. With his arm around Wendy, he told the assembly, 'This little lady started an all-in brawl at the tuck shop yesterday. She was sent to me to be punished for her behaviour. I have not, I will not, punish her for the reason she has given me. Wendy's brother, an ex-student of this high school, is currently in Vietnam as an Infantry soldier.

An uninformed fellow student described all soldiers in Vietnam as murderers. They are not! I ask you as the future leaders of our community, to read, watch and listen and take an interest in the world around us. Wendy Collins, I salute your bravery!'

*

Dad arrived home in the Valiant, sounding very much better with the manifold repaired, Barry and John had also appeared after work, and soon the whole family were all laughing and joking, throwing tea at each other, and laughing some more when suddenly the tears came; Mum was not there.

Dad said, 'All right, let's celebrate my boy being home. Have a beer with us, mate.' Thus, another XXXX was cracked open.

I had another day at home before going to Yelarbon, as a groomsman for my Army mate, Roger's, wedding. A Queensland bush wedding could take days!

When the family had all retired to their respective beds/homes, I was still wide awake. I headed to the White Horse in the Valiant. Dad was right, it sounded a lot better, and it ran better.

ROGER'S WEDDING, YELARBON, APRIL 1969

Remember Roger, the Queensland Standing Wood Chop Champion, who you met at the build of the sandbag bunker? Roger and his lady, Annie, had decided to be married before Roger left for Vietnam. It made no sense to me—why not wait? Roger asked me if I would be his groomsman, to which I readily agreed. Yelarbon is a small town in the bush, somewhere in the direction of Goondiwindi, close to the New South Wales border. My plan that day was to travel on bitumen roads via Pittsworth, Millmerran, Texas and Yelarbon. The plan was to meet the bride, her family and Roger's family and to get well and truly legless with Roger and his mates. It promised to be a long hard day and night. Fortunately, the wedding was late in the evening, necessary recovery time.

Roger was the second Army mate to bestow such an honour. The other was Alan who lived at the other end of Queensland in Mackay. It is interesting I believe, and a testament to the bond formed in the Army, that an honour such as this is bestowed upon a person of a short two-year relationship, an indication of care, trust and commitment, usually built up over a longer period.

I set off early morning from home in the Valiant, passed Pittsworth shortly after and stopped at Millmerran for brekkie. Coffee and coffee. The next little town was Texas. On the highway I came upon a large sign, a Queensland Government sign, indicating Texas to the right. I did not expect this, it was not on my map. It was a sealed road as far as I could see up a hill, so I turned right. After a few kilometres the bitumen stopped and became a graded gravel surface that was not too bad.

On I went, saw a signpost that read, "T 15". I remember thinking, *This must be a shortcut.* The gravel road became narrow and deteriorated into two-wheel tracks with a rather high centre. Another sign, "T 5". Then a thump on the floor of the car. What the fuck was that? The sealed surface reappeared, and so did the temperature warning light. I thought, *Have I hit the radiator again?*

Texas was in sight, so I kept going. I didn't know, but the thump was a rock hitting the sump hard enough to cut off the engine oil supply. The poor Valiant was rattling like an old steam train, and emitting steam like one, as I rolled down the Texas main street to come to rest at the local pub. I shut the engine down with a "thud", steam and oil smoke pouring out from under the bonnet.

Some very observant old codger said, 'Looks buggered to me, mate!'

I ignored this brilliant, informed observation, and went inside and ordered a beer. When I ordered another the publican, said 'On me, mate,' as he placed the beer on the bar. 'Your car sounded a bit crook when you pulled up.'

I thought to myself, *This town is full of expert mechanic*s, but I just said, 'Yeah, it's fucked!'

He laughed and said, 'Here, have another on the house. You deserve it.'

We got to talking about where I came from and where I was going. When I said I was going to Yelarbon for Roger's wedding he asked if I was an Army mate. When I replied I was and I was to be his groomsman, this guy let out an ear-piercing whistle. People appeared in every doorway.

The publican announced I was in the Army and that I was going to Yelarbon for Roger's wedding. A huge cheer went up. The publican said Roger was the favourite son of the district. I was overcome with offers of help. 'I'll drive you'; 'I'll tow your car'; 'Here's a beer. You want lunch?'

'I'll ring Roger and tell him where you are,' said Mike the publican.

The reception was incredible, the combination of being a mate of the local hero and the Army thing worked wonders for me that day. I would discover in later years as I travelled western Queensland as a company rep that such treatment was not unusual. The further west, the nicer the people. I was in the finance sector, lending money to a trusted, good cause. I grew to trust and respect these people who lived a tough life happily in the bush with only basic supporting infrastructure. They, I guess, are somewhat akin to the Army discipline and mutual support way of life.

Pretty soon Roger arrived to the cheers of the now growing crowd.

'You bloody beauty, Roger,' they yelled.

'Getting hitched, hey! That'll slow ya up a bit, mate.'

'We looked after your Army buddy. Blew up his car, he did, just outta town a bit.'

'Did a good job by the looks of it.'

I said, 'Sorry, Roger, for dragging you here. Had a few offers of a lift.'

'Pete, mate, I was really happy to get out of town for a rest. You gave me a perfect excuse. How about a beer?'

I told him I had not been without a beer since I arrived and admitted I would be legless pretty damn soon.

Roger replied with a huge grin, 'Pete, you'll be legless before bed tonight for sure.' His civvie mates had promised to do a job on us two Army wankers. And they did!

I woke up in a sorghum field with Roger nearby. Birds and wildlife looked on with disgust. Beside each of us was a XXXX stubbie wrapped in a cooler.

'Aha,' said Roger, 'bed and breakfast!'

'Here's to a fabulous fucking wedding day, Roger. Love ya, mate!'

It was a fabulous fucking wedding, as only the country people can do. No frills, but laughter by the tons, dancing to the max and gallons of beer. Roger's dad insisted I give a speech on our Army life together. I spoke of meeting Roger in recruit training and through the pains of all that shit. They enjoyed the story of Roger, Bernie, Dick and me building the sandbag castle at High Range.

By Monday morning I was feeling well enough to make arrangements to go home with the sick old Valiant in tow.

'You're not going in that grubby old tow truck. I'll drive you home,' insisted Roger's dad, Henry. Early next morning we left that great little town, Yelarbon, behind.

NEXT BIG THING IN MY LIFE: A VALIANT PACER

I had given the Towie a letter about the car addressed to the workshop foreman, Albie Collins, who was my uncle. I had asked Uncle Albie to contact Dad when the car arrived. Henry drove me to Dad's shop where the two men met for the first time. Both blew their respective trumpets about their sons. Dad had met Roger at the Battalion Trouping of the Colours Parade and the Regimental Ball in Townsville the previous year. In a teary threesome hug, they wished and prayed for Roger and me to return safely from the war.

15. Home again: Another long trip

That all over with, and Henry on his way home, the conversation turned to the car.

'Albie reckons you did "the business" on the engine. The bottom-end is totally stuffed,' Dad said. 'Australs (a local car dealership) are assessing the repairs or trade-in on something else in their used cars.'

I thought repair was a no-go considering the big bad bull episode of a few months ago, so we went to the showroom to talk to Arthur T in sales. Peter R, the used car manager, had proposed a deal on a 1964 Valiant AP5 sedan, a nice, plain white car. The finance deal was $85 per month for eighteen months. Sounded reasonable, I would have wheels again. Arthur had gained approval from Industrial Acceptance Corp (IAC), provided Dad was guarantor. Arthur would have the docs in about an hour.

As I entered the showroom a new car was being displayed. It was the latest model, the VF, in a dark blue (called "wild blue") with white stripes along the top of the doors. It stopped me in my tracks. In my head, I was saying *I want it!*

When Len, a.k.a. "High Pockets", saw Dad and me, he waddled over and said to Dad, 'What you reckon, Gordie? Nice, hey? Would suit you.'

I said without thinking, 'Pig's arse, it's mine.'

Len looked at me with a huge smile on his dial and said, 'Buy it then, Pete. It's the only one in Queensland and I have it here.' He rattled off the details: hotted-up engine, one hundred and seventy-five horsepower, three-speed floor change, high backed bucket seats, special wheels and tyres, 'It's called Pacer, Valiant Pacer ... Arthur, can we do it now? I will have the figures to you in five minutes. Go sit in your new car. It's effing awesome, mate.'

Thirty-six months at $80 a month for a new one-off car. Yes. Yes. Yes!!! The car would be registered and ready for delivery at three pm. Dad handled the insurance through his broker and of course consented to go guarantor for the finance. Love ya, Dad!

Dad drove me home where I lay on my bed and thought about my new car and how fortunate I was to have good friends in all aspects of life. I fell asleep until Wendy woke me and said I was wanted on the phone. The call was from Townsville, security something. I was told I would be going to Vietnam as part of the battalion advance party. I was to leave Townsville by air several days before the battalion departed by sea on the aircraft carrier HMAS Sydney, a journey which would take twenty-one days. The guys had a ball, I heard later. My trip on a Boeing 707 from Townsville to Saigon via Darwin, Singapore and Hong Kong, would take but a few hours.

My leave had been shortened by two days for the preparation briefings, etcetera. I was given flight details out of Brisbane. I had a week-and-a-bit left at home!

At 2:30 pm I started walking to pick-up my spanking new car. It was all I could think about, no one in town had seen this car, the colour would stand out among the white, green and beige that made up the car population. Ford Falcon and Holden Monaro had introduced their sporting models the previous year, but this was the first Chrysler Valiant to enter that market, and it was all mine!

There it sat in the showroom looking fantastic— number plate PKZ-974— all mine in a few minutes.

I went to Arthur's office. He had the documents ready to sign, the insurance details done, rego in my name and Dad had already signed the personal guarantee.

'Sign here and here, Pete, and you are on the road,' said Arthur. He handed me the keys and simply said, 'Enjoy, my friend.'

A young mechanic met me at the car with the words, 'Lucky bastard.' He showed me some important bits on the car then held the door open, 'Start her up, mate.' The front doors of the showroom raised, and I drove slowly out. At the door stood High Pockets who saluted and said, 'Thank you for the business. Enjoy your car, Pete!'

Austral Motors was situated on the southern end of the main drag, Ruthven Street. I headed north into the city centre. The new three-speed, floor change gearbox, was very different and I bunny hopped, or maybe kangaroo hopped a few times. The main street is slightly downhill, so I was eventually able to idle along in second gear. It was then I noticed that people were staring at me, and some young girls were running down the footpath to catch-up and wave. I sat there clutching the wheel feeling pleased with myself, and my new wheels. Other drivers blew the horn and gave a thumbs up. Amazing.

I reached the main intersection traffic lights, turned right, passed beautiful Queens Park, and instead of taking a right into Curzon Street as I once would have to reach number eighty-three, headed left, then right, and left again into Fairholme Street. That was the first time I experienced the performance of the Pacer! Albeit briefly. I drove up the steep driveway, tyres screeching. Wendy was home early and saw me from the balcony.

'Gee Pete, what's that?'

'My new car, li'l sister,' I said as I tossed her the keys. She was downstairs and in the car in a flash. A rev-head after living with me and my car mad mates, she was keen to see how the car performed so off we headed over to Sandra's house.

'Stick ya boot in, Pete,' Wendy said.

I could see Sandy at the kitchen window squealing with delight as she saw us arrive, obviously surprised to see the new wheels. Not a rev-head like Wendy and me, but she loved the car, especially the colour. After a brief visit with Sandy, who was busy preparing for a move to Rockhampton where Barry was taking up a new management position the following month, I dropped Wendy home and went to Dad's shop to tell him all had gone well at Austral's.

Dad was over the Moon to see the car and called Graham and cohort outside. They both recognised it as a "chick magnet", to which I said, from my brief experience, they were correct. It was nearly Karen's knock-off time, so I parked outside Falconer Motors, the local Ford dealer where she worked next door to Austral Motors. As the Ford mechanics left work they stood and stared at the Pacer, many saying what is it, hadn't seen it before. I thought, *Of course you haven't. It's the only one in Queensland.*

Karen emerged looking her radiant self and stood looking for my white car. With a few people still looking, I jumped out and called her. All heads turned, not unusual for Karen, as she saw me and trotted over as I opened the passenger's front door. There were wolf whistles, cheering and advice for Karen from the small group.

Carefully, I reversed out and drove away to the same whistles and cheers or jeers. Karen would tell me later about all the questions at work the next day. A rather hard-nosed boss had said, 'Karen, he should have bought a Ford, a Ford Falcon GT!'

Karen revelled in the reception, as I did. We drove around a bit before going to Karen's home. I stopped at a railway crossing on a red light when Karen suddenly saw boom gates coming down straight on top of the car. She screamed as I fumbled for reverse and madly accelerated backward, never thinking or having time to look behind. The train rumbled past and I, "shaking in my hush puppies", drove Karen home.

Karen had ballet school that night, so I left her at home and headed for the White Horse for a much-needed settling ale or two. Sitting in the quiet public bar nursing a nice cold XXXX pot, I was contemplating the near future. In a short couple of weeks, I would be in Vietnam. I had extensive training as an Infantry soldier, but really did not know what to expect. The last week had been busy; fun and normal. For the first time, I felt apprehensive.

'Hey, ya little Army wanker, what's up ya, mate?' It was Bill, my Ford mechanic mate. 'Have you seen that stonking blue Valiant outside?'

I tossed the keys to him and said, 'Yeah, here, take it for a run.'

'You are fuckin' jokin,' are you not?'

'Nah, Bill, got it this arvo. Like it, mate?'

He had heard about it at Falconer's, all the littlies (young guys) were raving on about the colour and the coolness.

I told Bill I had to soon return to Townsville, as I was part of the advance party of the battalion leaving in early May. Bill's response was, 'We had better get pissed then, li'l mate.'

'Before that, I had better take the Pacer home.'

'The fuckin' what?' said Bill.

'My car. You can drive it home, and I'll get Dad to bring us back here. Deal?'

'Suits me.'

Half an hour later we were back at the bar and settled in for a session. Before long everyone knew my latest news: the new car and the imminent departure to Vietnam. Everyone was shouting us beers, both mates and businessmen in dark suits. Bill and I did get pissed to the eyeballs and fell off our legs on a few occasions.

After spending time with Karen and the family, it came time to fly out of Brisbane to Townsville, via Mackay and Rockhampton.

16. PREPARATION AND DEPARTURE

An Army bus identified as 6RAR was waiting at Townsville Airport with a couple of corporals in attendance. They checked ID and, with twenty onboard, the bus headed for Lavarack Barracks. I had a weird feeling I recognised quickly. It was the same feeling of anticipation, of uncertainty, as my first day in the Army. The feeling passed as the driver delivered each passenger to their own digs with a hearty, 'Good luck, digger.'

The flight from Brisbane had taken forever. It was now 1800 hours and time for the ORs' mess to open. The mess hall was almost deserted. Only those in the advance party were there. However, the small crowd did not concern the cooks. They provided an excellent well-cooked steak and vegies. Again with, 'Good luck, digger!' well wishes.

I received details of briefings I was required to attend over the next three days leading up to departure from the airport. One blessing, I guess, I would not be subjected to the twenty-one-day not-so-pleasant ocean cruise on the HMAS Sydney, a retired aircraft carrier, the "Vietnam Express". I later heard the balance of the Battalion had good times, bad times and a lot of time on their trip.

My briefings entailed what to pack, how to pack and when to pack for the flight. The majority of the troops would be packing a large metal box (approximately one metre by half-a-metre by half-a-metre) that would form part of their wardroom in Nui Dat. This thing could accommodate a lot of stuff, both Army and personal. They were required to correctly identify their container with number,

16. Preparation and departure

rank, name, unit, and subunit. "Chicken Man c/o 6RAR" was not sufficient, Owen!

Me, I was given a green heavy-duty zip-up bag (I still have it) that could accommodate far, far, less than the metal box. Also, it was restricted to a weight that included my weapon, loaded on the plane separately, and of course me at about thirteen stone (82.6 kg). The bag and rifle had to be identified in two places with name, number, rank, destination, unit, and subunit.

The reason for the strict weight restrictions, we were told, was that the Boeing 707 taking us away had never flown out of Townsville. The airport was still an Airforce base. There were concerns about the take-off gross weight. Passenger-wise it was fully loaded, and I was told it would land at Darwin, Singapore and Hong Kong to refuel, accordingly lightening the departure load. And that it did. Back to that shortly.

As the D Company signalman (extraordinaire) it was my duty to select radios and equipment, spares, etcetera, for the company. This involved testing the operation, the condition of the accessories, ensuring new batteries were fitted, and that short and long aerials were included. A new M16 SLR was issued with instructions and relevant authority to use the rifle range to sight in the new little beast. The M16 was light, a 5.56 mm high-powered fully automatic weapon.

After issue of the latest Aussie "bush greens", new boots, etcetera, I packed my bag. Anything left in the barracks would be dealt with later. The final instruction was to retain a full uniform for the battalion parade through Townsville prior to departure. All this equipment, uniform, SLR rifle, bayonet and associated webbing was to be surrendered to the Q Store after the parade. This last instruction stated civilian clothes were to be worn on the flight out. This was to satisfy the Singapore authorities though what they were worried about, we could only surmise.

TOWNSVILLE: 6RAR TO MARCH TODAY

COME SAY GOODBYE, LOCAL BATTALION TO MARCH THROUGH THE CITY

Media coverage and support from the people of Townsville on that day— 1 May 1969— was amazing. The battalion, led by the CO, Lieutenant Colonel David Butler (retired Major General, deceased 2019), accompanied by the infantry support groups based at Lavarack Barracks, was an extensive column with two complete Army bands and associated motorised equipment included.

Emotion! The feeling on that day was simply indescribable. Thousands of Townsville people lined the streets on both sides. They carried Australian flags, green 6RAR flags, cheered, whistled and clapped their hands off. I can recall the day so vividly, how proud I felt to be a part of an historic event, the first time an Australian Army battalion had marched through a regional city with bayonets fixed. I was proud to be an Aussie and an Aussie soldier.

Being a midday Tuesday event had little effect on the attendance and, thankfully, there were no antiwar protesters to impose their thoughts on the Australian involvement in the Vietnam War.

The Lavarack Task Force base was new to Townsville and the Army had concerns about how the local people might react and accept the introduction of potentially thousands of military personnel. The 6th, being the first major unit established there, carried with it the future of local acceptance. The CO, Lieutenant Colonel Butler, was acutely aware of this task and put in place many guidelines for the troops to follow when off base, either in uniform while on duty or on leave in civvies. Even dressed in civilian clothes, the Army guy stood out from the crowd. The short hair was a standout— after all, it was the 1960s' era of those long-haired "louts", the Beatles— and clean-shaven into the bargain. "Army" was picked by every girl one ever met. They would be pleasant to dance with etcetera, but considering any future relationship was impossible. They were probably right!

16. Preparation and departure

D Company 6RAR, May 1969, prior to leaving for South Vietnam. I'm fourth from the right (facing), back row

The CO was a great boss. Fair and considerate of the behaviour of his men, he expected the best and was rewarded with many accolades and records for his battalion. 6RAR posted a record and unbeaten score at the renowned Enoggera Jungle Training Centre and its officers were commended for Operation Kangaroo at Shoalwater Bay training ground in Queensland.

A further initiative of his was to involve the Battalion in the local sports competitions. The most successful of these, although there were many sporting competitions involved, was Rugby Union which had a large public following. The rugby standard was quite high for a regional area and the premier team was held in high regard by the sporting community. The men from 6RAR, many of them National Service men from southern Queensland and northern New South Wales, were itching to play. When the opportunity arose to enter, the 6RAR Rugby Union team soon won the competition. Rugby was popular and enjoyed strong media coverage in print and on television.

The Army rugby team helped cement a good relationship with the Townsville community.

There had been concern about the acceptance of the Army in large numbers, but the efforts of the CO and his officers and men deflected all concern. The day the 6th Battalion Royal Australian Regiment marched through Townsville streets with fixed bayonets dispersed all concern.

There is a song, a wonderful song, that refers to the day I was only nineteen. Yes, I was, but have you heard the song by Redgum, titled *I was only nineteen?* Every time I hear that song, tears well up with both pride and sadness. A top hit, a fantastic song about my battalion. I marched through the streets of Townsville, I later knew Frankie who kicked the mine, I was there, and a bloody good mate lost half his leg in that incident. Thank you, John Schumann and your group, Redgum, for a wonderful memory. The parade was dismissed, and we boarded buses and trucks to return to Lavarack. I had tonight and tomorrow before "Leaving on a Jet Plane" late afternoon for Vietnam.

Jock decided he would give me a "send-off" in town with a few parting drinks at the Army's favourite watering hole, Lang's Hotel on the Strand. I was due to leave the Base at 1500 hours by bus to the airport. Jock and I were at Lang's at ten am (opening time). Jock, in his Scottish wisdom, decided the drink(s) of choice would be rum with five-ounce beer chasers. Approaching the bar, Jock yelled out, 'Two Bundy rums and two five-ounce beer chasers. Keep um cummin', ma li'l mate goes to Vietnam today.' Early drinkers— quite a few— cheered, many shouting us Jock's preferred drinks during the session.

About midday I told Jock I was starting to fall off my perch. 'Ookay mate, we will have a Scottish lunch.' His Scottish lunch meant the rum was replaced with a wee dram of scotch (a brew I had not heard of) and a piece of dry bread. After lunch? It was back to the rum and beer. A couple of hours later I was falling off my legs. 'Jock, you had better put me in a cab and send me to the base.' Somehow, he understood the dribble and drivel coming out of my mouth. So off I went in a cab. I knew I would not see Jock until he arrived in Vietnam with the Battalion in a few weeks' time. Even then our time together might be limited as I was now in company headquarters and he in a rifle platoon. Although in the same Company, we were set apart by location in the company base and were required to undertake different duties and responsibilities, especially so in Vietnam.

The advance party had been told to travel in civvie clothes. I was wearing a light blue long sleeved shirt rolled-up to just below the elbow. So, what, one might say. Part-way back to Lavarack Barracks, I upchucked, vomited, spewed, threw up, all this black shit out the window of the cab. 'Ah, you fuckin' Army guys can't handle it, hey?'

I thought, *Mate, you could not handle half of what I drank*. I didn't say anything because I was unable to think, speak or see. Fuck you, Jock ole mate, your time will come.

I arrived at the base, short of the guard post, and alighted the cab with grace and fell on my face. The cab drove off. Jock had maybe paid him, or the cabbie just could not be bothered with me. On my feet again, with legs moving in their own chosen directions, I began shuffling towards the guard post. One young guard, a cook who recognised me, had a big grin on his face and helped me to my digs. He said, 'You might change your shirt. The left arm is a bit ugly.'

All my stuff had been packed in a kit bag and sent to the airport earlier. All I had was some small personal things in a carry-all bag, but no shirt. I looked at the sleeve and it was ugly to say the least. Have you ever been "legless" trying to negotiate three flights of stairs to get to the laundry below? Eventually, I got there by encouraging each leg to do its job.

I have vivid memories of trying to wash my shirt, while I was wearing it. I could not stand in one spot without staggering backward or forward, sideways or upside down. Finally, a corporal turned up looking for me. I was late for the bus to the airport. Thank you, corporal ol'chap. 'Come on, digger, we heard about your little gig in town. Let's go catch a bus.' Assisted by the friendly corporal, I arrived at the Townsville Airport somewhat drunk, suffering jelly legs, poor vision and very little awareness.

The aircraft waiting on the tarmac to take us to Vietnam was a Boeing 707. In 1969, Townsville Airport was primarily an Air Force base also catering for local and interstate small and medium passenger craft. Apparently the 707 was the biggest plane to use the facility, hence a lot of townsfolk were there to watch it depart.

So, to the next chapter of this book and the next chapter of my life. A period that would change my life so dramatically.

17. LEAVING ON A JET PLANE: FOR WAR IN VIETNAM

With four wing-mounted jet engines, the 707 looked big and impressive. It was known in military circles as "The Freedom Bird". Qantas used the same aircraft to bring Aussie soldiers back home. I hoped in a few months I would be boarding the "Freedom Bird" to return home.

All our gear was on board, rifles unloaded and checked were in a secure section of the hold and marked clearly (in two places) with the custodian's details. I carried an identical claim check to use in Saigon. The boarding announcement came quickly. As we filed out of the terminal onto the tarmac, security details were checked and seat allocation given out. I was hoping for a window seat about midships, which was what I received. Could I take advantage of the window with my eyes still not in the best working order, I wondered as I settled down in the seat.

'Jock, you Scottish bastard, thanks for nothing. I hope you are suffering a huge hangover in the morning!' I vowed to get even when we met up back in Australia, as arranged, in twelve months, 'Good luck, mate, see ya!'

Take-off was a frightening experience. I had had a couple of flights since joining the Army and lots of training in helicopters, the famous Iroquois "Huey". This was my first on a jet plane. The biggest in service at that time. Pilots of prop engine aircraft rev-up their engines at the top of the runway before accelerating down the runway. This big thing, loaded to the hilt, facing a runway shorter than usual, did the rev-up of the engines thing. Then a bit more, then a bit more until everything was vibrating, shaking, rattling, and dare I say it: rolling! It left the standing position with a lurch forward and continued to accelerate until spearing into the sky on a steep climb. I saw Mt Stewart (behind Lavarack) disappear below as we banked right one-eighty degrees and headed for Darwin.

Troops of the 6RAR advance party board a chartered Boeing 707 at Townsville Airport for the flight to South Vietnam, May 1969. Photo by Bryan Rupert Dunne, public domain, Australian War Memorial.

In Vietnam, and since, I have travelled on many and varied aircraft; nothing measures up to that experience. A fully-fuelled 707 could safely reach Saigon on a nonstop flight. It was apparently the extra loading that required refuelling stops. However, once we were up there it was pleasant flying, and I fell asleep until a steward woke me for the Darwin landing. Another fuel stop, so we had to disembark and proceed to the terminal. I was not feeling so good after my sleep and felt a bit unsteady on my feet. I concentrated on staying upright down the stairs and across the tarmac. The security lights at the terminal were aimed at me, I reckon. I could see eff all and tried looking at the ground for some help.

I didn't see the bugger rush over and hit me in the forehead. A black, or maybe white, steel post stopped me in my tracks. I slid down the post and settled on the ground until a Qantas steward returning to the aircraft found me and loaded me back on the thing. A couple of mates asked, 'Where have you been, Pete? Thought you would have joined us in a last beer in Oz.'

I think I said in reply, 'I met a lovely tall slim Darwin girl who knocked me out.'

'Typical of a sig, I reckon. See ya, Pete.'

That is as much of Darwin as I have ever seen. Take-off was less dramatic, maybe a longer runway, or maybe I was becoming a seasoned traveller. Maybe that should be "pickled" traveller. Whatever, next stop was Singapore.

Arrival at Singapore was without incident. I had more recovery sleep and was feeling a bit better. The word came to disembark, but remain in the terminal, or else. I am starting to feel like a dunny lid, up down, up down all day and night.

Singapore these days is a clean, tidy city with strong regulations to keep it that way. But in 1969 things were very different. When I stepped off the plane I was met with a thick dark grey smog. I couldn't breathe the stuff. The foul smell was only part of the problem. At the bottom of the stairs, I found the smog extended down to about four feet above the ground. Everyone in front of me was stooped low and running to the terminal where hopefully the air would be better, and the bar would be open.

It was the quickest exit of an airport tarmac ever I reckon. Everyone settled down and dragged in a few deep breaths. The bar was open. The only beer available was Tiger Beer, obviously a local brew. A mate and I ordered a large one of these Tiger Beers.

'Looks okay to me,' my mate said, 'Good luck, Pete,' as we took a deep swallow.

In unison, our reaction was the same. 'Faaaack, that is shit, it is—just awful!' The reaction around the terminal, by most, was the same.

A loud voice— there are plenty of them in the Army ranks— called out, 'That's not Tiger Beer, that's TIGER PISS, and bloody warm into the bargain.'

I was offered a rum and Coke, which I refused while trying to control the stomach from retching at the thought of rum. I had a bottle of water instead.

Thankfully there was a re-boarding call in an Asian-sounding voice. Back to Qantas, maybe those Aussie stewards have a XXXX or VB left. Next stop was Hong Kong where, during a short refuel, we were to remain on board. I was starting to feel like an international tourist, not a soldier about to enter a war zone. Enjoy the moment, Pete!

I do not remember much about Hong Kong. How could I? We didn't disembark. What I do remember is the approach to the airport. It seemed to me the plane was heading for a bloody big mountain (as it was) and then the high-rise buildings seemed to be crowding in on us as they flashed by close outside my window. A scary and spectacular landing all in one moment. At the end of the runway, the pilot hauled us to a stop. As he turned the aircraft towards the terminal, I could see this huge sheer mountain rising straight up at the end of the wing. *Bloody good driving, hey what,* I thought. Soon it was take-off number four. Next stop, Vietnam.

DESTINATION: SAIGON, CAPITAL OF THE REPUBLIC OF SOUTH VIETNAM

As a young person in Australia, growing up in a peaceful country where crime was minimal and home security was basic, the last two years had opened my eyes to just some of the problems of the world. I would soon be landing in the midst of what was the world's biggest problem. I was being told by the government, and by the media, that I was part of the protection of our country, Australia. Against possible invasion by the communists of the north. I barely knew what a communist was. What did one look like, did he have two heads or what? I did not understand what "communism" was and why it posed a threat to our homeland.

Still, I had been trained to kill these communists and their supporters. No doubt the communists had trained their own supporters, who were perhaps just like me, and trained to kill me. I was about to arrive in a foreign land I had never heard of before the Army came by, not as a tourist to enjoy the land, but to possibly destroy parts of it and kill others I did not know.

I realise what a thorough job the Army training teams had done to prepare me for this task. They had instilled some fundamental human characteristics that combined to produce an effective soldier capable of following direction without question. The combination of self-discipline, group discipline and preservation of the lives of others through mateship had been the result. I felt safe, although apprehensive, about where I was about to go.

My thoughts were interrupted by the pilot saying, 'Approaching Tan Son Nuht Airforce Base, landing in ten. Fasten seatbelts.'

Then another voice, 'When the aircraft comes to a halt, do not leave your seats until called. Proceed to the front exit only. Follow ALL directions. Take cabin baggage with you. Your luggage and other items (guns) will follow you to your ultimate destination.'

Then the pilot announced, 'Good luck, guys. Thanks for flying Qantas, the Australian airline. See you all on the way home. Freedom Bird out.' A loud cheer erupted that could have burst the seams of the jet. Wow, well said, mate. The pilot was at the exit door to shake the hand of every passenger and wish him a safe return. Onya, Qantas!

18. VIETNAM. A LIFE-CHANGING EXPERIENCE!

DAY ONE IN COUNTRY

My first taste of Vietnam was hot, humid air filled with the smell of jet fuel and exhaust gas. It was stifling. I started to sweat heavily, and months later I was still sweating. It never stopped, even at night.

I was met by an American sergeant, armed with a clipboard, who directed me to a small tent nearby, with the instructions, 'Wait there!'

I had not seen any other USA Air Force bases. This was amazing. I stood watching hundreds of aircraft moving about and even more ground vehicles. Fighter jets were taxiing past within a couple of metres and taking off in unison. The noise was tremendous, punctuated by the scream of the Phantom F4 Fighter Bombers leaving fully loaded with 227 kg bombs.

I can remember shivering with fear and delight at the same time. For a moment I was back in Australia, at an air show with Dad and family, when a RAAF Sabre dived from nine miles above to break the sound barrier.

The tent had about a dozen men now, none of whom I knew. No one spoke, just watched and waited. I assumed some were replacements and others destined for one of the other two Australian battalions stationed in Nui Dat. A US food truck came past and offered a hot meal. I realised I was very hungry and eagerly ate the food. I do not remember what I ate, but as I ate, I looked around and saw I was the only one dressed in civvie clothes; the others were all in full battle clobber. No wonder no one spoke to me!

A giant five-axle, eighteen-wheel truck stopped outside. A spiffy captain leaped out (by parachute, you'd think, given the truck's height) onto the ground and by name ordered, or maybe asked, us to board his vehicle.

'I believe you are all bound for the Australian task force base at Nui Dat. Am I correct?'

'Yes, sa!'

Now I understand; they are all Yanks. I wonder where my guys are.

This truck is tall and wide open, affording a view of everything as we travel somewhere. The amount of equipment on this base is simply mind-blowing. Huge stuff of every conceivable use. Fixed-wing aircraft in the hundreds, single-engine, four engines and six engines, both jet and propeller-driven. Bulldozers, scrapers, excavators; little ones and the biggest in the world. I can't believe what I am seeing. There are Army and Air Force people everywhere. Service vehicles darting in and out of the rows of machines, fuel trucks constantly pumping their wares.

I think to myself, *What the fuck am I doing here? What can I do in this place?*

I am pondering that question when the truck stops. The spiffy captain asks us to proceed in a column of one to the right to a waiting aircraft, sitting with the tail towards us and engines running. It is a Fairchild C-123 which we always referred to as a Baby Herc (even though it isn't one), with two engines instead of four as seen on the larger C-130 Hercules. The rear cargo hatch is open, forming a ramp. We are to board immediately. During training, I travelled on these things, noisy little fuckers. Usually, seating is along the fuselage sides in the shape of slings. There was nothing in this thing. I soon realised the floor was moving backward and forward by about six inches (15 cm). These were loading platforms, several independent wide platforms which when loaded would be tied down, but not now. With every movement of the aircraft, these things jolted back and forth. Should make for a safe and comfortable trip to Nui Dat, not!

The pilot moved out into a wide taxiway; the rear door was still wide open giving a good view behind. As we crossed a major intersection a huge aircraft appeared behind. When I say huge, I mean fuckin' big. It looked like a giant moth, wings extending out from the top of the fuselage with jet engines strewn along their length, ending with wheels at the extremity of the wings. It loped along on a massive set of wheels, wings swaying up and down with the contours of the taxiway. The scariest aircraft I had ever seen. It was, as I soon learned from a fellow passenger, a B52, a.k.a. Stratofortress, long-range bomber. US Air Force, of course!

The Baby Herc made a left turn as the big B52 continued on, giving a further view of its size. Truly a magnificent thing. I wondered how it could fly. After another left turn, our plane came to a halt. Everything shook wildly, the sides rattled and the floor gyrated. I trembled, not sure whether from vibration or maybe fear. Then the thing lurched forward and lifted off within seconds, did a very quick steep bank to the left, and climbed quickly. The passengers grabbed anything nearby for the stability of sorts as the floor platforms moved violently.

It levelled off as we passed over Saigon. The rear door opened, affording a fantastic view of the city and surrounding countryside. Everything was green, the city crowded with buildings. Then the nose of the plane dipped down quite a lot until we levelled off just above the treetops. The rear door slammed shut and locked.

One of the pilots appeared in the doorway of the cockpit. I assumed he was one of the pilots, hoping someone was still up front flying this thing. He waved his arms to get attention and then said, 'Thank you for choosing Vietnam Budget Airways. We trust you are enjoying your trip, but we doubt you are!' He went on to say we would be flying at an average height of sixty metres, just above the treetops. It would be up and down depending on the tree height. He explained this tactic reduced the possible use of rocket-propelled grenades (RPGs) being fired by those "noggies" below. 'There will be rifle fire, there always is. But they are poor shots and don't hit any vital bits of the aircraft.'

'I am required under regulations to advise youse all about safety procedures for this aircraft.' He took a couple of steps forward, hanging onto an overhead handrail, 'There are escape doors positioned above each wing,' said with a rather neat hop skip and jump in each direction, with associated hand gestures. He obviously knew he had "newbies" on board and took every opportunity to be American.

'But,' he added loudly and in his best Yankee voice, 'this plane has been hit so many times, when it crashes the tail will fall off, so run out the big hole in the back! Enjoy the rest of the flight. Luscombe Field at Kangaroo Airport, Nui Dat, is about fifteen minutes.' There were a few rifle shots aimed at us apparently, but the annoying floating floor stopped any entry.

Suddenly it felt like we fell out of the sky. The wheels hit the deck with a screech of tyres as the engines reversed with a thunderous roar. The pilot was still braking when he turned right, dropping one wheel off the end of the runway. When you can't see an effing thing, it is scary. As it turned out there was nothing in front of us, just dirt for a couple of hundred metres. Not to mention dozens of helicopters of various sizes and a few fixed-wing aircraft.

HELLO VIETNAM: I'M HERE!

When the aircraft came to a halt there were some external thumps and crashes before the rear door opened. All the guys were up quickly and disappeared out the back. I was the only one left in this cavernous space. I picked myself up and walked down the plane and down the ramp. I was still dressed in civvies, dark blue pants and light blue long-sleeve shirt (with a dark stain on the left arm). I stood out in the sea of jungle greens like dogs' balls! Soldiers of various corps and ranks were doing their stuff quickly, unloading and reloading the plane, still with engines running. I clearly remember standing there at the end of the ramp thinking *What the fuck am I supposed to do now?* Some soldiers, mostly other ranks looked at me quizzically, nodded and continued with their task. I looked around for an officer with infantry insignia without success. I felt and looked out of place, no one approached me, everyone was unsure of this alien being.

From behind me, a voice said, 'Private Collins?'

I turned around to be met by a corporal, who was already carrying my bag, and he handed me my M16 rifle.

'Been expecting you, mate, but sorry I got caught up in a briefing for a TAOR patrol I am taking outside the wire tonight.' I had no idea at the time what a TAOR[14] was.

He introduced himself as Corporal Z, D Company 4RAR. As I was already aware, the 6RAR was replacing 4RAR. There was always an Anzac battalion as one of three stationed at Nui Dat. The Anzac battalions were either 2nd, 4th or 6th.

'Let's go, mate. I'll show you your new digs.' He picked up my bag. 'New issue, I see,' he said and threw it into the Land Rover. The next stop, quite some distance I think, was in the rubber trees. Nui Dat was a vast complex, a task force base of three infantry battalions plus all supporting Army corps. Each battalion deployed two companies on the frontline defence perimeter, while a third company was stationed behind in reserve. My Company, D Company, was in the reserve position the corporal told me.

'I hear you are the company sig, which means the comms bunker, over there, will be your territory.' He pointed to a spot in the trees. *There is nothing there*, I thought as I scanned the spot.

'Your home for a few months, Pete,' he said as he stopped outside the last tent in a long row. 'The rear left side is vacant, so settle in there. The other three men are on their last operation and will be back

---

14 Though I didn't know it at the time, a TAOR stands for a Tactical Area of Responsibility, a prescribed area for which a commanding officer is responsible.

18. Vietnam. A life-changing experience!

D Company 6RAR Battalion Headquarters, Nui Dat, South Vietnam, 1969

tomorrow around 1000 hours.' He said they would be pretty happy at the prospect of going home soon. 'You, mate, will be extremely welcome in the digs, a bit like being a physical confirmation of their RTA (return to Australia).'

I climbed out of the jeep, looked at my new home, and wondered could I handle this. *It was all bloody basic accommodation rated*, I thought, *at minus at least one hundred. Where is my ensuite, where is the bloody toilet, where do I shower?* As if reading my mind, the corporal said, 'Ah, Pete, the shitter is the fly-wire enclosed structure behind your digs, about twenty-five metres away, the ablution block (I fuck'n hate that term) is over there. Take all your own gear.'

'You will find a complete combat rig inside,' he informed me. Then he blew me out of the water with what he said next, 'Your mess time for dinner is 1800 hours. I will pick you up minus five. Be ready with full combat gear, loaded rifle and basic rations. Ammo and all you need is in the metal bedside locker.'

'Okay, corporal,' I squeaked, 'I'll be ready!'

Then came the cruncher, 'The boffins decided it would be a

stellar idea if you joined my TAOR patrol tonight, a sort of welcome to country, maybe?'

I looked at him in a daze, and said, 'What is a TAOR patrol?'

'Sorry, I will explain at the mess, okay?' said the corporal, starting the Land Rover and driving off.

I dragged my bag and friend (rifle) around the sandbag wall covering the entrance, noting a deep pit in front, that housed many beer cans. Inside was dim, the heavy tent and the sandbag walls were about 450 mm apart, like a big all-around window. The floor was duck boards. My little hidey-hole contained a narrow bed, beside a metal cabinet, the centre of the "room" was a combination of four large storage cabinets (minus doors). I tossed my bag on the little bed and sat down on a small metal chair, and I believe I said out loud, 'What the fuck?'

I wandered around the tent. The place was organised but not in any way neat and tidy. I was happy to see the lack of regimental bullshit. Mine was the only bed properly made; on the pillow was a note, 'Welcome, Pete!'

After unpacking my bag and stowing my civvies in it, I began sorting out my combat gear. Everything was modern-day stuff and, for a change, fitted quite well. My GP Boots had come from Townsville with me as had the Aussie slouch hat and the well-worn and weathered bush hat (giggle hat). I was ready to go once I loaded and prepared my rifle, my friend the Armalite AR M16, a vicious, very light and easy-to-operate automatic weapon. I am ready, communists and VC.

The corporal arrived five minutes before six, as he said he would, typical of the Army non-commissioned ranks. Officers, on the other hand, even more so the important high-ranked ones, could be a bit tardy sometimes when the event is not tactical or critical.

The Catering Corps did the usual fine job of preparing very decent food under trying conditions, so dinner was a pleasant event. The conversation was typically about my Army career so far. Max,

My "room" in Nui Dat, May 1969

the corporal, was very interested in what I had trained in and was surprised I was a nasho. He was a career regular currently with 4RAR D Company as a section commander. Soon he would be going home.

THE TRAPS, BUGS AND OTHER THINGS

'Pete,' the corporal said, 'out in the bush watch everything. Check out anything that seems out of place, take every step with immense care. The "Nogs" have stolen our land mines and used them against our guys. The large minefield laid by Australia to protect Nui Dat was a mistake. So, mate, take care of yourself and your mates. I wish you luck and will see you back home one Anzac Day.'

As I was soon to learn, Vietnam held many perils.

As well as using our own mines as booby traps, the VC used any unexploded ordinance they found. I saw an unexploded 340 kg bomb from a F4 Phantom fighter bomber wired with trip wires. Such a bomb would create a crater you could fit a three-bedroom house into with room to spare. I saw large trees standing upside down (roots in the air) in other trees. I often thanked our Lord that the enemy had no Air Force capability. More of those thoughts later. The VC rigged other dangerous traps set to kill or maim our soldiers in the rubber tree plantations and the dense jungle.

"Pansy Pits" we named one of these traps. A small hole in the ground on a jungle track, neatly camouflaged, contained sharpened bamboo sticks with poison, or animal or human excrement on the points. These were part of the reason my GP Boots contained steel sole protection. These booby traps were also part of the tactical decision of the Australian forces to never, never use the jungle tracks. It was difficult to move through the jungle avoiding tracks, but a hell of a lot safer.

I remember vicious booby traps, operated by a trip wire and usually set-up in very dense and difficult terrain at chest height to an Aussie. A piece of wood or bark, about 250 mm square contained several sharpened and poisoned bamboo sticks about 120 mm long. The piece of wood was attached to the "broomstick", a piece of springy strong sapling. The other end of the broomstick was fixed to trees beside a path, then a trip wire was attached to the piece of wood and pulled back tight and across the path at ankle height. When tripped, the poisoned "head" flew out at great speed. The result needs no description.

The natural vegetation and landscape were effectively used as weapons by the VC. When we think of bamboo, we think of the tall thick trunk and shady tops as an attractive garden addition. In Vietnam, a different variety of bamboo exists. The Australian soldiers named it the "wait-a-while bush". This horrible thing grew

18. Vietnam. A life-changing experience!

everywhere, about 2.5 m tall, 3.6 m round with arching branches reaching the ground. The branches had long curved needle-like thorns that latched onto everything passing. Trying to pull away from it caused the thorn to painfully dig deeper. Not only did this fucking thing catch arms and legs, it dug into backpacks disrupting tactical movement. 'Hey, mate, wait-a-while!'

The VC set-up camps in the middle of these bamboo patches. If Aussie infantry entered close to the area the VC often vanished leaving the area booby-trapped. It was an impossible task to surround a VC camp and effect a successful attack.

Once I entered such a camp at close to nightfall. We had been looking for this camp for some time. When we got there the fires were burning and rice was bubbling in pots. They had left quickly. Against a large tree near the edge of the camp, stood a 340 kg unexploded bomb from an aircraft raid. It was a booby trap! Dig in … ahhh, fuck these roots!

Tactically speaking, we dug in every night as a protection from rifle fire or mortar attack. Whether digging in a 450 mm shell-scrape might help survival if this baby exploded was doubtful. But we tried! The bamboo wait-a-while bush had the last say. It proved impossible to dig through the many roots with our small shovels. Thankfully the engineers found the bomb was unarmed, probably because the VC didn't have time to arm the trap before melting into the jungle as we arrived.

The Vietnam jungle was full of ugly things. Dangerous deadly snakes, leeches, mosquitoes and spiders. Plants such as the "Gympie" bush were sometimes used by the VC as a booby trap. This bush named, I think by the Aussies, was a tall thing with very large leaves. The topside of the leaves was smooth, the underside contained millions of tiny "stingers", that produced immense pain if they contacted with the skin. One day when I was talking on the radio, I failed to see a Gympie near the right elbow. It only contacted a small area, but the pain lasted for hours upon hours. The only relief, though short, was to pour cold water on the area. Some twenty-odd years later, when I experienced a significant change in the environment temperature, the pain would return.

The VC would tie a tree back on a trip wire in the hope of disabling an enemy soldier. There was a report of a significant incident involving the Gympie bush, but not VC instigated. In the jungle, an infantry soldier may be caught short of the necessary loo paper (bum wipe). The advice from the older experienced soldiers was, 'Use a large green leaf.' This, I learned on a Lord Howe Island discovery tour, was a historical fix for the problem. Just don't use a Gympie bush leaf, guys! Unfortunately, a soldier used the dreaded leaf on his arse. The poor bastard had to be flown out by chopper and ended up in a hospital in Malaya. Ouch!

I had never heard of "bird spiders". These things set-up their webs in trees to catch birds, which of course they eat. I was about to have an intimate lesson on the existence of these effing things. Shortly before stand to (sundown) the jungle we walked through was not as thick as usual. Suddenly I was hit in the face by a large sticky moving thing. With a left hook and a quick right, I almost knocked myself down, 'He's out ten seconds into first round!' It was a bird spider. I still dream about it. The thing was big enough to almost cover my whole face.

Maybe it was my early boxing training that disposed of it before it did whatever it did to its prey. Thanks to my lifelong friend, Bill B, who could catch flies in midflight, for improving my boxing skills. The Army didn't instruct me on bird spider survival techniques, so it is down to Bill B that this awful thing got swatted before it ate me.

Before we left Australia, we received vaccinations against many bugs and diseases. One injection was for malaria, carried by mosquitoes; those annoying little bastards that spend their lives buzzing around your head at night. As an extra precaution, we took quinine tablets in our water. The camp beds were covered by mosquito nets, and these were available for use in the bush. The Army supplied a rub-on repellent as well. Over time I became

18. Vietnam. A life-changing experience!

convinced this stuff was not a repellent but an attraction to the mozzies; we reckoned they loved the stuff.

These Vietnamese mozzies were from the superhero school of flying insects, big tough buggers. There were unsubstantiated stories of their exploits around Nui Dat: 'I swatted one and four of his mates came in and carried me outside where the troops waited to suck me dry'; 'One night four big mozzies were sitting beside my bed enjoying a large drink of my repellent'; 'They took my net and my blanket and threw it on the floor and had their way with me, I reckon. I woke up feeling rather drained'.

An encounter with a snake resides deep in my memory. I do not like snakes, they scare the shit out of me. On gun picket one early morning, lying prone on the ground, both hands in position on the M60, I heard a slight movement beside my left arm. I watched as a long snake's darting forked tongue appeared. The thing was long, black with white hoops around its body. Later I discovered it was a bamboo snake, highly dangerous, aggressive and venomous. The thing proceeded to slither across my arms slowly, tongue checking out everything. Hurry up you bastard, I was saying under my breath while transfixed and frozen to the spot. Finally, it was off me and slithering away but stopped and raised its head about 15 cm. I had to resist the temptation to fire a burst from the M60.

Tactical exercises in the tropical jungles of north Queensland in places like Mount Spec taught us a lot about leeches. The horrible little grub that lives to suck your blood. The latest GP Boots that had inbuilt steel soles as a protection from pansy pits, tied off tightly well above the ankle. The trousers were secured on or above the boot with an elastic tie, all designed for protection from the leech. Despite these efforts, the ugly little buggers would try. Often at the end of the day in a "wet" jungle we would find blood-soaked socks from a leech or two trying to get inside. As they expanded from sucking your blood, the constant movement squashed the little fuckers.

19. SETTLING IN: FIRST NIGHT IN VIETNAM

Max, a section corporal, began talking about the patrol his section, including myself, would undertake that night. We would be outside the wire all night. These patrols went out every night to patrol the perimeter of Nui Dat, and act as an early detection of an attack on the base, an early warning system. We would proceed outside the wire at stand to (sundown) and return at stand to in the morning (sunrise). There were specific spots in our area of responsibility where we would stop in a defence position and listen for movement in the surrounding area. If nothing was detected, we would move to the next position and perform the same tactics. Eventually, around midnight we would double back and repeat the tactics, finally entering the base through the wire at sunrise. Max assured me the troops inside would not shoot us as we would be expected to be in that place at that time. 'I sincerely hope so,' I said.

'Personally, Pete, I think it's pretty tough to send you out there tonight, having not yet been in the country for twelve hours. But I have heard a lot about the 6th, so I know you are very well prepared. Good luck, buddy.' With that, we headed back to the company lines to link up with the section.

Max introduced me to his men. They all commented on my "brand-new" appearance, suggesting a swap for their well-worn and faded gear. Acceptance into the close-knit section was immediate. I felt I was part of this group immediately.

'You'll be right, Pete,' they all said. 'We'll look after ya, mate!'

It was almost dark when we passed through the wire. The posted pickets wished us well and good hunting, 'Bring me back a couple of fresh noggie ears'; 'Be careful of the drop bears'; 'Have a good time, don't drink too much, see you all in the morning bright'.

I was thinking as we left, *God, this is the real deal. I am in the middle of this shit fight. The enemy could be only a few feet away, or one of those booby traps waiting for me.* All my months of infantry training flooded into my mind. Alert, stay alert, eyes wide open looking and comprehending. Stay in contact with your mate, in front and behind, watch and react; there are no second chances here.

The terrain was reasonably flat, although underfoot could be difficult. There was about one hundred metres from our position to the rubber tree line. After an hour or so we reached the first listening post. Half of the section took a defence position allowing the others to rest, but every one of us remained completely silent listening for any movement. The defence roles were reversed at the next stop, sleep was not really an option.

What I remember most of all is how fuckin' dark the night was, the only thing visible were the stars above. When Max asked me at the halfway point how I was coping, I said, 'Corporal, I cannot see a bloody thing.'

He assured me that was completely normal. 'In time your night vision will improve, by the time we get back you will see much better, just relax the eyes and let it happen.' He was right!

Our patrol was quite well armed with five M16 rifles, an M60 machine gun, five SLR rifles plus an M79 grenade launcher, and thirty-three hand grenades. Enough to make a bit of noise if required. Also, we had a radio to report our exit and entry as well as any suspicious movement detected.

Thankfully my first night in Vietnam on an overnight patrol went off without incident and at sunrise, our group was greeted by some fresh smart-arse guys on early picket, all of whom would have done the same duty more than once.

'Didn't get lost in the dark? That's a change for you lot.'

'Which bar have you been at all night? Get to the RAP and get checked out.'

'How come there are eleven, did you pick-up a stray?'

Max said, 'So sorry to disturb you lot, go back to sleep now children!'

The section was going to breakfast at the mess immediately. They insisted I tag along, almost frog-marched me actually. Not many were in the mess as it was an early sitting for the TAOR patrols. Food was good and plentiful. I passed on the scrambled eggs. *Pale and a bit runny*, I thought. Everyone did the same, except the M60 gunner. 'Him,' said Max, 'he will eat anything alive or dead.' They explained to me that egg supply was erratic at times so the cooks used either powdered eggs or etherised eggs. Eggs treated somehow to keep them longer. Neither tasted too good.

*

This conversation caused me to remember how during the 1950s my Mum kept eggs in a large can in a clear liquid, sticky and thick, called "keep egg". This was a time before we had a refrigerator, only an ice box, wood stove and a meat safe hanging in the breezeway. Mums throughout the neighbourhood boiled the copper to do the washing, stirring it with a long stick and wringing it out by hand. Radio but no television, how did we survive life and stay as happy as we were? Probably because everyone slept at night with windows open and doors unlocked. Crime was minimal and the police, especially in traffic control, tried to educate drivers rather than punish. Maybe a kick up the bum was the worst one would get, with an added, 'I will contact your parents next time, young fella.'

This attitude to community living was, one might think, a result of the end of six years of the turmoil of World War II. Community attitude since Australia entered the Vietnam War was very, very different. Led by a minority group of protesters who did not represent the overall sentiment of the people, but as in all protest movements, gained a voice through television, radio and newspapers. The media began to prioritise these protests over the sparse reports of the Australian armed forces' efforts battling in Vietnam. There were already several reports of returning troops being abused by protesters, but little attention was shown towards those men by the general community.

Conscription of young Australian men into the armed forces and the commitment of the Army, Navy and Air Force to the Vietnam War was a watershed event in Australian political growth. Until that time, young people remained "in their proper place". The voting age was twenty-one years, adulthood was twenty-one years, and the legal alcohol drinking age was twenty-one years, but the age for compulsory registration for National Service call-up was nineteen years.

Thus, young men who could not vote, could not drink alcohol and were considered minors could be forced to serve two years in the armed forces and potentially become involved in a war in a country far away that had little connection to Australia, a country involved in a war or conflict over centuries. It is no wonder many rose up and protested. The protests were fine in my mind, but the anger and disgust of the Vietnam War became something else when the returning troops were the target of protesters. Those men, myself included, deserved better!

*

Max said, 'Pete, you did the job well last night. You are off duty until stand to at sunset. Catch-up on some shut-eye and maybe later wander around and get your bearings of this place.'

NUI DAT: MY NEW HOME FOR NOW!

I went back to my tent and within a few minutes was sound asleep. I woke around 1100 hours when the three roommates arrived back from their stint in the bush. They quickly noticed me and proceeded to toss me out of bed onto the floor all yelling things at me: 'Get out of that fart sack, soldier'; 'Sleeping on-the-job, soldier, is naughty'; 'Welcome to our Palace de Shit, Pete'. All three grabbed me and embraced me in a wonderful welcome. Rob, Joe and Jack were my instant best friends. All privates, like me, they were the happiest they had been for a year.

'Pete, ol' mate,' said Joe, 'we've just finished our last "bush walk" and will be going home soon. We're happy to be still upright and walking about. Seeing you is confirmation. Sorry about the over-the-top welcome.'

Rob said, 'We'll look after you for the next few days. Anything you want to know, we'll help if we can. Just ask, okay?'

They were obviously, and rightly, excited about surviving here in this place. I wondered how they would "fit" back into the Australian environment after this extremely difficult and dangerous lifestyle I was about to experience.

Jack, the oldest of the three, asked 'When did you get in, Pete?'

'About this time yesterday, Jack.'

'Been sleeping ever since, have ya?' said Joe.

I answered him quietly in an offhanded manner, 'Last night I was on TAOR patrol with Corporal Max and his section.'

All three almost in unison said, 'Fucking hell, not even a half day in the country and they send you out there. Not good, not good, not good.'

'All is well. I'm still here,' I said.

They insisted I join them and their company buddies for lunch at the mess. They had been promised very decent food after enduring two weeks of ration pack meals. On entry to the mess my three new friends introduced me to the packed room, '6RAR has arrived. Private Pete is here, please welcome him.'

The 4RAR men cheered and hooted then broke into a song. I suspect one clever guy, who had the voice, led, 'You are here, you are here. Onya Pete. See ya, see ya, we are happy to see ya. Off we go, off we go, we'll be going hommme.' It went something like that, but it said again that a new person from a new battalion was sufficient confirmation for them they were going home.

My three new friends urged me to reply. I was not really confident about speaking in a group, but remembering something, an old joke about the English fighting the Scots, I decided to say a few words. I said, 'Thank you for the welcoming song, well done. I am but one of 6th Battalion, some say one 6th is enough to replace the 4th.'

The mess erupted in hoo-haas and laughter. They were so happy to be back in Nui Dat with the prospect of boarding HMAS Sydney in Vung Tau Harbour for the long voyage home in a matter of days that anything I said would be welcomed. Jack said, 'Well done, Pete, but a month or two ago you would be mincemeat by now.' I said to him I could feel the mood, the reaction when a replacement actually arrived. Luckily, I was right. The four of us talked Army stuff for over an hour. They gave me so much info about the jungle, the rubber tree plantations, rice paddies and the people. I was awash with new knowledge of this place.

'Do you like rain, Pete? Do you care about getting wet, fuckin' wet?' was one of the questions.

I said where we trained in Townsville heavy rain was a regular thing.

'Yeah, but over here it just fuckin' rains, if you get my drift. In the jungle everything is wet, slippery and waiting to get you off guard, watch every step, nothing is safe. Do not trust the locals, especially the young kids, be suspicious of everything and everyone.'

Joe, a really hard case (if you know the saying), talked about the "hotel accommodation" I would be living in for the next few months. He said nighttime was the most interesting, especially for mozzies and other wildlife, 'If you're woken up by a mongoose in bed with you, don't worry. It won't hurt you or bite, he will be looking for the snake he saw on the sandbag walls. It's a good thing!'

'Thanks for the heads up, Joe. Mongoose is welcome any time!'

'The bloody mozzies will get you no matter what. Ensure you use the net at night, buy some commercial spray for the night, and hope your quinine is up to scratch. Malaria is rife here. Forget the Army issue repellent, these mozzie bastards love it. Pour it on the top of your locker, they will go for it and not you, I reckon.'

'Mud, mud and mud! This place never dries out, the rubber tree canopy and regular rain take care of that. Make an effort to keep the digs as clean as possible. We have a chair near the sandbag entry. We use it to help remove the boots and get rid of as much mud as possible. Otherwise, the floor, as luxurious as it is, will be a fucking mess in a day. Stow your boots so nothing crawly can get in to surprise you in the morning or, worse still, in the middle of the night when there is a rocket attack.'

'A rocket attack?' I said in a lame surprised voice.

'Yeah, mate. A couple of times a month the nogs fire rockets at us, just to piss us off! You'll be ordered to stand to in the weapon pits outside, the ones with a layer of empty beer cans on the bottom. They're better than standing in the mud out there, hey guys?'

'My fur coat,' they replied in unison.

'As the company sig your job is different. There are radios in the comms bunker you will be required to man, stand to, at times. The orderly corporal will show you the ropes in the next day or so.'

Joe, the hard case, said. 'We had better tell him about the "shitter" out back!'

'You tell him, Joe, you're always hiding in there.'

Joe obliged, 'See that building with the fine mesh all over it? That is our luxurious toilet, shithole, a.k.a. "the shitter". It is a big deep hole in the dirt covered with a wooden platform on which sit a row of about ten thunder boxes. Each box has a wooden lid, we keep all lids shut. The big hole is populated by some flies. Millions of the little bastards. They live to bombard your arse when you sit down. I have acquired a small number of "smoke grenades". I toss one in and shut the seat. Helps to settle the little pricks down for a few minutes. Just be sure no one else is sitting at the time, could be uncomfortable.'

'Improves the odour, smell, aah stink, and kills some noggie-arse flies,' said Jack.

THE BOOZER: "THE SELDOM SEEN INN", NUI DAT, 1969

Back at the palatial digs, the other three guys collapsed on their feather beds. After a month in the bush, a rough dry camp bed feels like a feather bed. I was about to venture out on a discovery walk around the company base when a corporal arrived at the "door".

'Hi Pete, welcome. I'm Ian, the D Company clerk, come whatever go-do-it person.'

I was to spend many hours with Ian, who was a very pleasant, friendly person (not like some corporals I had met). The relationship between us underlings, officers and NCOs changed somewhat in Vietnam. For instance, I addressed the OC of D Company as Jock, while out on operations.

'Pete,' Ian said, 'you have certain responsibilities as a 6th advance party representative.' What he had to say next surprised me, but it was tongue-in-cheek stuff. 'The boozer,' he said, 'you have to take over the boozer until 4RAR leave and 6 arrives in a few days!'

As it turned out, it wasn't all beer and skittles, although beer was a major part of it— obvious, hey! There were some other things to learn. The skittles. These were, in order of importance (i.e., to me): (1) Supply—6RAR was basically a Queensland mob, wanting, no doubt, their favourite drop, the famous XXXX; (2) Money business; (3) Storage facilities, cold room etcetera; and (4) Rules of trade and timing.

'Normal opening time is 1700,' said Ian. 'However, the OC is allowing an early march at 1500, as recognition of a successful final operation. He added we could expect a full inn and mega sales. Ian was aware I had arrived yesterday and with the overnight patrol it was understandable if I was a bit "bushed".

'But, mate, you'll enjoy the experience. They're a bunch of good men who will accept you as one of them— although not as 4RAR. Expect a bit, no, a lot of fun to be had over your mess comments.'

Ian and I walked to the "Inn" as he pointed out the RAP, CHQ, the comms bunker, and the signs at the entrance to the D Company compound that read:

> Speed Limit 10 m.p.h.. See the sign, or see our OC.
> Boots Company (below which sat a pair of yellow GP Boots)
> D COMPANY 6RAR (below the Infantry Combat Badge)

D Company was known as "boots company" because it was us who walked, marched or ran everywhere, never in the luxury of an APC. Unlike the other AB3 or 12C mob.

19. Settling in: First night in Vietnam

Boots Company insignia (my own drawings)

The boozer was an open structure, concrete floor, partly closed sides, and closed rear. It was strewn with round metal tables and metal chairs, nothing extravagant. The bar area was covered and secured. Ian and I entered through a locked door behind the bar. Ian pointed out the roller door, the cold room and controls, the safe, the fridge controls and the bar roller door.

He opened a drawer under the bar and produced a dog-eared book. He handed me the keys and said, 'Sign here, here and here.'

'Pete, you now own the "Seldom Seen Inn", in Nui Dat, South Vietnam.'

It was my life's dream to own a small pub. Now I had one, but in effing Vietnam.

FIRST DAY OF TRADING AT THE INN

The 4th Battalion men had not seen a beer for a month. Ian said it would be a baptism of fire for me. The bar was manned by Ian, two volunteers and me. The Inn sold canned beer and soft drinks, but no spirits. The cost was US fifteen cents a can. Every can was opened by the bar staff. Payment was by cash or by Military Payment Certificate (MPC), a small paper currency based on US currency.

The MPC series changed without notice, rendering the current notes invalid. Only, the diggers could convert their holding to the new series within a limited period. The reason was to restrict the use of the currency by the Vietnamese. Some enterprising diggers, gamblers or whatever, also accumulated larger amounts than could be deemed savings of the regular allowance. When a unit was returning to Australia, a series change would occur at some time before troops departed.

After twelve months and little opportunity to spend, many men had reserves of MPCs they could find difficult to convert to Aussie dollars on departure. Many just didn't worry. Apart from buying a camera or TEAC M9 reel-to-reel stereo, the boozer was the place for spending.

At 1500 hours they descended upon the bar in droves. The experienced barkeeps among us had cartons open on the bar and the cans already opened. Money changed hands freely. 'Keep the change,' was a constant call. Beer flowed and the noise of happy laughing diggers increased. The frantic pace continued for an hour. The guys joined in a shout of two, four or six. The shout was a carton (twenty-four cans), all open and cold. Economical, you bet, at a discounted three dollars a carton. Ian was smart, he had realised the beer stocks would not be suitable for my guys. Courage and Victoria Bitter from Victoria, Reschs from New South Wales, Budweiser from the US, and a few other southern state drops would be discounted.

Discount or not, these men were relaxed. Happy at the prospect of going home they drank or wasted (tipped out, fell over, lost it, or poured it on a mate's head) "ton'za" beers. A large crowd of young men, every one of them pissed to the eyeballs, not an argument, just laugh, laugh and then fall asleep where they stood. They spent money like it didn't matter. The bar till, an ammunition box, was overflowing with MPCs. No one wanted change of $20 for a single beer or a carton. Occasionally when a $50 appeared, a change of $20 was requested. The bar soon had the $20 back anyway.

Ian and the volunteers had little opportunity to participate, although we did join in the ditty singing. Most, if not all of these, could not be repeated here, even if my old head could recall the words. Ian was happy with the night, especially the behaviour of his men. He would sort out the money and donate a sufficient amount to the 6RAR OR (other ranks) bar to get it up and running successfully.

'Pete,' he said, 'you were a hit with the men of the 4th at the mess today and they have remembered your good humour here. Thanks, mate.' Ian went on to say he would meet me at the mess for breakfast and continue his briefing on my responsibilities, 'At 0600, Pete. See you then. Goodnight.'

What an introduction to Vietnam that was, I thought, as I sought my way in the darkness to my tent.

The other three residents were soundly asleep, competing in the snoring Olympics, sounding like a bad production of Beethoven's 4th "Sympathy". I was so bushed I soon fell asleep listening to the "music"!

DAY TWO

After breakfast, Corporal Ian took me to the CHQ command bunker. Nothing but several aerials were visible above the ground. The partly concealed entrance led to a wide, heavy, wooden stairway leading down several metres into the large open space below. The floor, roof and walls were lined with heavy timber. Overall lighting was quite dull. The air was musty but cool.

Along one wall a heavy timber bench at seating height accommodated several field telephones, VHF and HF radios. Each position had a chair, individual lighting and writing equipment. Daily codes were in a closed box at the end of the bench. Also provided was a loudspeaker address system and alarm controls. The equipment was all top-of-the-tree stuff available in the 1960s. No computers, no videos, no cameras and no KFC. There was a radio tuned to US Radio Vietnam, so the latest episode of *Chicken Man* (the greatest crime fighter the world has ever known) would not be missed.

'You are responsible for communication with each platoon commander. There are landline phones to each platoon as well as VHF and HF radio. In addition, there are phones to the mortar platoon and artillery, including the American 88s next door. A lance corporal from battalion comms shares the responsibility for communication with Battalion staff and ATF (Australian Task Force) staff. Daily operating codes will be provided in hard copy in the code box I showed you earlier. You must ensure receipt of the codes by 0800 each day.

'Apart from that lot, Pete, all you have to do is ensure everything in the bunker is in perfect operating condition by radio check calls every day and also maintain the aerials above and the telephone connections. The lance corporal from battalion will be here tomorrow, I will introduce you then. The same person will be with you when the Company is out on operation,' Ian said.

'Seems I'll spend a lot of time in this hole in the ground, Ian,' I said.

'Not really, Pete. Maintaining the gear and checking the codes is a daily job but takes little time. If a stand to is called outside the dawn and sunset regular procedure, like a rocket attack, you will, you must, be in here asap and begin all comms with platoons.'

'Rocket attacks,' I said, 'how often do they occur?'

'Once or twice a month. Usually, they're attempting to hit Luscombe Airfield, or there will be mortars aimed closer inside the base.'

According to Ian, little was achieved by these bombardments.

The retaliation by the Aussie artillery or mortar fire was swift and devastating to the enemy. Australian radio monitors within the base HQ constantly listened for and tracked enemy radio positions. This information was relayed to the various defences within the base, allowing a quick response to an attack.

Surprisingly, it was almost lunch time. I went back to the tent to maybe get my area better organised. The "orchestra" were all awake. A little broken and busted, but awake. They were sorting through their gear, deciding what went and what stayed.

'Here, Pete, you can have this and this and another of those,' as they tossed bits of kit on my bed. There goes my plan to get organised. The bed was piled up with useful stuff, well, maybe useful. I have, after fifty-five years, a US battle jacket, worn and torn, hanging in my garage. The 4RAR soldier's name on it is now missing. Onya, mate!

Inspections of living quarters were a very rare thing. The officers relied upon our personal discipline in maintaining our personal space. For the most part, the policy worked. NCOs might visit on a random basis only to say, 'Clean up this brothel, you blokes!'

It was "munch time", so I went to the mess with the other three inmates of Palace de Shit who were a little hungry after missing breakfast.

At 1400 hours, I wandered over to the Inn. Ian was there, preparing for the 1700 opening. The beer stock was sufficient for the next few days, but something had to be done to obtain some XXXX for the Queensland troops.

'The Q Store has a pallet of XXXX you can have,' said Ian. 'The only problem is you have to take a pallet of Courage as well. And I've talked to my friend at 5RAR, who has a half pallet of XXXX he is willing to swap, but he wants the full pallet of Courage in exchange.'

There were rules governing the beer holding for each Inn. Ian went on to explain— if I had too much stock (of undesirables) and XXXX became available, I could not get it anyway. What Ian was saying was, 'If you have a pallet of Courage sitting ... '

I interrupted and said, 'So we, or I, take the offer from Five?'

'Exactly,' said Ian. 'Sell your men what they want, they deserve it here in this crappy place. Pete, I'll attend to the necessary arrangements and inform you in the morning.'

Back to the Manor. No one was there, called to some company briefing about logistics and the home to Australia adventure. On their return they'll be "happy little Vegemites, bright as bright as can be" and sticking it to me. Sure enough, they arrived dancing and singing, shit dancing and even shittier singing.

I said, 'Just fuck off home. Fuck off anywhere, I have work to do,' in the strongest voice I could muster.

'Listen to him, doesn't need any help from Four, can fight this war on his own.'

'Yeah, one Six should do it easily, I reckon. Look at you three—can't dance, can't sing,' I said in quick retaliation.

'Hey, Pete, the Inn is opening early again this arvo. Wanna come whiff us?'

'I'll be there. I'll be there before you and I'll be behind the bar, so be nice!'

'Well, whoo haa for you, cobber. Give us some freebies, hey.'

'No freebies, but there will be a "buy one get one free" on some of your crappy beer!'

Harvey Norman, consider this a modern marketing tool.

Ian was correct. This place, South Vietnam, was a crappy place. People who have visited the county in more recent years say it is a beautiful place. I have been asked by various groups of people to join a conducted tour, including visits to the Nui Dat site and The Battle of Long Tan precinct, including the Memorial Cross raised there in 1969 (although the cross there now is not the original). The Long Tan Cross commemorates the eighteen Australian soldiers of D Company 6RAR killed in a battle against the NVA regular soldiers and the D445 VC Battalion. I was there when the Cross was flown in, suspended from an Iroquois chopper. I have no interest in reliving that experience. The original Cross was taken by the conquering NVA and for years stored in a closed museum. Not a surprising reaction as The Battle of Long Tan was a major loss to the VC and NVA forces. Many years later the original cross was recovered by negotiation and is currently exhibited in the Australian War Memorial in Canberra.

The Vietnam War was an unconventional conflict. For the most part, in the Australian area of responsibility, Phouc Tuy province, the enemy was unrecognisable. The VC were ordinary village people during the day. At night, dressed in black (pyjamas), they were a dangerous enemy. Australian Army authorities, being aware of the situation, designed the training of its troops to suit that environment.

20. ANOTHER DAY IN PARADISE

an met me at breakfast at 0600 hours. He informed me he had requisitioned a Land Rover and trailer to pick-up supplies at the Q store as well as at 5RAR.

'Hi, Pete. You look like shit, mate. Didn't you sleep well?'

'I hardly slept, Ian. It was like a boom, crash opera all night.'

'The big American track-mounted artillery guns are stationed pretty close to your tent. They're noisy bastards,' said Ian. 'They operate at night quite often without notice to us. You'll hear them again!'

The Q Store was some distance away. *This base was a big place*, I was thinking as I passed all sorts of weaponry and service establishments. Ian ran a constant commentary on what was what. I was totally bushed by the time we reached the Q store.

I was introduced to the necessary staff, mostly corporals with a captain in charge. I signed off on our delivery and headed off to the D Company 5RAR boozer. The trailer was loaded by a handy little forklift. Again, totally confused, bushed, and sticking close to Ian at all times, we somehow found the Fifth's Inn.

'Unfortunately, Pete, there's no forklift available, so it is a carry job, mate!'

The Fifth had a half dozen "willing" helpers on hand, probably Courage drinkers, who unloaded our pallet in quick time. When the half pallet of XXXX was removed from the cold room, it was plain to see why they did the deal. The XXXX was the remnants of their supply.

Back at the Seldom Seen Inn, the job of unloading one and a half pallets of beer fell upon Ian and me. Several 4RAR guys laughingly refused to touch that XXXX shit! 'Unload the crap yoosself, you fookin Queenslander wanker.' Eventually, some two dozen men assisted, all laughing and joking about the XXXX beer crap they were having to carry.

Two things began to become clear to me around that time. The only thing that varied within the Aussie battalions was the faces of the men forming the unit. Everything else was similar. The attitude towards other men, the willingness to participate and help, the concern for another man's wellbeing, the Aussie sense of humour, all making up the most important ingredient in a successful group: mateship!

The other thing I noticed was the attitude towards me. These 4th Battalion men were on a high, they were soon heading home, but not once did I hear a comment, joke, etcetera, about, 'You have to stay. I'm going home, ha ha, dickhead!'

There is a lot to be said about the abilities of the Army personnel in charge of training and the formation of nine infantry battalions during the Vietnam War period, plus all the supporting groups. I said earlier what bastards we thought the recruit training corporals were and recalled why we formed that opinion. We, at that time, did not understand what these bastards were attempting to achieve. They formed the platform of spit, polish and discipline onto which the Army was able to build a reliable and cohesive fighting force.

MEETING OUR AMERICAN ALLIES

After the beer was squared away in the cold room, Ian took me to CHQ. I was introduced to the OC and the CSM. Two reasonable men, considering their rank. A war does have some equalising effect.

With the saluting done the major said, 'Private Collins, I have been told about you, all good I must add. Welcome to the 4th.' He went on to say (as an officer would) 'The 6th is, I hear, a fine battalion, but yet to prove itself over here.'

I replied, 'Sir, I am sure my unit will perform very well and follow on from the 1966 tour.'

The major looked at me in a way officers do and said, 'Thank you, Private. I believe you are meeting our American neighbours tonight. I suggest you keep your wits about you; they are a shrewd bunch. Thank you, Corporal. Dismiss.'

As we took the vehicle and trailer back to the transport pool, Ian said 'You handled that nicely, Pete. He can be difficult at times.'

On the 500 m walk back I asked Ian about the visit to the Yanks. Did he arrange it?

'Don't know anything about it, mate. Probably those three you share you digs with, I would guess. They've been over there before.'

Sure enough, when I entered the tent an hour later Joe leaped up, 'Pete, those Yankee guns upset you last night, hey mate?'

'They did, Joe, and kept doing it all night!'

Jack sat up in bed with some effort and said, 'We're all going over there tonight to sort them bloody Yanks out!'

'Yeah, Pete. Early din dins, we jump the fence and show them Yankees a thing or two about upsetting our new mate, so dress up in your oldest greens and we'll venture on.'

'Won't we be AWOL or something?' I said in a meek voice.

'Ahh, don't worry about it, she'll be right mate. No one will know.' Famous last words of many Aussie men!

Barely able to keep a straight face, I looked at these three guys in front of me and said, 'The OC and the CSM know. The major advised me to keep my wits about me over there.'

'We did get permission. The boss considers some interaction with our neighbours is a good thing,' said Rob. 'So, Pete, relax and enjoy these crazy Yanks; it'll be a long night.'

The American camp was very nicely set-up. Each big gun crew of four men lived in substantial framed tents immediately behind the gun. Sleeping quarters, separated into four large adjoining spaces, were somewhat more comfortable than our little bunks in an open-sided marquis tent. Radio, music and television were provided for these Americans.

Common infrastructure, administration, mess, bathrooms and the bar were situated in the centre of the complex. The bar was called "Fort Nott". Apparently, the name changed with each garrison change. It was a large, heavy tent with a steel structure at one end with lock-up entrance doors.

The four of us entered without challenge and went straight to the bar and ordered our first beer. 'G'Day,' said the barman in attempted Aussie.

Joe introduced me as one of the replacement battalions, 'Pete is on his own at the moment, the rest of them arrive in a few days.' The barman, who looked like Clint Eastwood, surprisingly had the name "Clint".

Clint, in his very best American, said, 'Welcome to our establishment, Pete. You are welcome here anytime.'

The place filled quickly. The music, the voice babble rose, and the beer flowed at an amazing rate. The price? 'To you, Aussie wankers, free,' was the direction of the "manager", who was a captain, I think.

These men had a good life by all accounts, interrupted by rotation of gun crews on full duty, and occasionally a call to arms, requiring some sobriety of the crews.

As the night wore on, the Aussie v Yankee conquests began. Among these was the beer can crushing challenge. In the year 1969, American beer cans were made of thin aluminium; our XXXX beer cans were made from steel. The challenge was to fold a can in half with one hand.

The American tins were pretty easy; even I could do it. The big Yank guys all but destroyed them. The XXXX can was a bit different. I had been shown the technique at the Seldom Seen Inn, so most attempts were successful. The technique requires a little preparation of the can. While drinking one should slowly crease the can on ONE side, and gradually increase the damage to the one side. The can will fold quite easily. When fully prepared, the Yanks are asked to fold a XXXX can.

It is all in the technique. It is the same business as being an effective soldier in a unit. Listen to the experts, the ones with experience, remember what they say and put it into practice on-the-job. If everyone is on the same wavelength and tuned in to a combined objective the result will be positive. Acting as an individual without regard for others, without discipline, will not achieve an objective.

What I saw that day fell in line with my thoughts of American military activity. Be the biggest, have the biggest Army numbers, the biggest artillery, more mortars than mozzies in the swamp, biggest fastest aircraft, enough helicopters to blacken the sky in daylight and an ego to match. Toss it all in at once against an enemy the US Intelligence people do not know anything about, let alone their exact location or their tactics of defence and attack.

The beer can "grand prix" was to be me (the smallest person in the crowd) and an American of their choice. The winner takes all! The American contender was not white-skinned and was a giant of a man, with arms like tree trunks and hands as big as a family Domino's pizza.

I was asked to go first. The can I was drinking was almost empty and fully prepared. Facing the opposition, I raised the can and in a delicate motion with forefinger and thumb, folded the can in half and tossed it in the air. My opponent, unimpressed, grabbed a XXXX can (a full one) and tried the same action without success. In frustration, he squeezed the fuck out of the can sending beer spray over the crowd. He grabbed me, lifted me above his bald head and said, 'You the fuckin' best, li'l Ozzie,' and dropped me from about three metres up.

These Yanks were a lot of fun, full of bravado, full of themselves as we Australians say, but I did not think they were very good soldiers, especially as infantry soldiers. They had praise for the Australian Army members they had met in South Vietnam, and several mentioned the earlier (1966) Battle of Long Tan, where a company of 108 men faced an estimated two and a half thousand NVA and VC and were successful.

There was a sort of amazement of how our infantry operated in the jungle and how we adapted operating procedures depending on the terrain. An officer with at least a year "in country" talked to me at length about the discipline of our forces. Actually, he didn't recognise it as discipline, but rather a learned procedure to be followed. I explained to him why discipline in company with training made the difference. Americans understood the idea of a team in gridiron and baseball, but did not, at that time, apply a team strategy to their defence forces.

I talked to him at length about how an infantry unit is formed. Once the various parts are formed, all training is undertaken as that unit. This forms a cohesion of the group and respect for the other bloke. The end result is what we Aussies refer to as mateship, which creates a watch your mate's back and work as a team ethos. Once a unit is effective, there will be no unnecessary changes to its membership.

The disciplines of not walking on tracks, not walking on roads, proceed in silence, communicate with understood hand signals, be ever vigilant, weapon always at the ready, no smoking, no odours foreign to the terrain (aftershave, etcetera) and no talking. When moving through the jungle or dense rubber tree plantations each step was taken with care. The sound of a breaking branch or twig carried in the silence of the bush.

The American forces fought major battles like Khe Sanh in the northern areas of South Vietnamese territory and along the de-militarised zone (DMZ). These battles were fought under heavy aircraft and artillery bombardment including support by US Navy ships in the vicinity. The opposition was comprised of both VC militia and NVA regulars in large numbers. Having fought wars over centuries against the Chinese, Japanese and French military, they had developed some sound defence and attack procedures.

Surprise and silent movements both in attack and withdrawal were a hallmark of their operation, particularly in the north. Reports indicate US ground troops arrived at a site "plastered" by air and artillery to find absolutely no evidence of the enemy occupation. As is said by military experts, "a battle is not won until the ground troops command the ground".

The war in the south was different. Australians were involved in infantry search and destroy operations involving the resilient and clever VC. Apart from available artillery support at all times, and occasional US air support, all action was by ground troops.

We did encounter the US infantry on such an operation. Our mission involved setting an ambush on a track used regularly, according to Intelligence in Saigon, by NVA moving through to Cambodia. The ambush site was manned by a platoon-size force and included Claymore mines. Forward lookouts alerted us of approaching unidentified soldiers. They were soon identified as American. To their surprise and horror, an Australian officer stepped out onto the track and challenged their forward leader. The rest of the Aussies stepped forward, weapons at the ready. These Yanks did not know which way to turn. They were totally unprepared. A sole VC machine gun could, and would, wipe them out. One mine or booby trap on the path would cause death and injury.

I was amazed at the lack of infantry skills, and I was only a conscript, not a professional soldier, marine or whatever. They were armed with all the latest weapons and sophisticated communication equipment. A lance corporal directly in front of me carried his rifle over his shoulder behind his back; he had a guitar to the front. They marched about a metre apart, nose to tail, oblivious, it seemed, to the surroundings, casually listening to music on their transistor radios. Many were smoking, others were talking and laughing out loud. They broke every rule in the book.

The American officer, a major I believe, stepped forward and saluted our officer who did not return the salute. That form of recognition alerts the enemy to the commander. Later in the debrief we heard the conversation went something like this:

'I guess we are all dead now.'

'Not yet, Major, but you soon will be in this neck of the woods, unless you smarten up.'

'I get your drift, sir. May we continue?'

Off they went, still in single file on the track. At least the guitar was now on his back. The incident proves the worth of training and discipline at all levels of a defence force.

But, back to my first night with the Yanks, I discovered that what these particular guys did best was entertain themselves and their guests. Most of the night was spent drinking, drinking some more, telling stories of the war kind, singing and laughing. During a brief interlude two local Vietnamese girls appeared on the small stage, did some tricks with beer bottles and ping pong balls and faded away into the night. No idea how or who got them inside the base.

I was involved with two guys talking about our national sport, cricket. The group grew to around ten, as did the questions and observations about the game and its language. As reported by Hardwick (2021), the conversation went something like this:

'There are some weird people playing cricket. One player had a slash outside off stump and the commentator reckoned he was also a compulsive hooker.'

'Yeah, and there are some other weirdos fielding in slips. Other players have two short legs or maybe a long square leg. There is a silly point and a silly gully. Does the wicket keeper own the wickets, or does he sleep with them under his pillow?'

'A bowler of note bowled a maiden over; where did she come from? He probably got no-balled for that.'

'Some bowlers are said to be a bit short of a good length. How do the commentators know that?'

'He bowled that excellent over without no balls. The umpire has no balled the bowler for overstepping the mark. Tough punishment.'

The night finished and a good part of the next day as well. The four of us helped drag each other through the fence and to our beds. So that was my first encounter with our American allied troops.

What a night!

21. THE 6TH ARRIVES: WORK BEGINS

The time had passed quickly as I had been busy, busy, busy. There had been lots of nitty-gritty bits and pieces of change over administration I attended to, much too boring to write about. With the imminent arrival of the balance of the battalion, things started to happen quickly.

To be totally honest, my recollections of this short period are very vague. My 4RAR tent mates all wished me the best, gave me so many handy bits and pieces of kit, even money (MPCs) and Joe handed over his stash of smoke grenades, or as he called them, "toilet cleaners".

The CO, Lieutenant Colonel Butler, was keen to have his men outside the wire as soon as possible and had organised the initial battalion operation quickly. Wanting to hit the ground running, so to speak.

RECOLLECTIONS OF OPERATIONS IN VIETNAM

The stories I tell here are true as I recall. They come from my memory of events of fifty plus years ago. Apart from where referenced, no research is involved, only my personal recollection, reaction, feelings of some traumatic events that occurred in a war where the enemy was often unseen and unknown.

The CO was keen to get the battalion out working in the field. Shortly after arriving in Phuoc Tuy province the full unit left the base at Nui Dat. The CO had named the operation "Lavarack", the name of the base at home in Townsville. The operation would be conducted over thirty days. Whoopee! Thirty days of camping in the bush, digging holes to sleep in, if sleeping was allowed, eating delicious rations out of little cans, no shower, no toilet, no bed, no table, no chair, no beer, warm water with shit in it, dirty clothes, flies, mosquitoes, snakes, rain by the bucket and unseen people trying to shoot you. Can't wait!

We were transported to the area by APCs, a fun trip with nine soldiers in complete combat gear jammed into this track-mounted machine that has no concept of how its cargo is faring as it charges across, over and through anything in its path. Eventually the soldiers exit their comfortable 120-degree ride as the rear door drops down like a ramp. The cramped knees are expected to exit bloody quickly and form a circle of protection for the stack of metal they just left. Mind you we often appreciated the stacks of metal as they extracted us from a bad situation.

That first night we dug in and prepared to move out at daylight the next day. No such thing as a good night's sleep in the Army. The night, or most of it, was consumed by briefings at each level of command (us private punks being the last) and preparing weapons and checking gear. I did not sleep at all. Besides all the other stuff, I needed to establish radio contact with the platoon sigs. The fucking radio and the house brick sized spare battery the sigs carried was heavy and took up a lot of room in the backpack. Leaving some stuff behind became a necessity. What I left behind depended on the length and type of operation we were doing. Often it was luxuries like food! Many times, for days on end, I ate only rice and strawberry jam out of a tube. I went to Vietnam very fit, healthy and weighing 82 kg. I came home weighing only 60 kg.

Apart from the radio, spare battery and extendable six metre long-distance aerial, my pack-housed bedding (ground sheet and mozzie net), hutchie, socks, undies, medication, dixies, small stove and fuel, rations (dependent on resupply or not). On the outside of the pack, we all carried a valuable tool, digging equipment, a small combination fold-up pick and shovel.

On the belt were four water bottles, two ammunition pouches with sixty rounds each. A third pouch for field message pads, pens, maps, compass and codes. A fourth pouch had a small supply of emergency medical stuff, weapon cleaning gear, dark and night glasses. Also, on the belt were three or four hand grenades (pineapples).

This load of shit was bloody heavy, Joyce. It was heavier than I was, I think. When I hit the deck, I might land on my back and be stranded like a turtle. The only way back up on my feet was to drop the pack, roll over and retrieve the effing thing.

Thankfully my rifle was a light M16, light but deadly accurate and powerful, I called mine "Suzie"! Most of our soldiers had names for their weapon. Some were very amusing, others their partner or girlfriend: 'I sleep with "Peggy" every night after I have cleaned her bits and pieces and put her to bed. In the jungle Peggy protects me and my mates from the nasty enemy all day and night.' These men, alone in a hostile foreign country, grabbed any opportunity to visit their home memories.

It was a bit weird, I guess, but to a group of lonely men it was a bit like writing home, or having a long-distance telephone conversation, impossible at the time, with their family. Nobody laughed at the tears, no one criticised, but often these times were an indication a mate might need a bit of extra support. 'Come on, mate, let's go to the boozer for a couple!'

LAVARACK, NUMBER ONE OP: I AM NOT SHOOTING THIS PERSON, WE ARE!

As is infantry practice, the day begins with stand to before dawn. History will show, I guess, that dawn is the prime time for an enemy to attack. So, like it or lump it, the infantry day begins predawn. You do adjust, fifty plus years later, I still wake and rise at dawn. But I am soon back in bed, TV on and a coffee in hand. Stand down is passed down the line when a threat is not evident. Forward pickets remain on watch during a quick brew and breakfast (of sorts).

This was the procedure on the battalion's first field operation. At 0630 hours the battalion moved forward on our first of several search and destroy missions. Search for the enemy strongholds, destroy their weapons and their resources. Australian soldiers had a difficult task in Vietnam. It was a very different war to World War I and World War II. The difference being recognition of who the enemy was, and what he or she looked like. The NVA wore a uniform. The VC, as I mentioned previously, wore "black pyjamas", but only at night. During the daytime they appeared as ordinary Vietnamese people. The VC controlled the villages with threats of violence and death. The villagers felt unable to assist the Australian soldiers due to this covert control. There were reported incidents of the VC burning villages and attempting to blame the Australian or American forces.

My own experience confirmed this complicity. One day our company was investigating reported activity of the VC in a particular village. An old frail looking Vietnamese peasant had a problem, a wheel had fallen off his cart. It was a large wheel; the cart was heavy. He obviously needed help. After some Aussie soldiers replaced the wheel he continued on his way, bowing, nattering and smiling. That same night we shot him dead! Dressed in the VC black PJs and armed with a rifle and booby trap makings, it was the same man!

The battalion moved in arrow formation into the area of operation. Soon the tree canopy became dense and underfoot was wet and slimy green. Water, about 50mm deep, covered a sludge of about the same depth.

Major S, OC D Company, turned to me and said in his droll Scottish tone, 'Do hope we won't have to hit the deck in this quagmire, Pete!'

I replied, 'Wet is better than dead, I guess.' The boss just smiled.

My job, as company sig, meant I was always close to the boss. He was a good man, a good soldier who cared greatly for the men he commanded. I, and the other members of D Company, held him in high esteem. He was a tall slim man with immense energy, his long legs carried him quickly across the ground. At times this presented a problem for me. The majority of his orders to the platoon commanders were conveyed by me, on the run, so to speak, over the radio. My problem occurred when he wished to speak directly on the radio. The handset, with a Pressel (i.e. press-to-talk) Switch, extended about two metres from the radio on my back. I had to keep up through long grass, over logs, under bushes, up and down gullies to maintain communication. The boss said, 'Sorry, mate. I will remember to slow down next time,' but he never did. But that was my job, and I was paid fuck all for doing it.

We had a couple of stop, look and listen episodes. Thankfully no "hit the deck" incidents in the wet area. By late afternoon the ground was dry. The terrain was flat with small trees and low scrub. The order was given to dig in for the night, stand to at sunset.

"Dig in" means dig a hole in the ground deep enough to cover your body and do it quickly. Yeah, mate, what about the tree roots, rocks and bitty things? I have a small shovel to assist, nothing substantial to help. They call this hole in the ground a "shell-scrape".

So, we all dug in, as best we could. I had a scraping about 150 mm deep at one end and a bit less on the other. I was sitting on the edge eating a small can of something from the ration pack. A rifle shot echoed in the distance and then another closer. I heard a "swack" on a tree beside my head as I leaped face down into my pit. I lay there, rifle ready for several minutes until all clear was called. Suddenly I felt a sharp pain in my abdomen area. *Fuck me*, I thought, *I've been hit*. I sat up to find the ration can hanging out of my body. I had a war wound, a tiny scar in my tummy from the sharp cut edge of the can. Better than a bullet, hey?

For three weeks we cruised around the dedicated area, checking out villages and their people, looking for evidence of the VC. We were welcomed, but in a reserved manner. They were simple people involved with farming and rubber tree plantations and collection of the sap from the trees. Any VC connected to the village disappeared before we arrived. They were warned by lookouts often high up in the bush canopy. The VC were a well organised force, they fought their battles at night and were very adept at jungle concealment, fast retreat, and surprise attacks. They left no evidence of their wounded and always removed any dead. The only evidence was sometimes a blood trail or two. This hidden Army was very large and well supplied by the communist north. They were inventive with booby traps, not the improvised explosive devices (IEDs) of later wars like Afghanistan, but nonetheless traps which inflicted devastating individual wounds to their enemies. I will refer to their tactics in detail as I describe several situations.

Nearing the end of the operation, D Company HQ, led by the support section, walked into an area heavily overgrown with bamboo with a small clearing in the centre. Most people think of bamboo as a tall rather attractive plant. Not this shitty wait-a-while variety. If the 50 mm long backward facing thorns grabbed an arm, leg, or part of the pack, anything, it was impossible to pull away. Just wait-a-while for someone to help unhook you. There were some awful, painful injuries inflicted by these bamboo thorns.

Suddenly the enemy hand signal was given by the forward scout. Something was amiss up front. We went to ground. The boss said, 'Come on, Pete, stay low,' as we both moved up to the support section commander, 'There appears to be a Cong camp up there, 50 m away!' The boss turned to me and said, 'Get all three platoon commanders.'

'Forty-one, Forty-two, Forty-three this is four, acknowledge.'

'Forty-one.'

'Forty-two.'

'Forty-three.'

'Number one on the phone now, please.' I handed the handset to the boss. Using Christian or nick names he ordered ten platoon to the right, eleven to the left and twelve to our rear. Within minutes I received "in position" messages.

The boss asked support section to move forward followed by CHQ with twelve platoon close up behind. Support section moved through the camp and took up position, twelve platoon surrounded the rest of the camp with orders to dig in. It was late in the day; we would be here for the night.

With the position secured as best we could, it was time to assess the situation. The boss said, 'With me, Pete.' We slowly circled the camp. There was no doubt this was a VC camp. Fires were still burning and rice bubbling on little stoves. No weapons, no personal objects, only their dinner remaining.

One particular object we found brought forward a response from the major I did not expect, but quickly understood his anger. In front of him was a large square shiny metal tin, now sporting a large boot print in the side. The round top came off to reveal its contents, pure white rice. The labels on the top, and all four sides, said it was from a protest group in Australia.

Those few moments live with me every day. Who, what are these people? My likeable boss, a major, a Scotsman in the Australian Army, was deeply upset and remained silent and consumed in his own thoughts for hours. Eventually he said, 'Fuck those bastards! Good night, Pete!'

But the drama of the day was not over. One of the medics attached to CHQ ventured a little outside the camp to the only substantial tree. He returned in a frenzy, a nice guy but a little soft in manner, 'Major, major, there's a bomb, there's a bomb!' Waving his arms and pointing to the tree, then sucking his fingers.

'Settle, petal,' said the major, 'show me.'

Standing upright beside the tree secured in position with some vines was a large aircraft bomb with some wires protruding from it. Later it was confirmed as a 340kg bomb dropped by an American F-4 Phantom fighter bomber. Immediately the major summoned an engineer to check it out. The engineer confirmed the bomb was active, but the wiring was as yet incomplete and not in immediate danger of exploding. It was later destroyed by a fly-in specialist group.

I would later see the results of an F-4 fighter bomber dropping these things. It left a hole big enough to bury a three-bedroom house. Trees were upside down in nearby trees. Bye, bye D Company!

A couple of days later the battalion was back in Nui Dat. It was like moving into a four-star hotel. Hot food, water, showers, toilets (of sorts), and a bed. A lumpy bed, but a dry and warm bed.

The Seldom Seen Inn was opened, and I was asked to help out at the bar. This presented the opportunity to tell our guys about the supply system. 'You are all Queenslanders, if not I am sorry for you. XXXX is your chosen brew.'

'Ya, ya, yyyya. Bloody oath, mate!'

'So, to give you XXXX, the other shit in the cold room has to be sold or whatever. This is cheap piss, men, so buy one XXXX, get another for the same price. Do whatever you wish with the other.' Ya know, it worked a treat!

The next night the Inn was packed. When everyone was pissed to the eyeballs (old jungle saying) one of the medics stood on a table and said, 'I have an announcement.'

'Ahh, shut the fuck up, doc. Go bandage ya head.'

'Sorry, chaps. This is important. The company medics have awarded the first injury recognition to our intrepid overworked sig, Private Collins, who received a devastating injury to his tummy from an errant empty can of beans left in his shell-scrape. Unconcerned, he dived in without thought of self-preservation to take up his position of defence of the company. Stabbed in the stomach by the sharp tin lid he did not complain until the alert was stood down. He has been awarded the "Purple Tart" in recognition of his injury. Get up here, Pete!'

The award was a reproduction of the "tin lid", coloured somehow, with the words in black permanent pen, "I am a tart"!

'Ya got that right,' was the call from the crowd, with a rendition of "For he's a jolly good fucker"! The guys continued drinking until the MPs closed the Inn. Every can of unwanted beer was sold. Most of the patrons were soaked from beer poured over their head. Small things amuse small minds.

Me at the Seldom Seen Inn after an operation, July 1969

Far from being small minded, this sort of behaviour— taking the piss— was an integral part of the friendship among these men subjected to a pressured life. It went beyond friendship and achieved an advanced level of care and support for others. I suppose it is what develops in an environment of reliance. In the Army it is called "mateship". Difficult to define or describe, mateship is something special. Fifty-six years later the feeling, the relationship, the closeness, the love of those men remains. It hurts like hell when one passes on, a deep sense of loss, yeah loss. This is what has made the Australian Army special throughout its history. Boer war, World War I, World War II, Korea, Vietnam, Afghanistan and all the other conflicts, our Aussie diggers have performed above their world station. I've got your back, mate. And I have got yours, mate.

The battalion remained in Nui Dat long enough for personal recovery. Gear repair or replacement, resupply and a chance to write home and, for the very lucky ones, to collect their mail. Notice of departure to places unknown was received putting the troops in ready mode, be ready to go within the hour, all bars (Inns) closed, remain at your station. That same night, I was introduced for the first time to a teeth-rattling, frightening experience.

THE VC KNOCKING AT OUR DOORSTEP

A pitch-black night, no Moon of course. At midnight rockets began exploding within Nui Dat. As the rockets continued, a mortar attack began from apparently a different location. The base artillery batteries responded almost immediately with high explosive (HE) rounds as did the mortar platoons. The big American 88s behind us soon joined the party, with a thunderous roar.

Sirens blared, putting the task force on stand to. A major attack on the base was feared. Intelligence units had been tracking radio communication episodes over a few days. Intelligence gained from the various locations plotted was that the enemy force was large. But the clever little buggers seemed to be everywhere. The radio recognition procedure used by Intelligence units indicated very quick movement of the radio operators.

Stand to meant I must sprint, battle ready, to the comms bunker. Remember it? The underground room with many radios and field telephones and, on a good night, some lighting. On arrival, I charged down the wooden steps purely on memory and a developing night vision. Instructors in Australia had told us night vision is known to improve when a person is constantly subjected to that environment.

21. The 6th arrives: Work begins

To some extent they were correct.

But down there, inside this comms bunker, nothing helped. It was just black, as black as an 8-ball with no eight. I retraced my steps up the stairs, feeling for light switches but found nothing. I mumbled to myself the OC will be here, 'I need light, Lord.' I remembered the emergency generator, it was supposed to switch on when necessary, but it had not.

I moved quickly up to the front of the bunker where the aerials and generator were placed. Above, I saw the bright trail of a rocket. Old jungle saying: 'If you see it, forget it, it is the bastard you don't see or hear that will kill you.' Seconds later, a hummmph as the rocket hits, probably aimed at Luscombe Airfield. After a bit of crawling about (one gets good at crawling in the Army) I found the generator. Oops! Another rocket and a mortar or two at the wire, head down for a moment, just in case. That rocket was closer.

Very hard to see much without the generator. This area is covered with rubber trees. The dense canopy keeps light out, even sunlight, but not the fucking rain, always some mud about. Feeling about, I located a switch. Turning it off, on, off, on; it gives no response, lazy bastard. I stood up, looked it in the eye and kicked the bastard as hard as I could. On the third kick it blinked at me, a tiny green light. One more kick in the guts, for good measure, and the prick of a thing started. Dim lights appeared on the stairs. 'Private Generator, I will see you tomorrow. You will be charged with dereliction of duty and sentenced to the dump.'

When I returned to the radio room, the OC was there, 'Private Collins, where have you been, my man?'

Always a worry when he addresses me that way, I responded in kind, 'Sorry, sir. I have been kicking the fuck out of a so-called emergency generator outside.'

'Well done, Pete. It's a bit derk and dimsel in here without lighting.'

That sorted, we proceeded to ensure our contacts were online. I radioed the platoons to have their commanders available. The boss was on the field phone to BHQ and ensured we had contact with the task force HQ.

Six RAR automatically went to stand to, triggered by the alarm. It would remain that way until the rockets ceased and any threat of invasion passed. It was possible the situation could remain until daybreak. SOPs would require stand to prior to dawn anyway.

The CO advised, ninety minutes later, to stand down. Forward pickets to be doubled until dawn and a full-scale alert at that time. 'Obviously,' said the major, 'they are worried about an attack on Nui Dat.' That did not happen! We remained on alert within Nui Dat for the next couple of days until Intelligence reports confirmed the threat of attack had passed. Platoon sized patrols outside the wire reported no enemy contact or sightings.

22. A HOLIDAY ON THE SOUTH CHINA SEA

Long Hai is a mountain range reaching to the beach of the South China Sea. The mountains were bare of most natural vegetation, a result of years of aerial, artillery and naval bombing. The Long Hai Hills were known to be a safe haven for the VC. There were many deep caves used by the VC as a protective base of a sort.

D Company was dispatched to secure an area in the sand dunes a few kilometres from the base of the Long Hai's. The remit was to observe movement in the mountains and investigate anything seen by immediate dispatch of a patrol section. Our position provided an excellent view of the southern side of the hills.

Army engineers had constructed a ten-metre high steel observation tower that was flown in and positioned by a Chinook chopper on the highest sand dune available. The top platform (two metres x two metres) of the tower was protected by sandbags on all four sides to chest height. The view of the surrounding area was excellent. The position provided a 360-degree uninterrupted view. I remember thinking, as I climbed up the tower ladder the first of many times, that I make a tempting target up here for a very good sniper with a fifty-calibre rifle. Later as, this operation developed, I had many other thoughts enter my head. *What if the VC had artillery? They do have rockets. What if they had aircraft and helicopters? If, if, if. Just get on with the job, ya mug!*

Our considerate engineers had also constructed a secure command post for the OC, me and my radio. Concern for the radio not me, I think. I would sleep in there with the radio and the boss.

The command post was dug into a sand dune near the base of the tower. Large timber posts (150 mm square) at each corner, with metal roofing material comprising the walls and roof, lined with a double layer of sandbags outside and then covered up with sand. Except for the entrance, of course. They were engineers after all. During my time in the Army I saw the regular use of sandbags. I began to wonder who had invented sandbags; imagine a royalty on every bag used!

The "Watch Tower" was manned twenty-four hours a day. A big part of the reason for surveillance was to prevent boats resupplying the enemy in the mountains by sea. The tower was positioned to easily observe any small craft moving across the restricted area at sea. The tower observer was authorised to take deterrent action at every sighting.

The observer carried his usual armament, a SLR or M16 rifle. Also available was a grenade launcher, the excellent M79. This little baby could launch a 40 mm HE grenade accurately up to 400m. A warning shot in front of a boat was required. If the boat failed to turn around, the next shots were meant to count. Shamefully, I admit this was fun. It was war, wasn't it?

Some part of this "fun" was the sudden reaction of the boat crew as the warning shot exploded nearby. Panic set in. One could imagine, 'Fuckie, 8ufncjveqwuhh', and over the side they went, splashing and spluttering. Their little boat became a target for M79 practice, until it was destroyed or ran ashore, where it was searched before destruction. All the local villages had been warned to remain behind a clearly defined line and that all vessels crossing into the restricted area would be challenged.

Dedicated supporters assumed they could successfully cross during the night. They were wrong. An early night-vision contraption called the "Starlight Scope" was used to detect night movements. The night-vision scope was a cumbersome instrument that used the star light to allow limited night vision. It was sufficiently effective to see any small craft offshore on a dark night. The boat people got the message and activity at sea stopped. I have no doubt the VC found other means of resupply.

With the boats under control, we were able to concentrate more on the mountains. The men in the tower had high-powered binoculars to constantly scan the mountains for any movement. Two Centurion tanks were deployed alongside our company. A field telephone in the tower was connected to the tank commander to quickly alert him to the target and its position. The tank boss designed a target recognition system used by the tower and the tank gunner. The system consisted of a plastic sheet (300 mm x 300 mm) with 25 mm squares drawn on it. A centre point on the sheet was aligned with a common (familiar to both) feature on the mountain. With the sheet centred on the common point, the tower would simply call, right two, down two and so on. It worked a treat.

The Centurion tank had a 50-calibre gun mounted above the main gun. It fired a tracer round that was fairly easy to see. Once this was fired, any correction could be made by the tower operator as he saw the impact position. 'On target,' or, 'Yeah Baby,' was the response. The tank gunner fired his main weapon to that exact spot. I saw this happen many times, the accuracy was amazing.

Very occasionally I would say, 'You missed.'

The response was, 'Wait for it!'

If the target was a deep cave, the tank gunner was so precise his shot would enter the cave and explode inside. A few seconds later the tell-tale dust and smoke would appear. 'Got him,' would be the response from the gunner.

SUN, SURF AND THE BEACH, NOT

This beach resort was extremely hot during the day, the white sand surrounding our base was a blinding white. My eyes suffered the constant glare and the constant wind whipping up the sand. There was no escaping either. We became brown as a bear from head to waist and welcomed the daily heavy rain. No running for cover here, hang it all out and enjoy the short respite, a chance to rid the hair and body of effing sand.

Occasionally the boss would allow a few of us to visit the ocean, about twenty or so with an armed escort. We dived into the waves, fully clothed, boots and all for a quick dip! It was like being at home, for a minute, at Surfers Paradise beach on one of my naughty weekends with Karen.

Randy Newman wrote a song that went "You Can Leave Your Hat On". In the Army it is "leave your boots on". An infantry soldier (a crunchy) is totally disabled without boots. When on operation the boots come off only to change socks, maybe every couple of weeks. No, I won't say it…. Pete, you change with…

On one beach visit, a low flying Iroquois helicopter flew over our group. It was an American chopper. The pilot, the only person on board, virtually stood the thing on its tail and plopped onto the sand burying the skids in the sand up to the fuselage. The pilot climbed out, then he leaned back into the cabin to retrieve a carton of Bud (Budweiser, an American beer). With a can in his hand and the beer carton under his arm he approached our security guards.

'Hi ya, Aussies, wanna beer?' He sat on the beach with the carton nearby.

'Thanks, old mate, we are on duty, so no thanks,' security said.

'I get ya. Tomorrie I get out of this shithole, saying goodbye to my li'l green wagon over there. Been together for eighteen months.'

We thought, tomorrow you will be going home either in a box or in chains. He finished his beer, opened another and said, 'See ya, Aussie. Look after each other.' The blades twirling— whoop, whoop— with max lift to escape the sand, our visitor dipped the nose and flew back the way he came.

The Yanks never ceased to amaze me with their casual soldierly attitude. They appeared to be a one-man show, a "look after me attitude, fuck the rest of you dickheads". It did appear this way to me when I saw American soldiers, in single file walking along a path, heads down, music in the ears, weapons over the shoulder and even that guy with a guitar in hand. Was anyone alert and looking out for an enemy ambush, a booby trap on the pathway, a sniper in the trees or even an Australian ambush? They seemed oblivious to the danger. They were not trained to recognise the jungle guerrilla warfare of this area.

I recognise the absolutely huge commitment of money and men the US made in the war. I recognise the immense cost in lives and dollars. Maybe rather than committing large numbers of soldiers and dollars, a better approach might have been to ensure the soldiers and officers alike (and maybe government leaders) were more aware of the task they were undertaking. Horrendous battles like Khe Sanh (21st January 1968) indicate a lack of knowledge of the enemy's abilities and strength. Four North Vietnamese Army infantry divisions, supported by two armoured regiments and two artillery regiments— forty thousand men in all— began converging on Khe Sanh, during the lunar new year festival period, to surprise the American leaders who were not sufficiently aware of the Vietnamese military capability and cunning tactics (Cawthorne 2010:116).

Statistics of human loss in Vietnam show the US lost fifty thousand men killed in action and three hundred thousand wounded in action. The South Vietnamese Army lost two hundred thousand killed in action and the North, nine hundred thousand killed in action, plus over one million Vietnamese citizens. The number of artillery shells fired, and the number of bombs dropped amounted to four times the total used during World War II. The cost in hardware loss and ammunition expended was estimated at $USD 300 Billion (Cawthorne 2010).

SOME EXAMPLES OF US BOMBINGS I SAW

I received a radio message from battalion early one morning. The message said to stand by for a coded message.

Armed with my field message notebook, code book and radio adjusted for the best reception possible, I sat in my deep command post and waited nervously for the message. The OC arrived and sat quietly in the corner and gave me the thumbs up signal. We sat in silence waiting. Both wondering, assuming or dreading what the forthcoming orders might contain. The radio made its familiar sound, 'Here we go, Pete.'

The coded message was long. It would take me several minutes to decode. I closed the radio conversation with, 'Message received, Four out.'

Battalion came back immediately, 'Four, reply message understood in fifteen, battalion out.' The message did take fifteen minutes to decode. I reported the content to the OC and proceeded to encode his orders to the platoons, before contacting my fellow sigs.

At dawn the next day, there was going to be a B52 Stratofortress bomber attack on the Long Hai Hills. This would be a full-scale all-out attack unleashing hundreds of bombs all at once covering a boxed area of one kilometre by three kilometres. Guided by radar, these huge planes attacked from a height of 14.5 km. The accuracy was, as we would see, extremely good.

On the day I arrived in Saigon, I saw one of these monsters as it followed our aircraft prior to take-off. With a wingspan of 54.6m, it required wheels at the wingtips when moving on the ground. The huge wings extending from the top of the 48m fuselage reminded me of a giant moth. Tomorrow, I would witness them in action.

Our orders required the company to move back at least one kilometre prior to the bombing scheduled for dawn the next day. The "retreat" was to be undertaken in a quiet manner, without any obvious signs of movement. The plan was to leave our tents and other obvious equipment in place. The two Centurion tanks and crews would form the security guard for twenty-four hours. We made temporary camp about three kilometres from the mountain target.

The company stood to at 0500 hours, all eyes fixed on the

mountains! The B52s were scheduled to arrive at 0600. My radio crackled a message, 'Take cover, three minutes, out.'

'Three minutes, major,' I said. He nodded and waved all heads down. No one took any notice, all eyes were glued to the target, but also well protected in shell scrapes and behind rocks.

Suddenly, spot-on 0600, huge flashes of light appeared on the mountains as the first load of 25 000 kg bombs exploded. A repeat attack followed in seconds. More and more explosions, blue and orange flashes. The sound arrived— a deep rumble punctuated with a sharp crack. The sound surrounded me as I thought, *Oh, you poor bastards*. Spectacular rings in black and other colours rose into the sky from each explosion— these were, I was told, shock waves carrying smoke into the sky.

I did manage a photograph with my state-of-the-art Kodak Instamatic, that 1960s photographic marvel. Preloaded with black and white film, take twelve shots, and surrender it to a Kodak processor who would print small 100 mm x 100 mm black and white photos. My expertise as a photographer was evident in the final print: a white nothing with a hint of a black circle. Maybe a camera with a five-millimetre lens at five kilometres distance is asking a bit much.

Eventually we received the all clear to move back to our original position. I settled back into my command post, cleared away some unwanted sand, and reset the radio with the outside antenna. Almost immediately, 'Four this is Forty-one, over.'

'Go ahead Forty-one.'

'We require replacement of several hutchies, over.'

'Forty-one, what is the problem? Over.'

'Four, the hutchies have been holed by shrapnel or whatever, over.'

'Forty-one, message understood, standby, Four out.'

Soon, the other frontline platoons reported similar problems. Despite being up to two kilometres from the target, our position had been peppered with "stuff" from the bombing. The man to handle this was the Company Second-in-Command Captain "Fixit", an all-round good guy. Within minutes he said, 'Pete, get the platoons to send a section up here to meet the resupply chopper at 1700 for their replacements.' I quickly relayed the message, receiving thanks for the service.

OFFSHORE US NAVAL ATTACKS

Information was received that certain US naval ships would be attacking the mountains during the next few days. Timing was, as yet, unclear due to weather condition reports offshore in the China Sea.

One attack would be by a US battleship from a position of something like forty-eight kilometres offshore. This ship, we were told, had 450 mm guns it would use to fire upon the Long Hai Hills. If it was to fire all its guns in one direction at once, it would capsize, such was the power of the guns. The timing of the attack totally depended on the weather conditions in the South China Sea, twenty-four kilometres out of sight beyond the horizon. The US Navy would advise when firing began and had requested we perform the task of a forward observer calling adjustments to range and direction if necessary. Fancy that, li'l ol' Private 1st Class Pete from Australia telling a US battleship commander what to do with his great big guns.

It was the 1960s remember, technology was basic so forward air control and forward observers were used regularly to direct artillery and mortar fire onto a target. The forward observer may provide a map grid reference, call fire (one shell) and then adjust the range (up two hundred or down one hundred, for instance). When on target the instruction is, 'Fire for effect,' maybe requesting a certain type: HE or incendiary, and the number of shells required.

On one occasion, I was perched on a rock outcrop high above a valley acting as radio operator for a lieutenant responsible for forward observation. We provided a grid reference to the Aussie artillery at Nui Dat. The grid reference was double-checked by both me and the lieutenant. As was normal practice, the reference was repeated by the artillery battery and confirmed. A siting shot was requested.

22. A holiday on the South China Sea

We requested, 'Down two hundred.' Accordingly, a second siting shot landed spot-on target.

I was about to call, 'Fire for effect,' when a third shot exploded extremely close to our very exposed position.

'Fuck me dead,' said the Louie officer as he dived behind a big rock.

'Cease fire. Cease fire!' I yelled on the radio.

The artillery commander came back, 'That wasn't ours.'

Adrian, the lieutenant, grabbed my radio and asked, 'Where the bloody hell did it come from? We nearly got blown off the bloody earth!'

The artillery commander came back with, 'Perhaps it was the New Zealand artillery guys.'

In typical officer speak, Adrian said, 'Tell them to cease and desist. Out.'

'Back to the task at hand,' I said. 'The last siting shot was on target. When ready, ten rounds HE. Fire for effect.'

After a few repeats that cleared a large patch of forest, we too did desist, with no further help from New Zealand artillery.

Battalion contacted me to confirm the battleship would begin firing at 0600 hours. I would receive a radio message at 0550, the connection was to remain open for the duration of the attack. I was required to act as a forward observer reporting to the battalion operator.

Bugger, I wouldn't get to tell the US Navy what to do with their big guns! But maybe I could add a bit of Aussie lingo to my observation comments. Can't imagine the boffins at battalion passing on, 'Yankee doodle, doodle, dandy, spot-on ole chap. Let 'em have it, mate.'

The message came in at 0550, and shortly after the US radio operator said, 'Incoming.' The first round was on its way. Having never seen a battleship fire in anger before in my life, I had no idea what to expect. I heard this strange whirring roar. My eyes followed the sound, and I was fucking amazed. I could actually see this thing in the clear sky heading for the mountain. It exploded a second later in the same spot the tanks had targeted earlier.

'Four, battalion, report.'

'Right on the knocker,' I said in reply.

'Four, use correct communication protocols, battalion out.'

Stick it, mate, I thought, *you did not see what I saw.* From out of sight, forty-eight kilometres away over the horizon, they were as accurate as our Centurion tanks from less than a mile. The whirring roar was back, but this time there were more things in the sky. Oh, you poor bastards!

The mountains erupted in a huge cloud of smoke, dust, rocks and probably human remains. We had heard of our men seeing lone survivors staggering out of the caves in a disoriented and frightened manner. I am not surprised after seeing the horrendous explosions from afar. Who will ever know how many men, women and children were killed and buried within those Long Hai Hills. All I know is the death toll in both North and South Vietnam, armies and civilians, was in the millions. For what benefit? Fucking none, nothing.

The attacks on Long Hai did not stop at that, the US Navy had another weapon to unleash. I received a message that a US Navy "rocket ship" (my words) would appear offshore within the next twenty-four hours. It did!

This ship looked like a converted cargo vessel. A bow structure high above the water, a water line midsection and a high control structure overlooking the vessel from the stern. The low midsection carried four rocket mounted batteries, each with twelve rockets. That was on the port side. I do not recall seeing the starboard view, but I suspect it was the same arrangement.

When it fired it was like Guy Fawkes Night. Twelve rockets burst forward instantaneously in a bright yellow and orange burst of flame, instantly followed by the next twelve. The rockets flew over our position close to the beach heading for, yeah right, the Long Hais. Forty-eight rockets in a matter of seconds. And they followed up with a few repeats for good measure. Poor bastards!

22. A holiday on the South China Sea

GOOD LUCK, DARBY, SEE YOU SOON

A day or two later a report was received that movement was detected on the mountains. D Company was asked to investigate. On that morning, early around 0600 hours, a good friend, Darby, a regular corporal on his second tour of Vietnam, who had been involved in The Battle of Long Tan in August 1966, was now in charge of our support section. He and his section were given the task to investigate. After breakfast Darby and I were playing darts with makeshift equipment when he was called out by the OC.

I was on our tower and could see Darby's section of ten highly trained men moving towards the mountains. In the lower rocky part of the site, the section began to be obscured by large rocky outcrops.

As they moved higher, I occasionally got sightings of them. Suddenly an explosion nearby, followed quickly by the section radio sig reporting a mine had exploded very close to the section leader. Following information confirmed a rifleman had stepped on the mine, a jumping jack, which injured both him and the section leader. I immediately requested a "dust off" at my location. The medivac helicopter arrived within minutes and was directed to the contact landing zone by yellow smoke dropped by the section sig. The wounded soldiers were flown immediately to the Aussie hospital at Vung Tau.

Both men survived their physical injuries but would have, without doubt, suffered much mental anguish. I did not see Darby again. I did hear many years later that he lost part of his leg in that incident. Fuck the war!

One last story of this operation involves something quite different. The US Air Force was at it again with their big planes and big bombs. This mission, however, involved only one aircraft. Not a huge fast jet, nor a squadron or two, but one single four-engine propellor driven aircraft. It, like all the other equipment, would be attacking the poor old devastated Long Hais.

This plane would be carrying a single bomb, we were told. The bomb was called a "daisy cutter". Designed to fall nose first, hit the earth, penetrate to a certain depth, turnabout and explode as it came back up.

Yeah, what? Don't ask me, that was the intelligence we received. This clever thing would weigh four thousand five hundred kilograms. Rather large for the 1960s, old chap, hey what? Eventually a four-engine aircraft chortled across the sky, did a few ever-diminishing circles above. 'Don't drop that thing on us, you crazy Yanks,' I mumbled to myself.

I was in the command post with the radio cable stretched to the limit to allow me to see the plane. Nothing happened, the plane chortled off into the distance, the radio was quiet, no messages nor confirmation of the bomb being dropped. I went into the command post and sat down.

Sand and other crap fell out of my roof, then a deep rumble and everything shook violently. Sand cascaded on top of me from the roof and the sides. Bloody hell, that bomb cut some daisies. Outside there was very little evidence of the impact of the blast, one could only think the explosion was underground as planned. Poor bastards!

23. ARMY TRANSPORT: A LOVE-HATE RELATIONSHIP

We developed a love-hate relationship with Army transport in Vietnam. Simply, if they were taking us somewhere, we hated them, but when we walked out of the jungle to find trucks or APCs, we "luuved" them. The walking was over and we could travel in style.

Who remembers a young man who became a rock hero of the 1960s? His name, Normie Rowe. Young Normie fell victim to the National Service call-up. Now Normie Rowe, unlike some high-profile victims (a.k.a. Elvis in the US) of the two-year commitment to serve in the defence force, made no fuss! He, like the rest of us thousands of nineteen-year-old men "copped it sweet". Private N Rowe, after completing recruit training just like the rest of us, was allocated to Armoured Corps for future training. Private N Rowe, now Corporal N Rowe, was a commander of an APC during the Vietnam War. So what?

Our company was on an operation for some weeks in thick, wet, slippery jungle. It was a particularly uncomfortable time, especially trying to sleep. Radio communication was poor, requiring me to replace the one metre flex radio aerial with the inflexible six-metre aerial. It was like carrying a 70kg Old English Sheepdog on your back. The bloody thing got stuck on every tree and vine in its path. Mozzies, fuckin' big grey bastards, stung like a bee, leeches fell on your head and Gympie bush tried to ruin your life forever. It was absolutely exhausting to move just one kilometre.

Why were we there? We were there because of reports of enemy activity. The VC used the difficult terrain to their advantage. My worst, very worst experience occurred in this area. Struggling through dense jungle, I was suddenly aware of movement on my left. I propped a man standing in shabby black, aiming a rifle at me. I fired my M16 instinctively from my waist without precise aim. The shabby man fell. The Aussies immediately went to ground expecting retaliation. Nothing happened. Support section proceeded to investigate and confirmed the person was dead, a young person, with a loaded and cocked weapon. 'Well done, Pete, as the radio man you were the target,' said the boss. Sure, it was him or me, but he was a human being, had a family and other relationships, most probably.

I was reminded of something someone said to me during training back home, 'Remember, "I am not shooting this person, we are!"'

At about 1700 hours that afternoon, we broke out of the jungle into a clearing where Armoured had secured an area circled by APCs. To see those APCs sitting there silently was truly a sight for anyone's sore eyes. I leaned against the tracks of the very first APC and slid to the ground, totally physically and mentally exhausted.

A soldier wearing a helmet appeared above over the side of the APC and said, 'Mate, you look like you could do with a brew!'

My reply was, 'Fucking oath, mate!' That big dixie of hot black coffee is still the best I have ever drunk. The soldier in the helmet was none other than Normie Rowe. I have spoken to him after two shows, forty years later, and expressed my appreciation. I was also able to talk to Norm in a more relaxed venue of the Vikings Currumbin Surf Lifesavers Club on Queensland's fabulous Gold Coast. It was a pleasant end to a mind- wrenching experience. I cannot remove either memory from my mind!

In Vietnam, though, the choppers were king of the road and of the skies. They rescued us, transported us, resupplied us and frightened the fuck out of us. Army Aviation and RAAF pilots and crew, for the most part, did their job efficiently and by the book. The Yankee guys, not all. They could and would act like "sky cowboys".

These are some of my experiences with the famous Iroquois chopper.

There were never any seats or doors, just a flat floor where about nine infantry fully loaded men would sit, crouch and hope. I was often, because of my oversized pack, the last to arrive and would get the "window seat". The window seat? The one with the best view. You sat on the edge of the floor with both feet firmly on the skids of the chopper. There was nothing to hang onto, except maybe the M60 machine gun floor mount, if in reach.

The American pilots sometimes suddenly banked the aircraft to port (where I was) and I would be staring at the ground in horror. They knew, I suppose, that the centrifugal forces would hold us inside. Maybe it was not a joke. I hope so.

One day we were flown by chopper into a "hot" landing zone (LZ) under fire. Helicopters are obviously expensive and important weapons that must be protected when and wherever possible. Because it was a hot LZ the choppers would not land but would unload their cargo from approximately three metres off the ground. We jumped!

Training says you hit the ground running and take cover in a circle below the chopper. The others all dispersed successfully. Because of my pack, I was stuck almost up to my knees in a patch of mud, unable to move. The enemy in the trees were firing and our guys were returning fire. I was a stuck duck! The trouble was this little black duck could not fly. I was a sideshow duck, a prime target.

A chopper crew must have seen me and realised my problem. Hovering just above, I was able to grab the skid as the chopper lifted me to solid ground. It felt like I was being dissected at the knees but safe. Thank you, whoever you were!

The choppers were to play a major role in revisiting Long Tan in August 1969.

THE BATTLE OF LONG TAN: REVISITED THREE YEARS ON IN AUGUST 1969

The celebrated Battle of Long Tan took place in a rubber plantation close to the ATF base at Nui Dat. Some have suggested the enemy forces encountered by D Company 6RAR on 18th August 1966 were part of a force building up to attack the Australian base. A mixture of VC battalions and North Vietnamese Army regulars comprised the force encountered by D Company (one hundred and eight men) on the day.

Estimates of the size of the enemy force range from two to two and a half thousand. D Company platoons were separated due to the operational orders to investigate enemy mortar attacks and detected enemy radio transmissions. The battle raged for several hours with the support of the artillery from Nui Dat. The D Company radio operator would eventually call for artillery to target his own position. The soldiers were quickly running out of ammunition and called for resupply from the base. A brave helicopter crew answered the call despite higher authority opposition, and, in driving rain, dropped ammunition supplies to the troops. So desperate was the situation, our men were fighting with their bayonets.

Finally, a troop of APCs arrived. D Company were down forty-two men (seventeen killed in action, and twenty-five wounded, with one later dying from his wounds). The enemy losses could not be reliably calculated though Major Harry Smith, OC D COY 1966, in his book *Long Tan: The Start of a Lifelong Battle* (Smith and McRae 2015), states an actual enemy body count of two hundred and forty-five, three prisoners and a further forty-eight graves counted the next day. In addition, the Vietnamese carried out their usual practice of removing their dead and wounded at night.

Delta Company 6RAR was later awarded the highest US Presidential Unit Citation for bravery. It is commonly known as the "Swimming Pool" due to the bright blue centre and gold surround. As part of the Company, I was presented with the award in Townsville by the US Ambassador in 1968.

Operation Long Tan would commence on 16th August 1969. The rebuilt Delta Company, on the second tour of Vietnam, would oversee the placement of a memorial cross at the battle site of 1966.

APCs transport 6RAR and NZ troops back to Long Tan for a commemorative service and the erection of the Long Tan Cross. Photo: C. J. Bellis, public domain, Australian War Memorial.

This would occur on the 18 August 1969, exactly three years after the battle commenced. The large, now famous and celebrated concrete cross was flown to the prepared site by an Iroquois helicopter. With surviving members of the 1966 battle forming the guard of honour, the Memorial Cross was blessed during a moving ceremony.

The cross remained in position until the end of the war, then removed by the new regime. It was discovered in a museum and some years later returned to Australia. It is now on display in the Vietnam War section of the Australian War Memorial in Canberra.

I surmise Army operations considered the VC might attack D Company in a sort of "get even" mind set. This time, however, D Company was supported by Alpha, Bravo and Charlie companies, plus the support of the Nui Dat Task Force not very far away. Even so, on that very, very dark night, under the cover of a mature rubber tree canopy, one could see very little. The darkness added to the situation and increased all emotions, especially apprehension and fear. I must admit, of all the operations conducted during my time in the war, I did not feel my life threatened as I did that night. The occasional

The Piper's Lament is played during the commemorative service to honour those lost in The Battle of Long Tan. I am there somewhere in the background group: Photo: C. J. Bellis, public domain, Australian War Memorial

rifle shot in the distance, in the wee hours, did not help either.

Being there on that historic military moment to honour the Australians killed in that battle and being a present member of the unit, D Company 6RAR, made me feel proud of what I was doing and what I was. I carry those feelings now. On Anzac Day and on Vietnam Veterans Day (18th August), I proudly show my allegiance.

I was only a National Service man, conscripted for two years Army service, as a wet behind the ears teenager. Still to assume much responsibility in life, sitting there in the dark, in a hostile foreign country I had not known existed, fearing I could be shot dead at any moment. "Shit 'appens", as they say, but it is how that shit is handled that makes the man or woman. The Army training staff, bless their fuckin' absent hearts, and the organisation itself somehow provided us with the tools to cope with these situations.

Operation Long Tan lasted about three days. The enemy was quiet and unseen. Perhaps the men of 1966 had taught them a lesson, "Don't mess with the 6th Battalion".

24. A NEW ADVENTURE: THE CAMBODIAN BORDER

We were about to embark on a new operation. The WO2 Loadmaster (responsible for the safe loading/unloading of aerial cargo, including personnel) called my group of about fifty men forward to board the next Chinook Helicopter hovering above. The Chinook is a large twin rotor machine, used mainly for equipment transport and, sometimes, troop deployment. The rotors at the front and rear operate from one engine through a complicated gearing system. Loading is through a large rear opening door that forms a ramp. It is not fast and manoeuvrable. The Chinook usually operates behind the battle front as a bulk reinforcement asset.

Chinook Helicopter flying in supplies to Australian troops, South Vietnam, July 1969 Photo: C. J. Bellis, public domain, Australian War Memorial

The Chinook landed close to us, and we began to move forward. Suddenly the WO2 Loadmaster stopped our progress saying, 'Stop. Next aircraft!' The rumbling big helicopter we were stopped from boarding was instead loaded with hardware and small ammunition and proceeded to take off. It flew very low for a few hundred metres and, as it began to rise, it blew up in a ball of flame and smoke. Pilot, co-pilot and two machine gunners lost!! That is the stupidity of this and other wars.

But the show, I mean war, must go on. The next Chinook arrived. The Loadmaster called us forward to board. I was one of the first on the aircraft. The WO2, with a reassuring hand on my shoulder, said, 'It's okay, buddy!' The reassuring hand of an old trooper at that moment supported my endeavour to carry on despite seeing this disaster. Everyone would be thinking, *I was nearly aboard that aircraft*.

We flew off somewhere, I knew not where, to do I did not know what. Inside this huge noisy and vibrating helicopter there was nothing to see but the glum faces of the other passengers. After a short flight, the big rear door opened as we landed. We were transferred to trucks.

Once on board the trucks, a packed lunch was handed out. The package included a fresh orange: so what? With open sides and rear, our view of the landscape was excellent, especially to the rear. As it turned out the rear view provided some entertainment as we cruised along the main connection road.

A somewhat unfortunate Vietnamese person appeared behind riding a bicycle. Silly person, following an Army truck full of soldiers armed with oranges is a no-no! Poor bugger, I bet he or she will not do that again real soon. The two guys at the tailgate began trying to bounce oranges off the road to hit the bike. They had some success as was indicated by the waving arms of the cyclist as he was sprayed with juice and peels.

With this encouragement, everyone joined in the bombardment of the unfortunate bastard until he disappeared into a ditch on the roadside. Small things amuse small minds, they say! Fun and laughter also act as a tension relief valve. Thanks, little Vietnamese cyclist, for your courage.

That day we passed through some larger villages or towns in the province. On occasion the drivers, familiar with the territory, actually increased speed through a village. This surprised me until something forced our truck to stop in the middle of a village. Below were the villagers tending to their wares for sale. Mounted on a flimsy rack of small branches were small fish drying in the sun. Other food, maybe duck or chicken were also on display. Ahhh!

The ground was a sloopy mud where ducks, chickens and skinny dogs wallowed. Soon the reason for speeding arrived. The stench was horrible. The locals smiled up at us with their poor teeth, offering the fish to eat. Each little house, separated by a low wire fence, was the same. 'Fuck, how do they live like that?' someone said.

Our journey continued to the town of Ba Ria, a larger place with sealed roads and a bloody lot of cars of sorts, bikes and rickshaws. The town appeared from the chorus of horns and whistles and crowded intersections where there were no rules. If rules existed no one obeyed, or just didn't know them.

Suddenly everything stopped and went quiet. Two men walked to the centre of the intersection. They were dressed in black with brilliant white leggings, white helmets and white gloves up to the top of the forearms. On the hip, their shiny black belt carried a holster housing a .32 pistol. These guys were known as the "White Mice".

The White Mice— Vietnamese National Police Officers— were feared by every road user. Follow their directions or risk being shot. They did not fool around, one direction ignored and the .32 pistol was fired through a windscreen at the driver or directly at a cyclist. A half dozen shots and the intersection was cleared. They actually fired into two cars there and then! The Mice directed our truck drivers through. We cheered the two White Mice who stood to attention and saluted as we passed. Beats traffic lights, I say!

AMBUSH, AMBUSH! BORDER PATROL

Soon after the White Mice experience, we left the trucks and began doing what Delta Company does best, walking. We were not known as "Boots Company" without reason. This was a hard slog through the jungle, mile after jungle mile. The only access through to our destination was on foot.

The boss informed me our destination was an ambush position on the banks of a creek very close to the border of Vietnam and Cambodia, on a known exit from the Ho Chi Min trail from North Vietnam. Our target was NVA regulars forming as a reserve force. He said, 'Well, that is what Army Intelligence informs us, Pete!'

After several kilometres of battling the jungle, we arrived at the creek. The major sent the support section to ensure the position was secure, then we moved across. There were indeed well-used crossings, duly noted by the boss and selected as machine gun posts. If someone was to cross, we held the high ground, a clear view of their approach and movement through the creek.

Trip wires connected to flares were placed opposite our position. Claymore mines were placed, armed and wired for use on the approaching creek bank. The order was given to dig in, trenches at least 1.2m deep, in pairs, with sufficient space between to sleep. A low hutchie should cover the trenches.

M60 machine guns were dug in and mounted at the identified crossings. These guns would be manned by two men, twenty-four hours a day. The machine gun pits contained the Claymore mine controls. The Claymore was a devastating weapon, the slightly curved face sprayed a large amount of shrapnel (like ball bearings) outwards. It was very effective in close-range encounters such as an ambush. The site of our position had only low bush growth and, in some spots like mine, some nice short green grass. For a welcome change, "diggin' in" was a little easier. Darryl, the battalion sig attached to the company, was my bed buddy for the duration. After calculating the correct position and alignment of our trenches,

24. A new adventure: The Cambodian border

we started diggin'. As usual, we had the Army issue "bucket and spade", a combination shovel and pick. It really was like digging on the beach as a kid, but a lot more bloody difficult. A large rock or a tree root almost always stuck its nose in to ruin progress. Of course, in Vietnam, the tropics, it always rains and when the rain comes, "Huey" does not muck about. As Mum and Dad used to say, 'Send it down, Huey,' and Huey obliged.

At times you could hear a chorus of, 'Fuck off, Huey.' Whoever Huey was, he or she could not hear very well.

Darryl and I had reached a depth of about 300 mm when the rain started. Heavy rain is both good and bad as far as infantry soldiers are concerned. Shower time, bath time, wash the clothes time, all in one action. Stand up, lie down, strip off, not the boots please, and enjoy the cool. Don't worry, in a few minutes, you will be dry and sweating again. Fill dixies (our small cooking/eating pots) with the sweet rainwater and top up the water bottles.

The bad bit about rain is mud! It's okay to get wet, but muddy wet sucks. Darryl and I returned to our trenches. 'Bloody hell, Pete, look at that.' Our trenches were more than half full of water! We both laughed out loud with disgust.

The water would drain away overnight, but digging out the mud left behind would, and did, piss us off. A Herculean effort the next day after breakfast achieved great results. The trenches were to the required depth, and drainage protected by brilliant engineering, even deeper at the rear to avoid standing in any water seepage. Our hutchies were joined and stretched across the entire engineering marvel. As the cover was low to the ground, the one and a half metre wide central area between the muddy trenches was sufficient for us to sleep in relative comfort without fear of rain.

Battling all the mud and slush, the war went on regardless. Darryl received coded messages from the battalion Intelligence unit at Nui Dat, passing on information about observed NVA movements along the Ho Chi Minh Trail. This information would be passed to the major who would instruct me to forward coded messages to the platoon commanders. Coding and decoding took time and accuracy. There were occasions in tight situations when I had to code and send instructions while on the move. Keeping pace with my long-legged boss was very difficult, but he understood the situation.

The Ho Chi Minh Trail began in 1959 as a network of trails that stretched from North Vietnam, through Laos and Cambodia as an eventual supply route for the war in the south. Colonel Bui Tin, the officer who accepted the surrender of the South in 1975, travelled the Trail in 1963. He concluded that to conduct a war in South Vietnam the Trail had to be turned into a logistical system, capable of moving thousands of men and tons of ammunition and supplies. With the use of Chinese and Soviet equipment, engineers built roads and bridges capable of carrying heavy loads. Barracks, hospitals, fuel depots and warehouses were built underground before the first US ground troops landed in 1965. An aircraft warning system allowed convoys to hide in specially cleared areas along the trail (Cawthorne 2010).

The US Air Force bombed the Ho Chi Minh Trail constantly without stopping supply to the south. Bui Tin was correct; the Trail would win the war with the assistance of the Vietnamese in fighting against enemies who invaded their country over centuries. The use of the amazing tunnel system throughout the country afforded their military leaders the ability to surprise the enemy and then vanish.

The tunnel system not only provided access without detection; it also provided hospitals, kitchens, dormitories, supply depots (food and weapons) and headquarters facilities. The tunnel networks in some areas, in use for centuries, sometimes extended for hundreds of miles. One tunnel ran from Cambodia to the gates of Saigon. Very few of these tunnels were discovered by allied forces during the war. The very first American base camp was erected above a manned tunnel. At night the VC emerged to sabotage US equipment and destroy whatever they could, then disappeared until the next opportunity arose. Tunnels discovered revealed the intricacies of the design, and protection from intruders and the concealed entry points. These cleverly concealed entries were also booby-trapped and provided a warning system to alert tunnel occupants of a breach. Single tunnels would end abruptly with no obvious exit. The continuation would be above, below, left or right, always cleverly concealed. Sometimes the continuation was a couple of metres back down the tunnel. If two continuations were obvious one would be booby-trapped. Tunnels were found to end with a single trapdoor, if opened the tunnel would be flooded from the river or dam on the other side.

The VC and the NVA used the immense tunnel system to great effect against the Australian, New Zealand and American troops. Often infantry forward scouts would be heard saying, 'Where the fuck did they come from?' Or 'Where did he go?' Their movement was quick, practised and effective.

Certain Australian soldiers, known as "Tunnel Rats", were a very brave small crew who entered these tunnels whenever one was located. Facing dark restricted space in fear of being confronted by the waiting enemy, or some diabolical booby trap, they entered to investigate and learn what they could. Any information was a valuable commodity.

Considering the unconventional enemy we faced, how successful would an ambush at a border creek crossing be?

WILL THE AMBUSH WORK?

The company was well prepared. Activity and movement had been restricted for the past three days. There was no radio traffic because a code of silence was imposed. The M60s were manned around the clock, as were other one-man listening and observation posts. Every member was involved and committed.

The evening of day three was wet and miserable. Darryl was on gun picket at 0400 hours. I would replace him at 0500. We both took the opportunity to take an early camp. The rain was bucketing down when I fell asleep under our low, secure dry tent strung between our trenches.

Sleeping in the bush as an infantry soldier is an art only other "crunchies" possess. It requires patience and know-how, and an ability to find a nice smooth rock pillow that allows the body to squirm in between the other rocks. Ah! What a life. When first returning home, my dad and sisters three were horrified to find me asleep on the floor. No pillow, not even a rock.

About 2230 hours, two or three flares suddenly went off. One M60 opened up in anger— the one nearest to us. Darryl and I reacted immediately and rolled sideways into our waterlogged trenches armed and ready. Silence for a few seconds, then Lance Corporal Darryl surfaced with, 'What the... What the... What the fuck!!!'

'Yeah, what the!' I replied as I tried to gain my feet and struggle back to my bed. Both our pits were full of cold muddy water. We looked at each other in the fading light of the flare and burst out laughing. Both of us scrambled to the high ground, totally soaked.

But, the M60 was still firing. We had no clue as to what was happening.

The Sarge ran past towards the gun post. 'The two medics are manning the gun,' he said as he passed. A few minutes later he returned and said, 'Stand down. Maybe an animal or something. The medics saw nothing. Go back to sleep, guys.' Yeah Sarge, great, but look at us. He walked away laughing his three-striped head off. Go to sleep, he said. My ground sheet and blanket had followed me into the trench as had Darryl's. There was nothing dry to sleep on or in.

Darryl said, 'Pete, you're not a poofter, hey?'

'No, Darryl!'

He said, 'Then we shall share body warmth for a couple of hours until my gun picket at 0400.'

At 0400 precisely we were woken by Roger, the forward scout.

'Gun picket, Darryl,' he said. He looked in under our low tent. 'I always thought you sigs were a bit queer,' he sniggered as he walked away. We were both still very wet and the early morning was getting a bit cool. We decided a joint two-hour picket was the way to go. Wrapped in a partly dry ground sheet we braved the elements for two very long hours. At 0600, I rousted the company for stand to.

After a coffee and a tin of something for brekkie, the major and sergeant came past heading to the gun post to investigate last night's contact.

'Good morning, chaps. I see you've had an early tub,' said the major as he bent over laughing. Struggling to keep a straight face he said, 'Come with us to work out what caused this disaster for you two.'

The Sarge added, 'I will never forget the sight I saw last night.'

'What was that, Sarge?' said the major.

'Tell ya later, boss.'

As events unfolded it seemed the two company medics had been on the gun at the time the flares went off. Support section had sent out a patrol to reset the flares and ascertain what had happened. They were on the way back towards the gun position when we arrived. Their report confirmed two flares had been triggered, via tripwires and that it was almost certainly a small animal responsible.

The M60 machine gun is loaded with a belt of two hundred rounds at all times. At least half of the belt was expended. From our position in the gun pit, it was clear where those one hundred bullets ended up. The wild growth of rubber trees on the other side of the creek clearly showed their wounds. Rubber trees when cut bleed white sap. Last night's wounds were clearly visible in the early morning sunshine.

'Well, they fired pretty straight,' said Sarge.

'Yep, straight up,' added the boss.

Every round had hit somewhere six metres up or above. The medics, exceptional medics they were, must have ducked their heads and pulled the trigger. 'Bless their hearts,' said Darryl, 'I wonder if they would like a bath?' indicating our trenches full of water.

Where did the engineering of the trench and tent go so wrong? Why did both trenches fill with water and cause us so much discomfort? In the bright light of day, we could see everything was standing, hutchies were intact, and the centre sleeping possie was dry. So where had all the water come from? We had no clue.

The leader of the support section came by to have a giggle at the two sigs seen in a midnight embrace.

'Eff off, Corporal Eff Wit,' said Darryl. These two had a bit of history. Each took every opportunity to "have a go" at the other. All in good humour, of course.

'So sorry, Lance Corporal Dickhead,' said Darby.

'Carry on, chaps, fight. That is why we are here. I hate peace,' I said.

Darby said he knew what our problem was; he had had a similar experience. He went on to explain how the material the hutchie was made of tended to cave in between two anchor points. Our combined hutchies did not cover our pits completely. During that night it had been raining very heavily for some hours. Every bit of water on our roof ended up in the pits. 'Just widen the tent, you pair of dickhead sigs,' he said as he left laughing.

Saddens me to say he was right. It was obvious what had happened.

'So what?' said Darryl in between sarcastic jibes. 'We are infantry sigs, not engineers.'

25. THE REAL DEAL

Did I mention that I suffered PTSD as a result of my service in Vietnam? Possibly not yet, but I expect you know it's coming. It was not an immediate problem, but one that festered within my mind over many years. My psychiatrist encouraged me to "face my tigers". I was asked to write down and describe incidents I remembered occurring in Vietnam. This happened many years after leaving the Army. My behaviour, anger and anxiety were affecting my work and the people around me. One tiger in particular is a recurring memory that haunts me to this day. It occurred in July 1969, just fifty-five years ago.

Coincidentally, a significant world event also happened on 20 July 1969. I was sitting in my trench with the radio tuned to the D Company network and listening for any traffic. I took the opportunity to write a rare letter to Karen back home. In the trench a dim torch light was not visible from above, so I was able to see reasonably well without showing any light outside.

Suddenly the US Armed Services radio station broke the silence of the night with the fantastic news that Neil Armstrong had walked on the Moon. I heard these famous words for the first time, 'One small step for man, one giant leap for mankind.'

I didn't see the television pictures until a few months later, but my memory of where I was when Neil Armstrong walked on the Moon is firmly entrenched. I will always remember the astronaut circling the Moon in the "mother ship" was Michael Collins, namesake of my son born seven years later.

Back to my tiger story.

Army Intelligence (some say, "Army what?") reported movement on the Trail near the border, expected to reach the border in twenty-four to thirty-six hours. The reports were generated by high-altitude aircraft sightings and gave no indication of the type of personnel involved. The OC sent patrols out to check all defences were secure and in working order. These patrols reported on anything visible within our position that may give warning to the approaching enemy— reflections of metal objects, an obvious alteration to the landscape, anything an enemy soldier might question as unusual. The company was ordered into a fifty per cent stand to, meaning one of each pair on the perimeter must be awake and in battle position around the clock.

Early the following morning, the Sarge moved me to a new position. He said the major would assume radio responsibility as I was needed on a right flank lookout post. A partially dug trench was my new possie at night until this shit fight was over. My new digs were about 60 cm deep on the outer end and 90 cm deep on the other. The deep end was muddy water. Fortunately, it was possible to do my job despite the muddy bit. I returned to my more comfortable digs during the day to catch-up on some sleep. Mind you, sleeping during the day is not easy with so many dickheads willing to help.

'Hey, Pete. Had any sleep buddy?'

'Piss off.'

'Sorry, mate, just checking!' Ha, fuckin' ha.

The second night in my watch position a strange thing occurred. I was wide awake, the night was dark. Lying in my trench I had a clear view of the tree line about one hundred metres out in front. Nothing existed between me and the trees. Staring into the darkness, the tree trunks were visible but a bit blurred. Suddenly I saw something smaller, lower but very still. I rubbed my eyes and re-focused on the image. 'Yes,' I said under my breath, 'someone, or something, is out there.' I switched the safety off on my Armalite and aimed at the fuzzy image. It was not moving. I lowered the rifle, looked away briefly with my eyes shut, counted to five and looked back. It had moved. *Had it moved, or just in my mind*, I thought. My training called for action. Again, I raised my rifle and aimed at the centre of the dark image.

If I fire the company will immediately react. If I do not, the company position could be overrun by whatever is out there. I fired four shots.

Within seconds the CSM was in the muddy end of my trench.

'What the fuck, Collins?'

This person did not seem to like me, and I know I did not like him. He was never involved with the troops as other officers were. I rolled over to face him and managed to push him further into the muddy bit. Not on purpose, of course.

I said, 'I suspected movement out there, I could see something, so I fired.'

I had fired four shots in rapid succession. 'Sorry I have disturbed your sleep, sir.' He sort of grunted and ran off back to where he came from, his bed I suspect.

The company headquarters sergeant lay down beside me and said, 'What's the go, Pete?'

I told him of my last few minutes watching a dark shape in the tree line. I convinced myself the shape had moved a bit, so I decided to fire knowing the company would go to stand to. I said I thought that would be better than being surprised.

He clapped me on the shoulder and said, 'Good stuff, Pete. Well done soldier.'

It was a false alarm. After thirty minutes, the guys were ordered to stand down. Me, well, I got to stay there until after dawn. As I dragged myself back to my bed, the smart-arse comments flowed thick and fast. All meant in good humour called "rubbishing" and taken as such. 'What a dreamer'; 'Seen any ghosts lately?'; 'Some say, he can see in the dark'; 'He can defeat an Army with his speeding bullets'; 'Accidental discharge four times. Put him in the box'; 'Some say his radio pack weighs more than he does— skinny little sod'; 'They call him "turtle", fucked on his back!'.

I ate two dry biscuits and a can of beans and said to Darryl, 'Only wake me if it's important, please.'

Someone was shaking my shoulder. 'Pete, wake up, mate,' the voice said.

What else would I say but 'Just fuck off and let me sleep?'

'Sorry, it's Major S, I need to talk.'

I sprang to my feet, or tried to, and said 'Sorry, sir.'

The major continued, 'Battalion want a report on last night's contact, I need your input, Pete.'

When we reached the site, the major stood up in the trench and asked, 'What direction from here?'

I stepped forward and pointed my rifle in the direction I had seen last night. He headed off in that direction until we entered the tree line. He stopped. 'A good one hundred metres by my reckoning, agree?' He looked forward, right and left and stepped a few paces forward. There in front of us was a large drum (forty-four gallon size), old and burned black. The Major examined the drum thoroughly and turned to me with a big smile on his face.

'You got him, Pete. How many shots did you fire?'

'Four, sir!'

'Look at this here, mate. A perfect grouping of four shots. Good shooting, I say.'

I thought, *Wow, effing wow, I shot a drum; that helps the war effort.* I was embarrassed and showed it, I guess. The Major went on to say his report to battalion would be favourable, and I should not worry.

'You did what every soldier should do, be alert and protect your mates,' he said as we left the scene.

The boss and I parted as the sledging started.

'How many days in the cooler, mate?'

The boss called me back and said in a rather loud voice, 'Ah Collins, about my recommendation for recognition... ,' then said softly, 'There is none. That was for their benefit, hope it helps.' As I said, he was a bloody good guy!

I settled back into my radio duties in the tent with Darryl. I had done my stint on the overnight watch and was in the routine of two hours on, two hours off on watch. It was a quiet night and the morning the same. There was no real expectation of any nighttime contact, the expectation was for daytime movement across the creek and the border.

At 1500 hours Darryl handed the watch to me. It was a hot and steamy afternoon, sweat oozed out of my body from everywhere. *Wish it would rain*, I thought. Then a Claymore exploded over to my right and the M60 Gun opened up and continued to fire. A flare exploded in the air to the left. That M60 burst into life again. I grabbed my rifle and radio and sprinted the few metres to the command post. By the time I got there I had called Forty-one, Forty-two, Forty-three and Forty-four to acknowledge and stand by!

The boss took the handset and in a very calm voice asked the sigs to have the platoon commanders report asap. One by one their replies came in. Still calm, the major offered suggestions to his junior officers. Each time he finished the conversation with, 'Do not risk the lives of your men.'

Meanwhile the M60s blazed away. There were several NVA soldiers escorting others and carrying goods of all kinds. The VC black pyjamas were also obvious in number. The North Vietnam soldiers tried aggressively to cross the creek but met huge resistance from us as they emerged from the deep creek banks.

During a lull in radio traffic the boss said, 'Pete, go and man your post. Come back at stand to if you will.'

'Yes, sir. Good luck.'

This shit fight carried on for some time. On both sides, the creek banks were steep, slippery and very difficult to negotiate. Our position was very dominant. The M60s all had a multifield of fire over the three partly established and well-used crossings. We were receiving some incoming machine gun and rifle fire with little effect. Our posts were well established and difficult to see. Occasionally a Claymore exploded as the enemy attempted to find a way across. As the sun set, darkness fell over the area quickly and soon everything was completely black.

I quickly moved back a few metres to the command post.

'Pete, you survived that "to do" all right, I see.'

He asked me to have the battalion guy bring his radio up, and for me to ask the platoons to go to stand to until 1900 hours and continue with fifty per cent watch until dawn.

Darryl headed to the command post while I issued the major's instructions to the platoon sigs. Forty-five minutes later, Darryl returned and passed on all the information to me. Stand to ended without further incident. Darryl took the first two-hour watch while I managed to make a brew in the trench and then settle down under a light blanket for some much-needed sleep. Just past 2100 Darryl woke me. He said I was snoring so loudly he put my bush hat over my face. I rummaged in my trench, found a Hershey Bar, then settled down for the next two hours watching and listening for anything, even a roaming forty-four-gallon drum!

Darryl had trouble settling, still kicking and groaning at 2200. Finally, he fell asleep; he also needed the bush hat treatment. When my watch said 2300 (actually it didn't say anything) I looked at Darryl sound asleep with a smile on his dial. I was enjoying the quietness of the jungle surrounding. I doubted I would sleep right now. *Sleep on mate, you are enjoying something*, I thought.

Approaching midnight, I heard sounds from the other side, soft groaning that steadily grew louder. Similar sounds came from other directions. I felt shivers go down my back as I realised what the sounds must be. People wounded and dying in the darkness, in pain and no imminent help available. The noise continued for the next two hours, increasing to screams at times. At 0200 I needed some support, another person to talk to.

I shook Darryl gently. He was awake quickly and asked, 'Is it 2300 already?'

'No mate it is actually 0200.'

'What, did I fall asleep?' I told him what had occurred; he was very grateful for the extra sleep.

'Darryl,' I said, 'The wailing and screams have been happening for the past two hours. I woke you for some company, it is freaking me out!' We stood and looked into the darkness for an hour. Nothing moved but the sounds continued.

Darryl suggested I try to get some sleep, 'Stick your socks in your ears and think of home, push this place out of your mind.' I did as he suggested sans the socks, and actually fell asleep. Darryl woke me at 0500. I manufactured a brew in the trench as stand to approached. What a bastard of a night, we agreed. The noise from the creek area had ceased at about 0400 and all was quiet as we entered stand to.

I moved up to the command post after stand to. The boss gave me instructions to send to the platoon commanders, basically a request for them to investigate outside their perimeter and report back as soon as possible.

This would be a hazardous task. Our soldiers were aware wounded or dead Vietnamese fighters could be lying on a live grenade set to detonate if the body was moved. They acted dead and fired point blank at anyone approaching. This was war, raw and brutal. Such a situation sometimes requires a reaction or action that in the normal world might be seen as unacceptable. This is typical of war. Only those exposed to these horrible events understand completely. Actions must, must be judged on this basis and definitely not on what the normal world would expect. In wars in the Middle East, following Vietnam, Australian soldiers have been criticised for what the general community has sadly labelled "war crimes". The labelling and self-righteous judgement of action in war is wrong. Those trusted men must retain the trust of the ones who sent them there. These circumstances require a high standard of proof and intent.

Vietnam veterans returning home were being treated like war criminals. These soldiers, veterans of one of the most difficult wars Australia has faced, faded "into the woodwork" as they tried to forget their experience. Why was this? Because an opposing group, a minority, were allowed to voice their objections to the war and conscription. They were promoted by the media, especially television. Coverage of demonstrations in the capital cities chanting "baby killers" and other accusations of mistreatment of Vietnamese civilians took precedence in news reports on all TV channels. It was all based on misinformation and a confusion with the behaviour of other armed forces.

The term "baby killers" arose from an attack on a Vietnamese Village by a US unit. Australian men were not involved in any way, but it was convenient for protest organisers to paint a different picture. An untrue picture, but one that viewers believed. Known as the My Lai massacre, on 16th March 1968, an American unit of twenty men led by a lieutenant, destroyed a small Vietnamese village killing everyone. Between 347 and 507 women, children and old men were killed. The lieutenant was convicted and found guilty in 1974 of the premeditated murder of twenty-two Vietnamese civilians (Childs 2014).

I knew, we all knew, there were dead and wounded men lying out there. Hopefully no further killing would be necessary as our men investigated and searched the creek banks. I advised the other sigs that the major preferred a face-to-face report, not a radio report. About ninety minutes later, the platoon commanders began to report. When the officers-only meeting was concluded, the boss explained to me that our operation had been successful. He did not reveal any numbers of enemy killed. He did say there was evidence of many wounded being dragged away, but some bodies, surmised to be couriers, remained. 'With no identification possible, they will be buried on site,' he said.

MY TIGER: THE ENDURING MEMORY

I have never talked about the burial of these people with anyone other than my psychiatrist, circa 2006. The only time I had ever written or spoken about it was for her "face your tigers" request. I was asked to write down a description of my memories of Vietnam. Most of what I have written about in this book so far was described in that face the tigers written exercise.

I recall much of Vietnam when in conversation with other veterans and friends. I laugh about being stuck in the mud after jumping from a helicopter under fire. I describe the B52 bombers over the Long Hais, but I have never talked about the memory that returns constantly even fifty-five years later. The human mind is a wonderful asset, but it also can be brutal. It has provided a picture that has not varied for fifty-five years.

The major said, 'Pete, I need a witness of your rank (i.e., the lowest, the bottom) to observe the disposal of the dead left behind last night. Will you accompany me?' He added it was not an order.

'Yes, sir,' I replied quietly.

We moved to the edge of the creek bank, the outer perimeter of the company defences. From there we were to view the disposal of some dead men and maybe women. All would take place on the other bank. The major explained that a large unused and dry well had been discovered on the far creek bank. This was to be used to dispose of the bodies.

In my head, I could hear the moaning and cries of the wounded from last night. These poor bastards had died a painful death, alone and in the darkness and in a few moments would be disposed of in an unmarked grave— a well in the jungle.

The first body appeared. Naked and appearing white, it was frozen in a grotesque posture. Arms spread wide and bent, the legs the same. I groaned in dismay. The boss placed his hand on my shoulder. I watched as two more in the same posture were dumped into the well. The fourth was the same, but the face was towards me, the expression was a depiction of pain and horror. This person, enemy, stranger, a fellow human being from a different world, now resides in my memory. I bowed my head. I did not want to see any more. The major squeezed my shoulder, 'Stick with me, mate. It is nearly over.'

The major acknowledged each further burial so I could, if necessary, attest to the number. Finally, the interment was done. Within seconds there was a large explosion as the well was collapsed by explosives in the walls. With tears in my eyes, I looked up at a clearly shaken officer beside me.

We returned to the command post without a word. I went to my trench, lay down on the grass, and saw the first image of this man, number one of many visions. The company remained in position for a further week before being deployed back to Nui Dat. The base, a hovel by anyone's standards, felt like home. I did, however, return with some extra baggage collected along the way.

26. PREPARATION FOR RTA

After a few days and a thousand beer cans back at base, we tenth intake blokes were told we had completed our last operation and would soon be flown home. A day or so later, a small camp of about five tents was established. We were banished from the company that had been our home for eighteen months. The wags of the group, quite a few of this variety, soon had signs around our camp. The first was "The RTA Club" followed a day or so later by "The Tenth OUT-TAKE". We were all part of the tenth intake of the National Service almost two years earlier.

The little group did pretty well. Whatever came to mind, which was drink, drink, drink and drink some more, no one ever bothered us. We volunteered to do mess duties, washing pots, pans and dishes daily. The cooks enjoyed our work and looked after us at mealtimes by serving us before the mob with plenty of food. Even the ever-cranky head cookie had a few laughs more than once. I was able to return to assist the bar staff of the Seldom Seen Inn, whenever it was open for business. I was able to keep in touch this way with some of my friends staying behind.

Instructions were issued to us on what was required for the flight home, including restrictions on some goods, cleanliness, weight and types of goods allowed. The Armoury Sergeant provided information on preparation of any weapons (i.e., memorabilia) we might wish to have back in Australia. Our current rifles and other combat items would be surrendered at Nui Dat prior to departure. Travel dress was Army dress uniform, no date for departure was provided.

I had acquired an AK-47 assault rifle (a Soviet built Kalashnikov)

The tenth out-take, me with Geoff Dartnell, Nui Dat, September 1969

Standing: Joe Alexander, Geoff Dartnell, Bernie Joyce, Dick Irons, Ian McKenzie and Frank Douglas. Seated: Trevor Harrison. Nui Dat, just before RTA, September 1969

26. Preparation for RTA

during one of our operations that I was keen (at that time) to take home. To do so, the Armoury had to disable the firing mechanism and fill the barrel with lead. I received confirmation all was completed and provided an Australian delivery address. It (the AK-47) never arrived. On that same operation I took a Browning .32 pistol from the body of a NVA officer. This pristine weapon was still wrapped in greased paper— it had never been fired. The Armoury Sergeant thought it should be retained in that condition, to which I agreed. It remained in the Armoury.

All of us had money to spend, the Army issued MPCs. The series of our MPCs would most likely be changed shortly before we departed, making it worth nothing and impossible to convert. Prices of electrical equipment, cameras, cigarettes and alcohol were very cheap. A reel-to-reel tape recorder, the Akai M-9, proved very popular. With speakers, it was a large unit and would be a problem to carry and transport. I gave it a miss!

I purchased a Yashica reflex camera. A brilliant, all bells and whistles job. Well, for the 1960s anyway. The thing got drowned a year later. I was trying to cross a flooded underpass when the Pacer started to float at the rear end. Three people jumped out the windows, a fourth opened the rear door. The Pacer sunk to the top of the wheels. The camera was between the front seats. It never worked again.

Smoking had become a habit, so I bought five thousand cigarettes in cartons made up of Benson and Hedges, Marlboro, Camel and Winston. Added to these bad guys was a bottle of Bacardi rum and one of whisky, both very large! *Money well spent*, I thought at the time. The bulky package of cigarettes was consigned direct to my home address. I would carry the bottles as hand luggage.

Everything being taken home had to be scrubbed clean, even my favourite Dunlop GP Boots, especially the boots, soles and all. Everything would be inspected before departure, anything unacceptable would be dumped.

WE SAY GOODBYE TO OUR MATES AT DELTA COMPANY

A few days before we were to fly out of Vietnam, D Company prepared to depart on a new operation. Early one morning a line of APCs formed at the entrance and the men of D Company climbed aboard. Our little group walked down the long line saying goodbye.

I found my old mate Jock perched atop an APC gun turret cuddling his beloved M60 machine gun. As it turned out, I had not seen him at all while in Vietnam. The battalion spent most of the time "in the bush" on operations, and with that and our different responsibilities, there was never an opportunity to get together. We spoke briefly about linking up in Australia, as previously arranged, in a few months' time. I wished him well, told him to be bloody careful and no bloody heroics. Jock's untidy face burst into a huge smile as he said, 'I love you, little mate. I'll be back, as they say. Take care, see ya at home.'

I tried to reply but the words didn't come out. I saluted him instead as the column began to move. I stood and watched with the other men until they were out of sight among the rubber trees. We returned to our camp in silence and sat alone reflecting on those special mates. After some time, someone said, 'That was hard. Harder than going with them!' Little did I know it then, but it was the last time I was to see Jock.

27. "FREEDOM BIRD" AWAITS

The RAAF flew us by chopper in groups from Kangaroo pad, the helicopter landing strip used by the Australians at Nui Dat, to Tan Son Nhut Air Force base at Saigon. The journey home would be a charter flight, only Army personnel aboard, flying direct from Saigon to Sydney. The Qantas 707 Aircraft was known as the "Freedom Bird" to Aussie diggers.

I do not recall much of that flight. I do remember the huge cry of 'Goodbye Vietnam'. Hardly, it was more a cry of, 'Go and get fucked, VC, see you next time.' The pilot came on the speaker and welcomed us on board. He asked us to be pleasant to the staff, all of whom were stewards, not female hosties! He gave some information on the flight time, etcetera. He then said, 'Enjoy your time with Qantas, the first drink is on us. See you in Sydney.' The huge cheer was deafening.

We drank the plane dry! On arrival in Sydney in the early morning, about 0200 hours, the cabin was pretty quiet, apart from the snoring of a few. The pilot came on the speaker and, after a few bars of "I Still Call Australia Home", broke in with a 'Welcome home, lads. Fasten seat belts, we land in Sydney in fifteen minutes.'

A steward, a big guy, came down the aisle with a spray can, waving it and spraying from side to side, spraying everyone. Didn't he cop it? Sure did, and some. He laughed all the way down the length of the plane.

We circled Sydney, a fantastic sight at any time, but coming home from a war was special. Perhaps because, unlike other overseas journeys, it was possible one may not have returned. An immense cheer went up as the plane's tyres screeched upon touching Australian soil. As the aircraft settled into taxi mode, the pilot announced, 'Men, you are home. Thank you for what you have done guys, and thank you for travelling Qantas,' followed by a loud giggle.

As we all moved towards the front exit door, emotions varied from one to the next. Some overjoyed to be home, others complaining about only the front door as an exit. When we did reach the front of the plane, the reason for the delay became obvious. The Qantas captain insisted on shaking the hand of every passenger, thanking each of us and wishing all the best. I wish I could remember his name. We would soon discover the captain's attitude towards us, and the Vietnam War in general, was not shared by everyone here in Australia.

HOME: STILL IN ONE PIECE

Once down the aircraft stairs, the arrival procedure was simple. In the terminal, deserted except for a few local well-wishers, we had to do our own thing, like it or not. All I had was my carry-on bag, my other stuff was pre-booked on a flight to Brisbane the following day at 1100 hours. I had a big bottle of scotch and a big bottle of rum, and not much else, to keep me company for the first night in Australia.

No Army or Defence people greeted us on arrival, nor on departure the next day. We had fulfilled every bit of our "contract" to serve in the Army for two years. Now, at the end, the organisation, so strict on discipline, just didn't give a shit about me. Just fuck off, mate.

Faced with a night of sleeping in the airport "lounge" I was overjoyed when Lindsay, Karen's young brother (remember Karen?), arrived to look after me. In the RAN, Lindsay was then based in Sydney. Despite the ups and downs of my relationship with his sister, Lindsay and I were bloody good mates.

'Hey, Private Collins. Shall we go get pissed?'

I could write another book on our drinking exploits.

'You bet, mate. lead the way to a boozer.'

Although a bit younger than I, Lindsay had developed a certain confidence. As noted, at the age of fifteen, he joined the Navy and headed to Perth for training. Even today, fifty-five years later, he reminds me the Navy is the "senior service". I don't argue. He served for twenty years, me only two years. But I remind him I walked, he didn't. Lindsay understands and appreciates my contribution to the Australian military, especially as a "crunchie", a.k.a. infantry gook.

'Where are you bunking down tonight, mate?'

'Here on the fucking airport chairs, I guess.'

'Don't see any help arriving, so fuck it, let's go have a drink to celebrate, cobber,' Lindsay said.

Lindsay suggested the Sydney Motor Club. He was a member, it was close by and would be open. We arrived at the front door, a sign requested members ring the bell, and show a current membership card, before entry was permitted. A single guest was allowed.

Lindsay walked in, but I was stopped and held back by the doorman. Despite Lindsay taking all responsibility for me as his guest, the refusal of entry stood firmly. Asked by Lindsay under what protocol was I being refused, the reply was, 'Mr Shanks, your guest fails to meet the Club dress code.'

Lindsay erupted in a loud voice, 'What the fuck do you mean, dickhead. He is dressed in the Australian Army dress uniform. Is that not good enough for this establishment?'

'Mr Shanks, I am sorry, but it is Club management's decision to exclude uniformed visitors.'

'My visitor, as you refer to him, is in Australian Army uniform, because just forty-five minutes ago he landed in Sydney from Saigon, Vietnam, where he has for many months been an infantry soldier risking life and limb for the Australian people, like you!'

'I suggest a change of apparel would have been appropriate,' said the dickhead.

Waving arms and pacing about in anger Lindsay said, 'He has what he stands up in, nothing else. He has been in the country for forty-five minutes!'

I urged Lindsay to leave, no way could I celebrate in this joint.

The real kicker in this visit to the Motor Club that night was, as we walked along outside the bar, we could see men in uniform. They were American MPs in white belts, caps and gaiters over their spit-polished boots. There were four of them in full view and others around the corner.

'What a fuckin' croc of shit,' said Lindsay. 'I am going back to give that bastard on the door a gob full.'

I urged Lindsay not to stir up any shit. I was tired and the urge to have a drink with Lindsay had waned somewhat, and I just wanted to sleep, lying down on a bed preferably.

Lindsay said, 'Yeah, okay, but tomorrow I am coming here in my "whites" and I will shove my membership card up their what's its, sideways.' He went on to say, 'I'll look after you, private. The senior service to the rescue of the Army yet again.'

He took me to the Royal Naval House where I was given, gratefully I might add, a comfortable bed for the night. The steward told me breakfast was at four bells (0600 hours) in the dining room. A driver would be available to take me to the Airport at 0700 hours, just wait at the front door.

WELL DONE, AUSTRALIAN NAVY.

I woke early the next morning. I looked around at the strange surroundings for a while and wondered where I was. There was a strong odour of alcohol— rum— around me. I don't normally drink rum, so it was weird. I bent down to pick-up my bag. Bugger! There is the reason. Somehow last night the large bottle of white rum got broken. Everything was soaked. The only dry clothes left was the uniform I was not keen to wear on the flight home today. I managed to dump the broken glass and rinse some of my gear hoping I would not smell like a distillery on the plane.

I gave breakfast a miss and sat in the sun for a while at the front door. I began to think about going home, but then started to worry about getting to the airport. What if the driver doesn't turn up, I don't even know where in Sydney I am, have no Aussie dollars to speak of and a taxi would be expensive. I checked my new Seiko World Time watch. Big, heavy and bright it was, and cheap at the post exchange (PX) in Nui Dat. The time was 0630. I had thirty minutes of anxious waiting. People started to move about, Navy officers coming and going, all saying, 'Good morning, sir,' to each other.

A smart looking WRAN came up the stairs and headed towards me. 'Going to the Airport?' she asked.

'Ahh yes, I hope so,' I sort of stammered.

She smiled, said her name was Mel, and said, 'You are?'

I explained my circumstances. Then she said, 'Wait here, I'll be back in a few minutes.'

My Seiko told me it was 0645. I suddenly felt good, really good and thought of home. *In a few hours I will be back to a new life or starting up the old one again.* I tried not to think about Karen, she has moved on most likely. I do know Dad will be at the Brisbane Airport to meet me, who else, I don't know. Sure would be nice if Karen was there. Mel did come back as promised with a Navy rank in tow.

'Pete, this is Able Seaman Rick, he will drive you to the airport, good luck and welcome home.'

Mel handed a bunch of keys to Rick, turned on her heel and marched off. Rick said, 'Mate, you must be special. Follow me to the car, it's in the officer's car park.'

Once we were under way Rick told me it was Mel's "work" car, which was the reason he thought me special; it was unusual. I told him I had arrived from Vietnam last night and, after spending the night at Naval House, I was told there would be transport to the airport. Your officer saw me waiting, asked me some questions and here we are. 'Please convey my appreciation to Mel when you return the car.'

The flight to Brisbane was pleasant enough, better (just) than military planes (no quiet jets in 1969). We landed at Kingsford Smith terminal, Brisbane, on time.

28. COMING HOME: NOT SO EASY!

As expected, Dad was there to meet me. With tears running down his face he wrapped me in his arms and held on tight. When he relaxed after some time he introduced the woman with him; her name was Margaret. I had not met her before.

'Pete, this is my new wife, your new mother!'

I mentioned before that Dad was very lonely in the months after Mum was killed. I had no problem with him doing his own thing if he was happy. He and Margaret were married in July (while I was in Vietnam) and had travelled on their honeymoon to the Gold Coast in my new Pacer.

Maybe I was tired, but my reply was not what they expected.

'Margaret, I am pleased to meet you. I do wish you both all the best. But you are not my mother, though I accept you as my father's wife.'

Poor Dad, he straightened to his maximum height and said, 'Well, Son, let's collect your bag and head home.'

There was another person there to meet me. My little sister Wendy. So anxious to have me home, Wendy had asked the school principal if she could leave school early to meet her big brother in Brisbane on his arrival from Vietnam. In her young eyes I was a hero, she was so proud of me and remained so all of her life. It was a delight to see her tears of joy.

Dad drove, I was not up to it. I sat in the back seat of my Pacer enjoying the ride. We stopped at a hotel in Goodna, the Weeroona, for a drink and food. Dad got me a T-Bone steak (he thought I was skinny) and a pot of XXXX. I could not eat the steak and had one sip of the beer. I could see Dad was concerned. The last time he saw me I was fit, healthy and weighed thirteen stone (82.6 kg). Now I was but a shadow of my former self! Skinny as a rake, as they say, with a dark, unhappy expression.

I sat in the rear comfortable seat and my mind went everywhere. Karen had not come to meet me, so I thought that relationship was "kaput". It is funny how the mind works, maybe it was the thought of Karen, but a joke came to mind: *A fellow nasho on his way to Mackay picked up a hitchhiker near Brisbane. He noticed she was wearing a very short skirt. Just past Gympie, he plucked up the courage to rest his hand on her knee. Looking at him with a knowing smile, she cooed, "You can go further if you want." So he drove on to Townsville!*

We had arrived at the bottom of the Toowoomba Range, part of Australia's Great Dividing Range, which is a fairly steep road. Dad said, 'Pete, this car is magic. It just flattens the hills; you are going to love it.'

'I'm looking forward to showing off downtown. It looks bloody smart,' I said.

As we stopped at the top of Dad's steep driveway, I climbed out and looked around. The house towered above and, to the right, I could see for miles out into the Lockyer Valley. After Vietnam, the bush and such gave a feeling of freedom. I just stood leaning on the roof of the car, and all felt good.

Excited, Wendy dragged me up the internal stairs, down the hall to my room. With its new bed, built-in everything, two windows and polished floor it looked so luxurious after Vietnam. Li'l Wendy said, 'Pete, there's a big parcel in the cupboard.'

'Yes, my cigarettes probably, a lot of them.'

Dad appeared at the door carrying all my stuff, he dropped it at the door and with tears rolling down his face and said, 'Thank God you are home, Son.'

The three of us had a big cry in a group hug then fell on the bed; tears turned to laughter. Nice, hey! They left me and closed the door.

I sat there on the bed a bit confused. No, a lot confused. I felt strange in my own home, like I was visiting someone and staying in their home, something I always avoided previously. But here I was with my family, and I felt completely out of place. I threw my few Army belongings in the wardrobe and ventured out to reacquaint myself with Dad's house.

The family was in the step-down lounge room with large windows and a deck out to the side. It faced the east, and the view was amazing, uninterrupted for miles. I turned to Dad and said, 'This outlook must be something else at stand to.'

He walked over to me, put his hand on my arm and gently said, 'Pretty good at sunrise, yes.'

We had a look around the rest of the house and, in the downstairs rumpus room, Dad handed me the Pacer keys and said, 'Son, just go and enjoy yourself. Don't bend the car and we'll see you tomorrow. Dinner will be at six if you want to come home.'

LOOK OUT, I'M BACK

Dad had told me that Karen did want to come to meet me in Brisbane but had a work commitment. She had, as I would discover, been promoted to secretary to the boss man, Edsel Falconer. I thought I would drive down to Falconer Motors, the Ford dealership where she worked, at five o'clock and pick her up. I had a few hours to look up some old mates, civvie mates. I went to the ANZ to get some cash. The tellers were all new, as seemed were a lot of the staff that I could see. I asked a teller the balance of my account, I said it may be in the staff section. He looked at me strangely, took my details, asked for ID and headed out the back where I knew the ledger department was situated. Almost immediately the rear door flew open and Lyn, one of the ledger machine operators, emerged. I knew Lyn pretty well. Unfortunately, I also knew her boyfriend, so hands off. Lyn had taught me, or tried to teach me, the ledger machine operation. She spent lots of time fixing my errors.

She came outside the counter, gave me a big hug and a passionate kiss (well I thought so) and said, 'Great to see you back all in one piece. But a little thinner.'

She organised my cash and said she would send out a bank statement, then asked, 'When can we meet up for a drink? All the guys and gals have a drink next door on Friday arvo. They'll be happy to see you.' I said I would be there.

Feeling on top of the world with that reception, I walked up the lane beside the bank and into the rear entrance of my favourite "watering hole", the White Horse Hotel. It had been five months since I'd last visited the pub on my leave before Vietnam. Walking through the now closed disco, a loud voice came from behind.

'Hey you! Get the fuck out of my pub now or I'll throw you out!'

I turned around and there was Ron, pub owner with a huge grin on his face, 'You home for good?'

'Yeah, Ron, I hope so. Not yet discharged, on leave for a few weeks, then ...'

'Come on, let's have a beer. Takings have been down since you left. Good to have you back, mate.'

One after the other old friends, acquaintances and mates turned up. It was the same deal every time:

'Good to see ya, mate. Have a beer, blah blah blah.'

MEETING UP WITH KAREN: IS THIS RELATIONSHIP FOR REAL?

I was beginning to think this was a bad idea coming to the pub. I'll be pissed before 5 o'clock, Karen will not be impressed. I slowed down the consumption. At one stage, I had three pots on the bar. I asked the barman to remove a couple. Shortly before five o'clock I fired up the Pacer and drove up the street about a mile or so and parked outside Falconer's. I was feeling a bit, a lot, apprehensive, maybe even scared of seeing Karen. I'd seen her each time I'd been home on leave but that amounted to very little time spent with her over the past two years. Coming home was different, and permanent. And there was no doubt I was a very different person to the one she had known.

I sat slumped back in my seat and watched as people started leaving, then she appeared with a work mate, looking gorgeous as always. I tooted the horn. Several people looked up. The blue Valiant Pacer parked in front of the Ford dealership stood out like the proverbial sore thumb. Karen recognised me, or maybe just the car. A few young mechanics were standing looking at the car, it was the first Pacer sold in Queensland, but had been hidden in the garage at home most of the time I was away. Perhaps they hadn't seen one before. I looked back and Karen was at the door trying to get in. Her female work mates were watching and screamed and giggled when we kissed and embraced.

As we drove away the girls all waved and the boys stared, waiting for a smoking tyres demo (a "wheelie"). Sorry guys, I have other things to do right now.

Karen said she did not want to go home, could we drive through the city and cruise around a little bit. Quick as a flash I said, 'Why not come home with me? You can have dinner with us, and we can catch-up in comfort.' Agreed, I set a course for home. Dad, Margaret and Li'l Wendy were overjoyed to see us arrive.

'No, one more for dinner is not a problem at all,' Margaret said.

After dinner we were all sitting in the lounge room enjoying the view over the valley. Dad trotted out some good liquors with coffee. All was good, really good, and Dad sensed I was happy. To my surprise Dad said, 'Karen why don't you stay the night?' He continued by saying, 'Pete is really down, he has had a dreadful experience and needs us all to give him time. Since being with you, Karen, he is happier.'

Karen was as surprised as I was but managed to say, 'But I don't have any clothes.'

Typically for a male, I said, 'You won't need clothes!'

Dad smiled and said, 'Pete will drive you home to get what you need. It's Saturday tomorrow, so you can enjoy the weekend together. If he won't drive you, I will.'

Karen said, 'How can I refuse? Thank you, Mr Collins.'

28. Coming home: Not so easy!

'Karen, it's Gordon and Margaret, okay?'

Karen and I left soon after to get some overnight gear from Karen's home. It was about 6:30 pm. She lived with her grandmother, mother, brother and sister in a small house close to the CBD. I asked Karen how she was getting on with her mum, Elsie. I knew Elsie could be a bit scratchy about Karen's relationships at times.

'Never know, Pete. Changes daily, but don't worry, all will be well,' she said.

'Why don't I talk to her, tell her the story that Dad asked you to stay. Elsie gets on well with Dad, it might soften the shock.'

'Okey dokey, you talk to her while I pack a bag. I'll be as quick as I can.'

Before I went away my relationship with Elsie was quite good, and she said she trusted me with her daughter. Silly woman, hey! But I hadn't seen her since my twenty-first birthday, which seemed like a lifetime ago. After the welcome back stuff was done, I told her Gordon had asked Karen to stay over tonight, maybe for the weekend.

'Pete, I trust you, just look after her and please say hello to your dad for me.'

'Bye, Mum!' Karen said.

Back in the car Karen commented on how quiet I was and also how co-operative her mum was about staying over. 'I'm just a nice guy who likes to get what or whom he wants.'

Karen giggled, 'Yeah!'

From Karen's street, I turned left into Margaret Street, and crossed Ruthven as Karen said, 'There's your bank.'

I immediately remembered my promise to Lyn to meet the staff at the pub. I said, 'Karen, darling, do you perhaps feel like a celebratory drink at our watering hole?' I did a quick U-turn and parked outside the White Horse. I quickly explained the situation to Karen, so, hoping they were all still there, we entered the lounge bar.

Heaps of the staff were there, the boss, Ted, Norm, Lyn and several of the (out the back) girls from ledgers. No computers then, everything was hard copy stuff, done on the large rattly National Ledger Machines.

*

The first computers would not appear until the early 80s. When they did arrive in offices, they were huge monstrosities with limited capability. By then I was working for a finance company who had a Honeywell mainframe computer in Sydney's CBD, which was to be moved across the Harbour Bridge to Crows Nest. The thing was so massive it would take a weekend to complete the move. A young electrician working at the new site asked, 'What sort of computer is it?'

'A Honeywell 660,' was the reply.

Standing in the large, air-conditioned room the "leckie" said casually, 'It won't fit in here!' Computers generated a lot of heat and stood on a grated air-conditioned floor. The 660 would be too tall because of the raised floor to accommodate the air-conditioning outlet. Luckily this was discovered before the thing was decommissioned and moved. The company would be in a data processing mess considering the time it would take to rectify the new site. One young head stood tall, others rolled!

*

The staff were over the Moon to welcome me back in one piece. Everyone wanted to know, 'When are you starting work?' They had a dreadful time balancing the remittances (or REMS, which were the cheques being returned to other ANZ branches and banks). The total of all REMs sent to other banks and branches must be equal to the acceptance record. I wrote about this in an earlier chapter. They wanted my help. Sorry, guys, I'm in the Army for another month, on leave until discharged.

We had a wonderful time catching up on marriages, births,

transfers and resignations. There were no deaths in this little circle. Norm had just received notice of his transfer to Mount Hagen, Papua New Guinea. He at least was happy, though the Papua New Guinea highlands were not the safest place at that time, or perhaps at any time.

I had a long conversation with the boss who said, 'Pete, I'm personally looking forward to your return to my branch. A lot has happened with us and with you in two years. In the meantime, think about what you would like to do in the bank. I will do my best to help.'

I knew I would need to assimilate back into the workforce, into civilian life for that matter. I didn't know how difficult it would be. At work, for instance, I had lost two years' training, two-years' experience, two-years' advancement and two-years' seniority. It was a lot to make up. The National Service Act of 1964 required employers to keep employment open. The ANZ Banking Group did so and made up my income from the low Army pay. The politicians made an effort, but failed to consider many important aspects, interested only in quickly increasing the armed forces with fit, healthy young men.

When I did get back to the bank after being discharged from the Army, they didn't have a position for me. At that time ANZ had two branches and a sub-branch in Toowoomba. I worked at whichever needed help. Then the bank boffins in Brisbane transferred me to Crows Nest (Queensland this time, not New South Wales), a small branch of about six staff. I would be number three in the pecking order. Crows Nest, named after Jimmy Crow, an indigenous Australian who made his "nest" there a century or so ago, is about 40 km from Toowoomba. I hated the bloody place. I didn't like the manager, and he didn't like me. Part of his reasoning was that I wouldn't live in the town. I drove in and out every day in the Pacer. The local boys always followed me out of town trying to get a race going. Sorry, fellas, I did not want to embarrass you.

One afternoon a promotional man from Esanda Finance visited

the branch. Esanda was part of the old ES&A Bank company that had merged with the ANZ. I took a real and genuine interest in this mode of finance (hire purchase) and asked the manager to transfer me. He flat out refused. I was really pissed off.

I would have resigned, but I had commitments. It so happened, as it can, I met up with John who started at the same ANZ branch as I had on the same day in 1964. He now worked for The AGC, then the largest finance company in Australia. John suggested I apply to join AGC.

I did, and soon I was an AGC collection officer in Toowoomba. I progressed in the company to become a District Credit Manager with a staff of about fifty, responsible for financing about one hundred and fifty motor dealerships throughout the Darling Downs. It was a very high-pressure job that I enjoyed, far removed from the hum drum of Crows Nest, Queensland.

Meanwhile, Karen and I continued together for a short while. Initially it was okay, but Karen thought I was pretty "dark" most of the time. I found this difficult, and I did not understand my behaviour. I was a lucky bastard to have such an attractive girl by my side. I had culled every bit of money I could muster and bought an engagement ring for $2000, a lot of cash in 1970. She accepted. I was at this time still working at Crows Nest when I got an interview with the state manager of AGC. On arrival back from Brisbane, I called in to tell Karen the news that, luckily, I had got the job! That night my world fell apart. Karen informed me someone from her past had come back into her life. The engagement was over, and she handed me back the ring. Fucking wonderful. I needed a beer. I needed lots of beers. I left her house and went to the White Horse Hotel clinic where, when I wasn't working, I stayed on and off for couple of years drowning my sorrows.

Karen would quickly regret her decision. On the day of her wedding, she sent her brother to me with a message she wanted to see me. She regretted her decision and felt overawed by the circumstances surrounding this other person's sudden arrival. She felt she wanted to opt out but did not know how. Despite my willingness to spirit her away, she went ahead and married the bloke who had ratted me out and moved to Sydney while I got on with my life.

29. ENTERING THE FINANCIAL WORLD

My new AGC manager, Lance, was enthusiastic about my work and soon invited me to the more senior staff Friday booze sessions, including state executives and dealer principals. I met High Pockets again on such an occasion. Remember him?

'For a young bloke, you can hold your booze,' an executive from state office commented. *Practice makes perfect*, I thought.

In those days of competitive finance business, long lunches and long after work drinking sessions with clients and car dealers was the norm. I fell into line heart and soul. I loved what I was doing, my work performance was noticed where it counted: at state office. The executives at state office were a bunch of tough guys, ruthless and demanding. Regular surprise office inspections were feared. The State Credit Manager, Vince P, would walk up to your desk, sit in front of you and turn the in-tray and the out-tray upside down. He would question you about every bit of paper in the trays. 'What is this? Why do that? This is two days ago,' and on and on. He would stand up, the victim would breathe again, but it is not over yet!

'Move out, let me sit there!' He would then empty every drawer or shelf in the desk, more questions, then get up and leave without comment. We, us plebs, the collection officers, four of us, waited to be called for the report at the end of the day. What an effing drama. My patience and personal discipline paid off about eighteen months after joining AGC. The state office boffins were convinced by my manager, Lance, that I should be promoted.

29. Entering the financial world

This was early 1971 and the Darling Downs and beyond was devastated by a prolonged drought. Lance had been the manager of AGC Warwick but was transferred to Toowoomba to administratively ready us for the closure of the Warwick branch in six months. The Dalby office was scheduled (confidentially) to close six months later. The problem was both branches had unacceptable levels of overdue accounts. The company standard for thirty days overdue was 1.5 per cent of the total branch accounts. Warwick and Dalby were reporting way over the standard.

I was summoned to see the manager by his secretary "immediately". I must admit I was shitting myself. Such a sudden request was unusual. Lance smiled and asked me to sit. He stood and said, 'Not there, Pete, over here,' pointing to the small "good" customer reception area. 'Pete, I have been given authority by state office to offer you the position of District Credit Manager of this Toowoomba branch. You would work alongside the branch accountant and answer only to me.'

I think I passed out in my chair. I looked blankly at the boss and said, 'Huh?' Lance just laughed, opened his fridge and handed me a XXXX beer.

George, the current District Credit Manager of Toowoomba, short in height, big in stature and blond-headed, was to retire. I had worked closely with George on many difficult high-balance accounts in an effort to find a resolution and present a reasonable report to state office. George and I would arrive at the office before dawn and hit the phones in an attempt to contact the clients, mainly farmers. In the later hours, we contacted bank managers to negotiate a share of the risk. Conversations often went like this, 'Your customer X is in arrears $25 000 on his grain harvester. He has a crop of wheat planted and expects a reasonable return. Without a fifty per cent payment, we will be repossessing the equipment.'

'He owes the bank money too, you realise.'

'The difference, Mr Bank Manager, is you have security, a

mortgage over the farm. Without our machinery, he will not pay you either.'

'All right, I will authorise ten ($10 000).'

'Fifteen, or we move today.'

George and I had a lot of success with this approach, but we did, unfortunately, repossess a lot of farm machinery.

George came into Lance's office, sat down and opened a stubby, 'Congratulations, Pete, you have supported Lance and I, and you deserve this promotion. I wish you well, mate.'

The new job was exceptionally demanding. My first time being a staff boss. My first time at everything associated with the new job. A demanding aspect was having lending authority. Initially, I called on my Army experience and emulated the officers and NCOs who gained my respect. Approval authority was something else. Considering I could buy a packet of Marlboro Red for twenty-three cents and a pot of beer for eighteen cents, an authority to approve a hire purchase contract to a limit of $10 000 was a mega responsibility.

To this point, I had put my heart and soul into the job. On weekends I played up with the mates. I loved Friday nights at the discos and also on Saturday nights, if fit and able. There was, however, a distraction. The very attractive young lady, wearing a mini skirt daily, was cashier and customer receptionist at the office. Her name was Janine.

Janine and I were married in mid-1973, almost three years after my breakup with Karen. Unfortunately, when we were engaged Janine, despite her own career aspirations, had to resign due to an archaic company policy of not allowing a married couple to work together in the same office. I wonder what the current women's lobby would have thought. Maybe it was the catalyst that eventually set Janine on a long study journey culminating in doctoral studies in the area of women's rights.

In the 1970s, a change in the financial world of lending to business was occurring. Leasing of business equipment, as opposed to owning equipment, was quickly becoming a preferred form of business finance. The rationale was preservation of business capital, ease of renewing equipment and taxation advantages. For example: A newsagent requires a new cash register at a cost of $3 000. He/she could pay cash and claim depreciation. Working capital of the business is reduced by $3 000. Or, the agent could lease the cash register and pay monthly rentals over an agreed period, e.g., thirty-six months. As a business expense, the payments (100 per cent) become an income tax deduction. Three thousand dollars of working capital is retained and could be used to increase stock for sale.

Leasing soon became the preferred finance for capital equipment of all types. I became interested in this avenue of business and eventually I was given the position of District Sales Manager Leasing. With a brand-new product to sell I quickly made an impression on the local motor vehicle, truck and machinery dealers. Local opposition finance organisations reacted to business "leaks" from dealers.

The manager of a small but fast-growing company reacted by offering me a deal I could not refuse. Mercantile Credits Limited had a small staff when I arrived as Office Manager. Within a few years the staff grew to around thirty and was housed in new modern premises. We even had the then Queensland Premier, Joh Bjelke Petersen, perform an opening ceremony.

Nineteen-eighty saw a new era in my working life. The company wished to expand its services to central Queensland, specifically Rockhampton on the Capricorn Coast. I was asked to take the position of branch manager of a new office to be established in Rockhampton. In February 1981 (my 34th birthday) my family— wife Janine, Michael aged four and Angie aged two— arrived in Rockhampton.

It was an exciting but daunting task. I had an office space, bare bones in the middle of the CBD, but the location was very good. Janine and I knew our priority was to settle the family in secure, comfortable accommodation and begin looking for a home to buy.

The Chief General Manager in Sydney had agreed to pay for the new property until the Toowoomba home was sold. A staff loan would then be arranged.

With the assistance of a young real estate agent, whose office was next door to mine, we quickly found a very suitable home and began the purchase process. With accommodation settled I began putting the office on the map. Bit by bit it came together—furniture, telephones, and finding staff. Gary, a staff member of the Toowoomba office had asked for a transfer to Rockhampton. He was to be an exceptional assistant in developing the customer base and later assisting in development of new financial products. The new office performed very well, even returned a profit in the first year.

At the end of the 1983 financial year (September), I was advised the Chief General Manager, Warren T., would be visiting the office. I was concerned for a couple of reasons; the premises had not been developed sufficiently to suit our corporate image and what did the big boss have in mind?

Dressed in my best suit and tie I met the boss at the airport. I liked this man. He had a great attitude towards his people, and I felt he liked me. He too was dressed in a dark suit, standard uniform for Sydney Execs. Before we reached my car he said, 'Pete, it's fucking hot, mate.' I replied, 'Typical of Rocky Warren,' and added 'Why don't I take you to your hotel?'

'Good thinking. I can dump this coat and tie,' he said. At the hotel Warren said, 'Give me a half hour and meet me in the lounge bar for a drink or two, okay?'

The office was about a hundred metres from the hotel, so I hiked it to there, got rid of the coat and tie and checked all was well. Mobile phones did not exist then, so I informed my "girl Friday" where to contact me. At 2:30 pm I sat waiting. I knew many of the staff at Duthies Hotel and had accessed the room that morning to ensure all was well. I had a thick bottomed glass, plenty of ice and a bottle of Glenfiddich on the bar. Petty cash can pay!

Dressed in smart casual clobber, but with a business flavour, Warren sat down opposite me. Immediately a waiter sprang from somewhere. 'Drink Sir?'

'Scotch on the rocks, the best you have, same for my mate.' My mate. That sounds pretty good I mused.

Warren looked at me quizzically and said, 'Relax Pete, you and your staff are not in trouble. Far from it actually.' He said: 'Tomorrow there will be a memo to all branches from my office. It was my wish to personally deliver that memo to Rockhampton branch. The memo carries congratulations to your office from Head Office and Brisbane State Office for the achievement of posting a profit in the very first full year of operation. This is this first time in the history of the Company.'

'Waiter, another scotch, a double, I think. Good stuff, well done Rocky!'

'Pete, it's 4:30. Please ring your office and ask them to close up early and come to this place immediately. I want to meet each of these record-setting people personally.' He explained he had an unavoidable commitment that night but would be in the office by 9:00 am tomorrow and would like me to show him some of the local area before flying out later that day.

Family life in Rocky was good after we became accustomed to the weather. Heavy rain at midday every day, then hot and humid. Our new house, upstairs and down in the Rocky style, and the garden were nicely done. Wife and kids were enjoying the new adventure. Schools were close by, the outlook was treed and green, unlike some of Rockhampton. It was a pleasant environment.

Central Queensland is a major cattle area, and Rockhampton is the centre or capital (as some say) of the beef industry. Gary and I soon became interested in this thriving industry. We had discovered a lot about the cattle people, about the farming community, about their honesty especially in business commitment. We saw this as a valuable source of business. I approved Gary's desire to travel to the west, to Emerald and all in between. I had given Gary the new position of Sales Manager to ease my load and allow me to service the growth in town.

Our interest in the cattle industry led to an outstanding coup. I spoke about leasing of equipment, trucks etcetera, earlier. Leasing counted for much of the office success. Now we were about to enter a whole new era of finance in the cattle breeding industry: Stud Stock Leasing. But first I had to convince the State and Head Office boffins not only of the security, but I would need to develop a new procedure and new specific documentation. It happened!

The first Stud Stock Leasing deal came at the Annual Brahman Stud sale during the Rockhampton Beef Week. Our preapproved client was successful in the furious bidding for the top bull offering. He paid a hefty $85 000, an all-time record price.

In an interview on local television, the buyer revealed his source of finance and named the company, Gary and myself. The level of enquiry went through the roof over the next few months. The most well-known Brahman breeder in central Queensland became a major client in the following months. The service even extended to a trusted client's racehorses.

An established client made an appointment to see me. This led to the biggest, most involved finance deal I would write. This client had been with our company for many years as a Brisbane customer. His organisation operated a ferry and a barge service from Yeppoon to the Great Kepple Island Resort in Kepple Bay. After a Sydney Harbour Hydrofoil had been decommissioned, they purchased it, refurbished it and were carrying people to the resort several times daily. Their business operation, carrying tourists from the Rosslyn Bay Boat Harbour to Great Kepple Island resort, was growing rapidly. An updated vessel was required. Their plan was to have a large triple deck, diesel powered catamaran built by a Perth, Western Australian, shipbuilder. The landed cost estimated at about three million dollars.

'What do you think, Pete?' the senior partner asked. The company was made up of the father (who operated the barge) and two sons. I replied, 'You just blew me out of the water, guys. Give me a moment please.' In Toowoomba I was successful in gaining approval to purchase four prime movers and eight tri-axle trailers in the late 1970s valued close to a million dollars. But that was road transport, and the company understood that business. This was different.

After recovering I said, 'How long do I have to answer that question?'

The answer was helpful. The shipbuilder would not be able to begin construction for five or six months. I instructed them to each write a proposal setting out their current operation, how they saw this working, their individual future plans and to justify any predictions from research of the industry.

Eventually, some weeks later, after overtime and weekends in preparation, my 30 mm thick submission went to Brisbane for the endorsement of the Queensland State Manager. Two days later he (Tony) rang me. His initial comment was 'I have never seen anything like this. It's so comprehensive and thorough I have no choice but to forward it on to Sydney. Mind you it will take time for their decision.'

The decision was delivered verbally to me when the State Manager Queensland and Operations Manager Sydney visited the office in person. My submission was approved as submitted. Some months later I was invited to fly to Perth to sail the new vessel across the Great Australian Bight and up the east coast to Yeppoon in central Queensland. Sadly, I could not go. What a wonderful world of finance.

30. BIG CHANGES AHEAD

Nineteen-eighty-three saw a momentous change in the Australian financial world. In late October 1983, Treasurer Paul Keating announced the government's decision to "float" the Australian dollar on the international financial market. The managed exchange rate of the $AU had been ninety-plus cents (Carew 1988). A managed system was said to make any government economic fiscal policy almost impossible to manage. Further de-regulation of the Australian financial system flowed on from the float of the dollar. Foreign banks were admitted as new bank licences were handed out by the government. Local institutions felt the need to consolidate, causing mergers and takeovers of profitable smaller market players. Mercantile Credits Limited, my employer, was a prime target for the sharks of the financial world.

There were some rumblings in higher management circles, but at my level, little was said. I continued doing my job. My office premises had been completely renovated and I had the best office in town, complete with company logo carpet, and a computer—unfortunately! One of those machine things that takes all emotion, feeling and care out of all interaction.

Something else was occurring in my mind. Occasionally I had an odd feeling, difficult to describe. Early one afternoon I was sitting in my plush, lay-back, office chair and suddenly thought, *I don't want to be here.* I picked up the keys to my new company car, said to my secretary 'Be back soon,' and left the office. Soon I found myself on the highway to Yeppoon, about a forty-kilometre drive east of Rockhampton. Yeppoon in the 1980s was a small, quiet, coastal village on the shore of Kepple Bay. I stopped at the main beach, a wide flat brown beach with mostly small waves. Hidden behind the southern bits of the Great Barrier Reef, there was usually no surf.

Dressed in my dark suit and black leather shoes, I walked for several kilometres along the beach. I passed the Iwasaki Resort being built in the dunes and touted to become a large holiday destination for Japanese tourists. It became famous, or infamous, when a local activist blew up part of the structure. As I walked, and for the first time in about twelve years, thoughts of the Army and Vietnam came back into my mind. These thoughts were fleeting, momentary recollections, I did not understand why. Today I realise this was the very first indication of post-traumatic stress.

I talked earlier about the changes in Australian economic policies, floating the dollar and allowing new banks to be formed. Fears I expressed then began to materialise during the mid-eighties. I knew this was going to have a severe impact on my job and my life. Warren, the Chief General Manager, rang me, as he did all his managers to provide an update on what he understood would occur. It seemed, after various takeovers, my office would be consumed by Esanda, who had a sizeable outlet in Rockhampton, and my job as Manager and the jobs of my staff would be no more.

Rightly or wrongly, when the State Manager visited to discuss the future, I refused his offer of a transfer to Brisbane and after speaking with the Chief General Manager, I resigned my position with a reasonable package. I informed my staff and left to a whole new world of uncertainty where I have been ever since.

I looked for a suitable job in town until I realised the last thing I wanted was a job that kept me indoors. Things were not brilliant at home— my job had entailed a lot of socialising, drinking and late nights with clients. These activities invariably put pressure on a relationship. Eventually Janine and I purchased a milk run, a licensed and dedicated area in North Rockhampton. I was the first truck to pull out of the factory loading dock at midnight six days a week.

Deliveries were completed about 8:00 am the next day. At home I slept at odd times while everyone tiptoed around me.

BUSINESS DISASTER STRIKES: TWICE.

I had bought the business in 1985. The bank loan interest rate climbed from six per cent to eighteen per cent in a matter of months, all due to the looming financial crash of 1987. To add their own bit of misery, the Queensland Government decided to deregulate the milk industry. Coupled with this decision was a move to withdraw glass milk bottles from the retail market. The 600 ml bottle was replaced by a one litre cardboard carton. Supermarkets had wanted to enter the retail milk market but were unable to accommodate bottle returns. The impact on home delivery on the milko was immense, both in sales and in the goodwill value of the business.

Meanwhile, unsuccessful in finding work that accommodated the children's needs, Janine had enrolled in a university degree, a long-time dream of hers. Government Austudy payments enabled her to study full-time, contribute to the household and be there for the children. While everyone in the family did their bit with the milk run, our much-loved family home sadly went on the market in an effort to shore up the business.

We struggled on for a while. Eventually the government agreed to buy back vendor licences. The payout was based on the last period of trading, which of course was not too flash given the loss of glass bottles and the supermarket competition. We received a little above half the original purchase price.

By that time Janine had finished her honours degree and, after accepting a PhD scholarship offer, we eventually packed the kids, dog, cat and bird into the Rover and headed to Brisbane. It was 1992. A fresh start. Or so we thought.

Our lives had been tipped upside down and given a good shake. Following the loss of my management career, huge, unexpected rises in interest rates on our loans and the deregulation of the retail milk industry, the move to Brisbane gave us some hope of positive change.

Janine was very committed to the need to find suitable schooling for the children as well as completing her university arrangements to begin her study. Thankfully she had visited the Uni prior to our move and at that time arranged a home to rent. Apart from sleeping on the floor for a night or two before our furniture arrived, the move was done and dusted.

My major task was to find a job as quickly as possible. Daily I collected every relevant newspaper available. After completing a comprehensive resume, I started making applications. My world lit up when I was successful with the first application. A position in finance dealing with the farming sector. But!!! Twenty-four hours later the employer withdrew the approval stating the position would be filled internally. 'Why the fuck did you advertise?' I wanted to say but didn't.

In total, I submitted seventy-nine applications. I had some interviews which amounted to nothing. Interviews with large employment agencies were embarrassing and belittling.

After becoming increasingly depressed at not being able to find a job in Brisbane and finding that prospective employers required tertiary education, Janine suggested I try university. It seemed universities were very interested in enrolling mature age students. I started university studies in 1995. I began a commerce degree, majoring in politics and public policy.

My results that year saw me offered a move to the newly established Griffith Law School, then only in its second year. I willingly accepted this offer and, two-years later, was asked by the university if I would like to join the honours program. I accepted this challenge under encouragement from staff and fellow students. I eventually gained a degree, a Bachelor of Politics and Public Policy, but not without a few hiccups.

Janine's and my marriage survived for twenty-three years, until

I became an arsehole. My behaviour towards my first wife, whom I still love and respect, came from my PTSD beginning to show its ugly face and the arrogance of studying (as I was at the time) law, particularly old English law cases and arguing the value of them in a modern changing world.

At this point (the late 1990s), I had not been diagnosed with PTSD, but I knew something was wrong. I would launch into an argumentative rage with anyone and everyone. It was not regular but occurred often enough to impact on the family. Herself the daughter of a self-medicated, traumatised World War II veteran, Janine was adept at sidestepping confrontation and conflict, which of course meant we never addressed, or resolved, our problems. While continuing to support the family, it was not long before she moved out on her own and then onto a new life. I was deeply disappointed, more so in myself for not being able to save the family situation. I suppose I just gave up emotionally. I also lost emotional contact with my daughter for many years after she, too, moved out and on with her life. My son stuck by me despite suffering some bad times. Fortunately, I never became physically violent towards anyone.

31. STARTING A NEW LIFE

It was the year 2000. For the previous year I had put my whole life into my study. Long nights and early days, and lots of white wine to keep me company. My grades were good. A grade point average (GPA) of 6.8 of 7.0, but my honours thesis was a shambles. I had three supervisors come and go. I was getting pissed off.

My study buddy was a young man straight from high school. He was brilliant. He said if he read something twice, he retained it. Andrew and I hit it off pretty well. He appreciated an older person's opinion. As a team we were successful in public policy projects, political presentations and in law court moots[15] — except for one where we appeared as senior and junior counsel on an international law issue: the Mabo Case High Court decision. The moot was heard in the actual Supreme Court in Brisbane. I was second chair and was on my feet when the moot judge asked a question regarding a comment by Chief Justice Brennan. I had difficulty understanding how to answer.

The moot judge said, 'Perhaps you might defer to your senior council.'

'Yes, your honour.'

I stepped back and turned to find Andrew, head back, mouth open and sound asleep.

'Your honour, my senior has nothing to add.'

'Case dismissed,' the judge said with a chuckle.

So endeth the Supreme Court adventure (though we got a good grade anyway).

---

15 Where students argue points of law in front of a simulated law court.

A week later I was sitting beside Andrew in a rather boring research methods lecture (part of the honours course) when I suddenly closed my folder of notes and said, 'Andrew, I can't handle this crap,' stood up and left. That was the end of my university career and the last time I would speak to my study buddy, Andrew, who went on to become treasurer and deputy premier in a Queensland Labour Government.

While at Uni, I had a casual job detailing cars for auction at Fowles Auction Group in Archerfield. The company was moving to purpose-built premises at Eagle Farm and looking for full-time staff. I became one of the supervisors in charge of thirty plus detailers. Weekly auctions were conducted for Ford, Nissan and Holden as well as public sales of damaged vehicles involving hundreds of vehicles.

Late one afternoon after work, my son Michael handed me a letter. I looked at it and said, 'Looks like Dad's writing,' and put it aside.

After dinner Michael said, 'What did Grandad have to say?'

I had forgotten about it. I found it and opened the envelope. Inside was a card. I read the card, and nearly fell off my chair saying something like, 'Effing hell!'

Michael picked up the card. 'Who is Karen, Dad?'

BACK TO THE FUTURE

Yes, the same Karen. She had married the Sydney guy and moved there to live but divorced him in 1981 for marital transgressions. Circa 1996, she moved back to Toowoomba. She now had a keen interest in dog showing— Old English Sheepdogs. The card said a dog show was being held at Durack in southwest Brisbane, would I like to meet with her there?

'Bloody hell,' I said to Michael, 'that's a blast from the past.' Briefly I told my son about my traumatic life before meeting his mother.

'Are you going to the show, Dad?'

That night I could think of nothing else. I remembered how devastated I was way back then. I also recalled the good times we had and fell asleep undecided. For ten days it was on my mind. Finally, I said to Michael, 'I can't go. I don't have a car.'

Michael soon solved that problem and borrowed a mate's hotted-up Ford Laser fitted with a turbo-charged rotary engine. A beast! That excuse gone, I thought, *How difficult this would have been for Karen to approach me after what had happened thirty years ago?* I did meet her, and we exchanged numbers, etcetera. The relationship grew. Discussions of course about that time in 1970. Visits, outings and weekends away at her dog shows. Emma, Karen's number one sheepdog, loved me. By then Michael had moved out with some mates, so I packed up and moved back to Toowoomba where Karen was now living. On Karen's birthday in 2001, we were married and still are. Although it's shaky at times. The local paper, *The Toowoomba Chronicle* (Hardwick 2021), featured an article on me giving the same 1970 engagement ring back to Karen thirty years later. Mush, mush!

WHAT WAR DOES TO US

Within a year Karen noticed I was different, acting differently to the past. She saw a newspaper article about a meeting of Vietnam veterans, wives and partners. The meeting focused on the veterans' behaviour and pointed to PTSD as being the cause of behavioural change. Soon I was visiting a psychiatrist who specialised in treatment of Vietnam veterans. Treatment involved writing down my experiences in Vietnam, which, as I've already mentioned, the psychiatrist called "facing my tigers". I had several tigers to face, some of which I have recounted in previous chapters. It was a difficult and emotional process remembering stuff suppressed for years. Recollection was easy enough; dealing with the memories was not.

I was subsequently diagnosed as suffering severe PTSD, a mental illness that appears to stay (almost) hidden for many years, showing only the slightest of symptoms over time. But it is there, and it has a devastating effect on human relationships. Today, the government accepts a person registering a GARP (a guide to assessment of rates of veterans' pensions) score of thirty or above as being mentally injured. My GARP score was forty-eight.

This was the last thing I expected when I was called up for service in the Army, to end up with an incurable mental affliction that has dominated my life and unfortunately that of others. I was unaware it was happening to me, but it is an explanation of the eventual change of behaviour. Anxiety is forever present, a constant feeling of dread, of something (I know not what) about to happen. Any argument or emotional upset causes an immediate downward slide into depression.

The other aspect of this remembering stuff was the re-establishment of contact with other Vietnam veterans. The support and encouragement I received led me to make an application to the Department of Veterans Affairs for support. With the help of professional advocates, in 2006, thirty-seven years after returning from Vietnam, I was awarded a Special Rate Disability Pension (SRDP) as totally and permanently incapacitated (TPI)—what a drastic description of a person.

Two years prior to that, I had joined the RSL as a member and began attending Anzac Day dawn services and parades. I even forgave the Army for telling me, 'If you want your medals, apply for them,' which I did, receiving four at varying times across the years, depending on the length of the official approval process. All were presented to me by the local federal member, Ian MacFarlane, affectionately known as "Chainsaw" because of his deep rough voice, who had become a friend and supporter.

Not long after I joined the RSL, members of the Toowoomba sub-branch approached me to stand for a management committee position at an upcoming Annual General Meeting. I did and worked with the Vietnam Veterans Association of Australia (VVAA) to ensure we were well represented at Anzac Day celebration services

Medal presentation by local MP Ian MacFarlane at Toowoomba, 2009

and marches. It was a real honour to be an OC the Vietnam contingent on Anzac Day. But I did have my dramas with this job. My right banner bearer, Jim, was somewhat deaf as I discovered. One year, the Vietnam vets were leading the parade and marching directly behind the Harristown RSL brass band. The band was to turn off early, as I knew. The banner bearers followed the band ignoring my screamed orders from further back. I sprinted to the head of the group, but it was too late to follow the correct path. I guided the banner bearers across the lawn, down the slope in front of the Mothers' Memorial and emerged at the correct place. The MC of the service ran towards me in a panic, waving his arms. 'Just taking a shortcut, Bill,' I said. The crowd nearby cheered. I was asked later if it was a planned demonstration to have Vietnam vets recognised. 'No mate, just a deaf bastard up the front!'

Me, with the rolled-up banner, leading the Toowoomba Anzac Day Parade, 2009

During my time on the RSL committee, I assisted members of the funeral team in the conduct of a remembrance tribute service at the funeral of each veteran passing in the sub-branch district (and for particular mates outside the district, such as at Trevor Harrison's funeral). To ensure new members of the RSL were cognisant of the correct procedure, I was commissioned to write the guiding procedure. Relatives of these vets were very appreciative of the RSL team and presentation of the Australian flag draped over the casket along with an official record of service. The funeral team continues to provide a service today.

In 2009, I was elected treasurer of the sub-branch. Our team built up a very healthy bank balance before the rot that afflicts many committees, backbench unrest, caused the resignation of the whole executive in 2013. As a wonderful general manager once said to me, 'Pete, the best committee is a committee of one.'

Those two years of Army service had come back thirty years

later to bite me on the arse. They had a huge and lasting detrimental impact on my life. Thankfully, though, I have the support of many other veterans and, after diagnosis in 2006, the Australian Government, through the Department of Veterans Affairs (DVA), has continued to look after me. My medical team, general practitioner (GP), psychiatrist and psychologist have provided me with substantial daily medication to combat the depression. I keep myself going by relying on the consumption of alcohol; my preference is white wine, in particular, Verdelho. I know this is wrong, as Karen constantly reminds me, but my GP monitors my liver function which is currently normal. What the hell, I say. Something has to finish me; it may as well be something I enjoy. Anyway, I intend being around annoying people with my cynical attitude for a few more years yet. Maybe my family longevity will help as my grandmother, father and his brother Bill lived to ninety-eight, ninety-six and one hundred respectively. See you around, guys, in 2047!

32. ONE LAST BATTLE

At the time of finishing this book an important Army issue was resolved, at least for me. In 1965 the Republic of South Vietnam issued an award for service in the country by foreign armed forces. In 1966 Queen Elizabeth II graciously gave Royal Assent allowing Australian forces to wear the award (Directorate of Honours and Awards Appeals Tribunal) (DHAAT 2014). The award was the Republic of Vietnam Campaign Medal (RVCM). Members of my National Service intake (tenth) were denied the award.

The Republic of Vietnam Armed Forces Directive (RVNAF Directive, 1965) contained eligibility provisions, one of which required an applicant to have served a minimum number of days in Vietnam defending against an armed enemy force. The tenth intake group of approximately one hundred men had fallen short of the number of days required. The group members maintained the reason for not qualifying was beyond their control and they should therefore qualify. They had "marched in" in October 1967 and were to be discharged in October 1969. By returning, of necessity, to Australia in time for discharge, the number of days served in country would fall short.

Despite many appeals by various groups (myself among them), regarding eligibility of the tenth intake of National Servicemen, the government maintained its firm negative position. However, the Secretary of Defence ordered an inquiry be conducted by the DHAAT to identify any avenues available to make the award. The 2014 DHAAT inquiry reported no avenues were available. Under considerable pressure, in 2015 the Secretary ordered a second inquiry by DHAAT to investigate if the Australian Government had the power to amend the criteria of a foreign award given that nation no longer existed. DHAAT reported the government did not have the power to amend the criteria (DHAAT 2015).

One of the tenth intake members, Richard Barry OAM, who had been lobbying the government Department for many years, suggested others should make application for the medal. I decided it was worth a try as I did believe in our entitlement. I devised a list of twelve points that needed to be considered, all of which in my opinion supported my argument, and, in January 2019, lodged my submission with the Directorate of Honours and Awards (DH&A) in Canberra. Three weeks later I received a short letter asking for my patience as workload in Canberra was heavy. In March, a letter arrived advising that my application had been rejected.

I then received information from Canberra that an avenue of appeal through DHAAT was available. I took this opportunity and submitted the appeal in January 2020. DH&A were required to provided me with reasons for rejection which I was required to answer in detail. A time limit was placed on my reply to the forty-plus questions/comments. After requesting a seven-day extension, I sent a comprehensive reply to DHAAT.

A short time later I received a letter from the Tribunal advising my application was to be "reviewed". I was informed by others that this was rare— a good sign. The review would be in the form of a face-to-face interview at the Tribunal in Canberra. I would be advised of the time and date.

Covid 19 arrived in Australia. The scheduled June 2020 visit to Canberra was cancelled and replaced by a telephone interview. I was very disappointed as I felt impersonal telephone contact was a disadvantage. After a debacle of a telephone interview, in September 2020, I received a long, involved, rejection letter.

WHERE TO NOW: GIVE UP OR FIGHT ON?

DHAAT, in the rejection information, advised I had twenty-eight days to appeal the decision to the Federal Court of Australia. Although a daunting task, I dragged out a copy of Federal Court Rules from my university days and attempted to form an appeal. I considered I had developed a reasonable case.

It did not go well. The Registrar of the Brisbane Federal Court chastised me on all aspects of my submission. She did, however, understand my pleadings and suggested I find a lawyer. I decided I was suitably embarrassed and left it there. I then realised my Federal Court Rules were well out of date.

I maintained contact with other members fighting for the same cause in the hope something new might arise. I had an idea partly formed in my mind that I was convinced would be successful. The government ministers constantly rejected any submissions based on equity and fairness. Only legal reasons would be listened too. My partly formed idea was based on legal documentation of the time.

In 2021, the Minister for Defence Personnel had asked the DHAAT Tribunal to inquire into and report on recognition into 'members and families of members of the Australian Defence Force who are injured, wounded or killed in or as a result of service' (DHAAT 2022:101). The report (DHAAT 2022) recommended PTSD be recognised as an injury provided the injury occurred in service and occurred in honourable circumstances. In addition, disability must be assessed at or above thirty impairment points based on a GARP score (DHAAT 2022). The Department of Veteran Affairs in 2006 had accepted my PTSD was caused by service in Vietnam. My GARP score was 48.

I realised that being wounded/injured came under an exception to the minimum number of days required as service in the RVNAF Directive (1968). There was one hurdle remaining. This was in the form of a Military Board Instruction (MBI).

32. One last battle

On 23rd December 1968, the Australian Military Board issued an Instruction regarding the introduction of the RVCM (MBI 1024 23, 1968). The instruction added to the exception in Article 2 (RVNAF Directive, 1965) that any WIA be reported to Canberra via a "notification". This had not occurred in my case of PTSD. How could this disease/injury be notified? In 1969, PTSD had not even been recognised by the medical fraternity.

The Tribunal had referred to this MBI on previous occasions and would do so again. I waited in hope of something, anything, to help.

In an email from a fellow Vet, I received a poor-quality photocopy of correspondence from the Australian Government Solicitor (AGS 2021). The printing was dark and so small I read it with a magnifying glass. The "something" I needed was here in this messy document.

The AGS (2021) was replying to an inquiry from the Department of Defence regarding reassessment of an individual's eligibility for the RVCM. The reply stated: 'It may be correct that there are no legal impediments in reassessing an individual's eligibility for the award of the RVCM provided the assessment is against the criteria stipulated by the republic of Vietnam.'

This was exactly what I had been looking for. This comment would defeat the MBI provision requiring "notification of wounding/injury". The criteria stated a simple "wounded in action".

In May 2022, I quickly put together a new submission for the Department of Defence, Directorate of Honours and Awards to consider. I was very confident, convinced of success at last.

I waited 267 days— no contact. On the 268th day the Directorate requested confirmation of my address. Two weeks later my RVCM, dated 27 February 2023, arrived in the mail with congratulations from the Director. What a battle! Fifty-four years after leaving Vietnam, and seventeen years after first joining others of my intake in the battle for the award, I had won.

A small number of the Tenth Intake now proudly wear the RVCM. Since receiving mine, I have helped eight mates get the award, including Richard Barry OAM.

33. ROBERT (JOCK) BUCHAN

Beside me as I write this is a little friend, a yellow cockatiel parrot named Jock. Every morning, when I uncover him, he says repeatedly, 'Hello Jock, hello Jock,' in his cute little voice. I just love him, this constant reminder of my friend I have not seen now for fifty-five years. Jock and I were once daily companions.

Very recently, as part of a cleanup and declutter, I unpacked an old metal trunk in the shed. It was full of memories, birthday cards made by the kids, and a few photographs. At the bottom was a small yellow box full of photographic slides. I viewed them later using a small viewfinder. They appeared to be taken in Vietnam. Karen went and had them printed.

The prized photo was one I took of Jock as Delta Company was leaving Nui Dat on operation. It was taken with that famous drowned Yashica camera just before I flew home. In the photo, Jock is sitting atop an APC nursing his beloved M60 machine gun. I clearly remember taking that photo fifty-five years ago. From under that bush hat, I can see the remnants of the smile he blasted me with as we said our goodbyes.

For thirty or so years I had had nothing to do with the Army. I think that's because of the way Vietnam vets were treated, the abuse they received. I completely forgot the Army thing existed in my life. It was too painful a subject even after the official Australian Vietnam Forces Welcome Home Parade of 1987 began the process of restoring honour and dignity to the veterans. I had a happy and engaging career, coupled with an equally happy home life. Having taken on a managerial role, where no one knew about Vietnam,

*My friend Robert "Jock" Buchan the last time
I spoke to him in Vietnam, September 1969*

meant it was never mentioned. I had not thought of meeting Jock very much at all during that time and had not attempted to find him; nor had he contacted me.

One day in the early 1990s, Janine (my now ex-wife) rang me from Canberra where she was attending a conference on behalf of Griffith University. She had taken the opportunity to visit the Australian War Memorial and had seen, and been impressed by, the Memorial Wall displaying the names of all Australian servicemen and servicewomen killed in action in all wars. Janine and I had discussed my time in Vietnam before we were married and I had told her of my friend, Jock. She had remembered his name.

'Pete, your mate in the Army, his name was Robert Buchan, wasn't it?'

'Yes, it was.'

'I am so sorry, Pete. I've just seen his name on the wall. I thought you would want to know.'

Because of my self-distancing from the Army, I had no knowledge

Jock had been killed in action. I was shocked and deeply saddened by this news.

Eventually, I obtained information about what had occurred and what had become of my mate. I thank Lieutenant Colonel Fred Fairhead (Retired) for the information contained in his book, *The History of 6th Battalion the Royal Australian Regiment* (Fairhead 2021:140):

> Jock was killed in action on 11 December 1969 during Operation Marsden, in a contact on the Nui May Tao. He was the acting section commander of the lead section of 12 Platoon (Lt Paul Jackson) and when ambushed ahead, he went forward to deploy the section. As he did, the enemy opened fire hitting him in the chest, fatally wounding him.

Just twenty-two when he died, Jock is considered a hero by military historians who believed that many of his men would have died in the attack had he 'not stopped his platoon from going forward' (Pitogo 2014).

A memorial on Monument Australia also describes the incident:

> On the morning of 11 December 1969 soldiers of 12 Platoon, Delta Company, 6RAR, patrolled along well-worn track in an area known to contain VC. As the acting commander of the lead section, Lance Corporal Buchan was called to the front of the patrol to investigate the discovery of a suspected enemy bunker when the group was ambushed. The opening volleys hit Buchan in the chest, wounding both him and the forward scout. After an intense firefight the section was able to withdraw and regroup, but Buchan succumbed to his wounds before it ended.

The extraction of Jock's body by helicopter to the Australian field hospital in Vung Tau was photographed by Army photographer

Sergeant Peter Ward. The photographs now reside at the Australian War Memorial. They are too painful to show here. Jock was flown to Malaya, RAAF Butterworth, where he was cremated after a military funeral. His ashes were repatriated to his parents in Dundee, Scotland, where Jock (Robbie) was born. He is interred with his mother, Jane Davidson, and father, Robert Buchan. As a postscript, Fairhead (2021: 143) added

> At a meeting of the City of Dundee Branch of the Royal British Legion Scotland on 1 September, Jock's details were added to the Acts of Remembrance, and it intends to visit his grave on the second Sunday in December each year to lay a wreath. He is being cared for.

That pleases me greatly. My fervent wish is to attend myself, one day in the future.

The Jock Buchan Memorial Track at RSL Grounds, Toogum, Queensland

Jock is similarly honoured at a small town on Queensland's Fraser Coast where a beautiful bush walk, The Jock Buchan Memorial Track, nestles peacefully besides a replica of the Long Tan Cross in the RSL grounds at Toogum, once the hometown of Jock's forward scout, Ken Higgins (OAM), who, badly wounded himself, watched Jock die beside him.

As a proud member of the 6RAR Association, in 2015 I attended the fiftieth anniversary of the battalion's formation in 1965. Included in the three-day celebration was a visit to the Enoggera Barracks, where my Army time began. At Enoggera, veterans of the battalion have grown trees and formed a memorial walk. Each tree marks a lost Aussie soldier. On this day the lost 6RAR men were marked with a green battalion flag. I walked the walk, with tears in my eyes, as I recognised names. I saw a group of ten men around a flag. I joined the group.

'Hi, Pete. This is your mate, Jock, over here,' someone said.

I had written a story for the 6RAR Association quarterly newsletter, *Stand To*, that had been well received. In it, I described my first encounter and early association with Jock. Although not many people knew me, they did know the story. Tears welled and I bowed my head to become the centre of a ten-man group hug. Emerging from the scrum, everyone had tears in their eyes. Someone asked about that first morning when I discovered 'This hairy monster snorting on the bed.' Not quite the story, but it softened the mood.

Lieutenant Colonel Fred Fairhead was also there. He spoke to me quietly and said how sorry he was at the loss of my friend. Fred had taken over the command of D Company the day after Jock died and had visited the contact point. I sincerely thank Lieutenant Colonel Fairhead for his commitment to the battalion and especially for his efforts in finding Jock.

Remembered as 'an independent and respected member' of his platoon (Pegram 2015), Jock was honoured in a moving Last Post ceremony at the Australian War Memorial in 2015. Having lived in Perth, Western Australia, prior to enlistment in the Army, Jock is also commemorated at the Perth War Cemetery.

Rest in peace, Jock, my friend, LEST WE FORGET!

34. THE 6TH BATTALION

I am very proud to have been a member of this great institution. I wear the Colours and badges with pride on Anzac Day each April and on Vietnam Veterans Day, a.k.a. Long Tan Day, on 18 August.

Following Delta Company's horrific Battle of Long Tan on 18th August 1966 which resulted in the deaths of eighteen Aussie soldiers, the US President awarded the company the Presidential Unit Citation (Army) for extraordinary heroism. As noted, I was part of the battalion parade for the presentation and I proudly wore the "swimming pool", as it was affectionately called, while serving with D Company.

The Long Tan battle brought the battalion into sharp focus within the Army. Being part of the "new" 6th from February 1968, it was up to us to carry on the tradition. My intake of National Service men formed the first part of the rebuilding of the battalion. The CO was to comment on the integration and expertise of the National Service personnel within his unit. He insisted these men were too valuable to his unit to leave at home when the battalion was posted to Vietnam in May 1969.

Referring to Operation Lavarack, 31st May–30th June 1969 (the first operation), Lieutenant Colonel David Butler (CO) wrote, 'Everyone is saying nice things about the battalion, we had preserved the hard-won reputation gained on the first tour. Maybe we even made a few runs of our own' (Fairhead 2021: 149).

The task force also wrote about the battalion, 'From the very first successful operation 6RAR showed they would be the finest battalion in Vietnam.' A practical and conservative man, the CO simply said, 'There is much to be proud of,' Fairhead (2021:150).

Almost two years later in April 1970 the ATF Commander Brigadier S P Weir DSO, MC, made a statement at the final battalion parade in Vietnam that the 6th was, 'The finest infantry battalion he had ever seen' (Fairhead 2021:136). High praise from a veteran of four wars.

David Butler was a CO, loved and respected by all ranks under his command. Always prepared to do himself whatever he asked of his men. Wounded by shrapnel from an exploding mine, he carried on regardless.

Major General David Butler, AO, DSO, Silver Star, was laid to rest on 7 December 2020.

35. THE THORNY QUESTION OF CONSCRIPTION

HOW IT WORKED

At the time conscription began, Australians were told the ballot for selection for "call-up" would be based on birthdays. And so it was, but that did not mean everyone with a birthday on the 16th would be called up. Based on registration information (all nineteen-year-old males had to register) the military boffins would make their final selection. When I arrived at 3TB in Singleton, New South Wales, for recruit training, thirty-one of the thirty-two men in my hut were currently employed in banking, finance or insurance.

Number thirty-two was a woodchopper who was soon sent home. We all loved Billy; he was unique. Having spent his entire life with older men, he was overjoyed to be with men his own age. He was a tough little nut who excelled in any physical activity, was a crack shot and fitter than all of us town boys. The Army needed, according to their opinion, intelligent men to train for the Infantry Corps. Despite lodging requests for other Army corps, we all ended up in the Infantry. So much for choice, hey?

What of Billy then, you ask? Yeah, the Army boffins tossed him out. Not for any lack of courtesy or discipline, or untidy room or uniform, but for his poor marching style on the parade ground. We all realised, eventually, that parade drill was a part of discipline; group discipline is important in all infantry operations. One member stuffed up, and the corporals took joy in punishing everyone. Billy caused many stuff ups. The rest of us supported him and tried after-hours training without success.

Billy "square gaited"— he swung his arm in time with the same leg.

Left leg forward, left arm forward and so on. Try it, it is difficult to maintain. Not for Billy though, he kept reverting. Everyone in the hut took turns marching Billy up and down the corridor of the hut. Not because he was causing us problems— we all wanted him to succeed.

But because of Billy's parade marching performance, the Army tossed a career soldier on their scrap heap. Billy was so keen, loved the Army life and would have excelled in the right environment. All thirty-one of us would have trusted him to "have our back". So sad!

It was a similar story with the "other Billy", my friend Bill, the Ford mechanic and lifelong mate whom I celebrated long and hard with when we found he'd also been drafted.

Bill lived just around the corner. He and I started primary school on the same day at Toowoomba East State School and attended the same high school. We remain the best of mates to this present day. Bill lived at home with his mum, dad and two brothers. Bill was the youngest. The family was English and had lived through World War II in London. As I mentioned previously, Vic, the father, served in the Royal Navy during the war. Being awarded the British Empire Medal impressed his young sons. The oldest joined the RAN and eventually served in Vietnam in Navy helicopters. The second eldest joined the Army and rose to the rank of Warrant Officer Class One, the top non-commissioned rank. Bill was excited to get an opportunity to follow the family military tradition.

Bill was a crash-hot motor mechanic and a good honest employee. He was my best man and a friend for life. Unfortunately, the Army medical professionals decided he had "flat feet", so they sent him home, rejected on medical grounds. This was yet another ill-considered decision. I agree Bill's feet would have caused him problems, but I know the only person who would know was Bill himself. He was ten times fitter than I was, could survive ten three-minute rounds, and win, in the boxing ring. He could crush a person in a single hug.

Despite his pleadings, they stuck to their guns and lost another career soldier who would have excelled in any other Army corp. Today, fifty-five years later, he turns up dressed in his best for Anzac Day, pleased to recognise all those who were in our forces. Good on you, friend.

The other side of this coin is some of the recruits they did keep. I am speaking of attitude. Sure, we were all apprehensive and a little scared, but not disruptive. These were the slack arses who caused groups to suffer repeat after repeat on the parade ground, or in other team exploits, or going AWOL. But the Army stuck to its task of conversion of a useless soldier. After all is said and done, discipline is the key to Army performance, especially in combat.

DO I SUPPORT CONSCRIPTION TODAY?

Despite the trauma of PTSD, when I, like most other "nasho" comrades, have been asked (on many occasions), "Should National Service be reintroduced?" my firm answer has always been, yes, it should. But in a different format. Australia's first National Service Scheme was in the 1950s as a reaction to the Korean War. The term was six months. The National Service Scheme of the 1960s was a term of twenty-four months, being predicated on twelve months training and twelve months service in the war zone of Vietnam.

My contention is we, Australia, need a six-month period where recruits are taught basic Army skills in weapons and defence. Even more important is the self-discipline and team commitment, realising the value of caring for, and consideration of, others. After my experience in 1967, even a period of three months would be beneficial to the community. Perhaps it is economically unsustainable, but this "conscription" (I detest that word) would benefit all Australian youth both male, female and any other denomination. Why? There exists a problem within our society as a whole. A rise in crime against fellow human beings. The jails are full, the courts are overwhelmed. The crime continues because the punishment is weak and the recidivist has no fear of the establishment, no concern for the repercussions of the crime. Young girls are as involved as their male counterparts. The situation is getting worse by the day. What to do?

I was not a bad kid, no different from all the other kids in the community. I, and all the other kids who were having fun outside, had respect for our parents and for what those parents taught us. I remember my Mum saying at 2.00 am, 'I am glad you are home, Pete.' I was seventeen years old and aware of my responsibility to my Mum and Dad. That was in 1964.

In 2024, the media reports almost every day it seems of groups of thirteen-year-olds stealing cars and causing death, damage and heartache. My friends have had their homes invaded by four children stealing jewellery in the middle of the day. Old and defenceless men and women are attacked regularly by "kids" stealing whatever they think is valuable. I cannot help thinking these "gangs" are organised by adults who choose the target, retrieve the kids, and dispose of their bounty.

The overworked police force, more often than not know the "perps" and arrest them quickly, only to have the courts allow them to go free without any significant punishment. Some have been arrested the very next night committing the same offences.

In 1960, the Australian Government decided that even though I was considered a minor, unable to vote and unable to drink alcohol legally, that I could fight in a foreign country risking life, limb, and peace of mind. If I refused, I would go to jail for two years. These grubby little recidivists are younger than I was, but I was not a criminal in either the eyes of the community or the law. I learned so much self-discipline in Army recruit training. In three months, it made me a better person, a person I was proud of, and a son my dad was proud of and respected.

This early intervention into my life, a change I did not want, taught me things as a young person I needed to learn. The Australian community experiences behaviour that most of us see as unacceptable from young people, as young as ten-years old. The basic reason for such behaviour is the lack of discipline. Discipline is a learned attribute— it comes from many people, life experiences and events. A community devoid of discipline will not prosper.

As I said before, 'What to do?' Here is what I would do. It is simple in form, difficult in achievement. Teach them discipline! Personal discipline! Reintroduce National Service. Pass the law! It has been done to help other nations. I was expected to kill people in another country (one I had never heard of before) and that committed me to learn proper discipline.

Australia has the facilities, unused Army training camps and many, many capable Army and ex-Army personnel very capable of carrying out the necessary re-training. I'm up for it! I can be a "bastard" if necessary.

36. POSITIVES AND NEGATIVES

There are no positives to be gained from war, any war. There are many negatives. So many people were affected by the Vietnam War. The soldiers— including the enemy— airmen and naval personnel. Of course, the cost to the civilians caught within the conflict was also high.

The Vietnam War was lost. The might of the Americans, British, Dutch, Australians, New Zealanders and others was comprehensively beaten after ten long years of fighting, costing untold loss of life. Watching the enemy tanks plough through the gates of Saigon was a devastating sight. Nothing had been gained, much had been given!

The whole Army experience, especially Vietnam, had a very negative impact on my personal life and business relationships. The loss of my first wife, I believe, can be traced to my changing outlook and behaviour, attributed now to the unknown, untreated onset of PTSD.

The next greatest negative is the loss of my friend Jock. I think of Jock every day, my little bird reminding me first thing every morning with his "Hello Jock" greeting. Coupled with the loss of Jock are the memories of other mates killed and others who suffered devastating wounds. My friend Darby, with whom I was playing makeshift darts when he was called out to lead a search mission in the Long Hai Hills. He never returned. Instead, he was evacuated to Australia, minus a leg. Darby performed major charity work until he died in 1994, of cancer, I believe.

Trevor, one of my sigs, became a loner and travelled in his little van throughout Australia. Trevor was found dead in his van at the side of the road in Victoria in 2009.

Roger, a strong happy twenty-year old, an Australian junior woodchopping champion, the guy I was best man for in 1968, became a gibbering mess. He lived in his Toyota Landcruiser ute, drank rum, and searched for emeralds in western Queensland. There are others who have passed, many suffering the same severe anxiety bought on by PTSD as a result of their experiences in the war.

Post-traumatic stress is a negative, high on my list. Not only my personal situation, but how so many of my mates have been affected by the same disorder. I have detailed earlier how PTSD impacted my life. I am not alone. I do not know how different my life would now be if Vietnam had not featured. Ask the same question if the Army National Service had not intervened. The answer would be quite different I'm sure. For one thing, I would have had more certainty of what my future held.

That question leads me to the positives of the experience. The National Service experience, minus Vietnam, reveals a few important positives. As I have said, the first is "discipline", and the role it plays in Army life, perhaps all life. The Army pushed us to the limit to instil a sense of discipline required within their organisation. They achieved that, and we understood the tactics— eventually. The other aspect was the personal discipline we carried back with us into our civilian lives.

Another high-ranking positive was the relationships founded through hard times and good times, in other words "our mates"! People who have been there for over fifty years now, and the relationships have not changed. Our particular intake of "Nashos", the tenth, is held in high regard still due to the firm bond created fifty-five years ago. The relationship is supported by an annual, well supported, reunion.

Experience is a further positive. I refer not only to the experience of Army training in weapons, self-defence and awareness, but also to other opportunities to expand one's world. Everyday experiences now, but I had never been in a plane or helicopter before. My situation changed dramatically. I have not flown in a chopper since leaving the Army and have no desire to do so. Before Army life, my world was quite small geographically. I saw and experienced much more of Australia, especially Queensland, than I have seen since.

Despite the cost of Vietnam, I am proud to be a veteran. I am pleased to be recognised by other vets, especially by past and present 6RAR Battalion members, through the Association activities. On Anzac Day the cheers of the public and the many greetings and offers of a drink are much appreciated. The support given and shown to the veterans in this country is simply the best. Unfortunately, it was not always this way for Vietnam vets due to protests against Australian involvement in the war, and the protesters blamed the diggers. As I have reiterated before, 'I am not shooting this person, we are!'

I thank the Australian Government for the support shown to myself and other veterans. The tenth intake still has some issues, yet to be resolved, with Department of Defence bureaucrats. These issues are simple enough, but the ongoing dialogue provides me with an interesting legal-based contest to keep me on the ball and interested.

The legislation enabling conscription provided employment protection for those men providing two years' service to the country. Although appreciated, the provision fell short of returning the individual to his rightful employment status. I mean, to return to a job after two years absence had a major effect on knowledge, seniority, position and remuneration. As I have said earlier, I was "used" by the three branches of the bank to do jobs no one wanted to do and had not done. Routine boring tasks like calculating savings bank interest on hundreds of accounts or finding a balance error in existence for a year. Hey! And I did solve the problem. In the end, I obtained a new position based on my perceived abilities and quickly moved up the management ladder.

That life is all in the past now. At seventy-seven years old, I am happy to live in my quiet leafy street sitting on the veranda overlooking the city of Toowoomba, being acknowledged by neighbours and passers-by. I am known to have a white wine as company as I read, write or play cards. I am kept busy with the extensive garden and hedges I planted (oh, why did I do that?).

I love cars, and fiddle with my 1973 Toyota Celica Coupe often. I built a scale model Formula One race car with gas engine and remote control. It's capable of 60 km/h and cost $2 500. Recently Karen bought me a subscription to build a model Ferrari F40, 56 cm long when complete.

A neighbour, next door, has three restored Cadillacs: a four door 1954, a two-door 1947 and a 1959 pink coupe. In addition, there is a 1968 Chev Camaro convertible and a prize winning 600hp Nissan GTR coupe. Seems like heaven to any rev-head.

The downside of my life is still the PTSD, or more correctly, the side effects of the heavy medication I require to control depression and anxiety. The daily doses over the past eighteen years have had a dramatic effect on my relationship with Karen. She is an emotional person. Myself, I seem to have steadily lost the ability to show any outward emotion. That is not to say I don't feel anything, I just cannot show it. As an extension of that, I have grown to be most relaxed on my own with Maggie, my King Charles spaniel, always beside me.

Under my doctor's supervision I experimented reducing the medication. The result was nightmares and thrashing about in bed. A loss of sleep for both of us, and anger bought on by tiredness. I reverted to the correct dosage. Post-traumatic stress is the enduring negative of my past and present life and threatens my second marriage of twenty-three years.

37. SPIT POLISH DISCIPLINE: HOW DOES IT ALL END?

Through most of this book thing I have had a "handle" on what I wanted to say. I am at a bit of a loss at the present time just how to end it all. That is a good phrase, "end it all". In 2021, I made a submission to the Royal Commission into Defence and Veteran Suicide (2024) which has subsequently found that, on average, three serving or ex-serving Defence members die by their own hand every fortnight across Australia. I hope this Commission finds the answer, but I doubt it will. The reasons for ending one's life are too diverse to put in a box. The only answer for the future is, I think, not to commit our defence people to any wars in other countries.

I regularly attend the local (Toowoomba) Anzac Day march and Remembrance Service and, afterwards, the hotel of veteran choice, Fibbers. In 2022, however, I noticed a marked change in this experience. For various reasons (wet weather, Covid and age), I was alone. I sat at a small table on my own surrounded by young men, all dressed neatly in their seemingly undersized blue suits with one, maybe two, medals over the heart (which of course means they have earned those medals themselves). Not once did one of them either acknowledge or speak to me. I was confused. Other people were different, friendly and prepared to speak and wish me a good day. Young women offered to buy me a drink. Young men in shorts and thongs asked, actually insisted, that I join them. They showed interest in me and wanted to hear my Army story. When the two-up started, I went home. The next day I asked the question about the young servicemen's lack of interest of a friend, an Afghanistan Vet, who said, 'Pete, I think they feel they have missed the opportunity to "go to war". Australia is out of the Mideast and there are no plans to participate in another war soon. We will be committed to home security, I believe!'

These young men should be proud to be part of a security force protecting their own country and grateful not to have been to war. Our major wars, World War I, World War II, Korea, Vietnam and Afghanistan where Australian lives have been given, were all in the interest of another sovereign nation. Our future should be different. Our people will be best served in the protection of our home, Australia. Current government reports indicate there will be ample opportunity for the current Defence Force members to earn their stripes on home ground.

Being in the Defence Force is about learning what to do, how to do it and when to do it. It is about a team, not a group of individuals. A disciplined group with a connection formed out of reliance on each other to understand how to do the job together. I am not shooting this person; we are!

The title for this book began as *Here we go*. I changed it to *Spit polish discipline* (with spit and polish being the precursors of discipline) as I moved through my thoughts and memories of that time. As much as I paint a gloomy picture during the early recruit training period of punishment for seemingly minor things, it was all about discipline as I have emphasised throughout. Not only self-discipline, but discipline within the entire group.

Discipline is what sets the Australian Defence Force apart from others. Discipline is the base for the formation of the renowned, difficult to explain to many, institution of mateship.

My closing thought, at least for now:

'Only the dead have seen the end of war' (Santayana 1922).

APPENDIX 1.
NATIONAL SERVICE MEMORIES
BY PETER CULLEN

ANOTHER NATIONAL SERVICE MAN'S OPINION

Karen and I met an older couple while walking our Old English Sheepdogs in the park. They too had an Old English Sheepdog, an old rescue dog. Long story short, Karen discovered Peter was her form teacher at high school many years ago. Peter's wife, Lenore, was also a high school teacher. Peter recognised me as a Vietnam veteran through newspapers and TV news reports. He divulged he was a nasho of the 1950s call-up, the conscription program for the Korean War. Eventually I asked him to write his opinion of his experience.

Peter is a local historian, often on ABC radio, and has been conducting regular historical tours of the Toowoomba Cemetery, providing interesting historical background.

In his story here Peter mentions another coincidence, this time relating to the replacement corporal, Corporal Shanks who was, amazingly, Karen's father. Alan served in the RAN as a clearance diver, a very dangerous occupation. After leaving the Navy he joined the Army and became a recruit instructor of some notoriety, being tough and expecting only the best. He died in 1967 and rests in the Toowoomba Cemetery.

I asked Peter to comment on his time in the Army as a National Service man to gauge his reaction and that of his cohorts, to the "new" life thrust upon them about ten-years earlier than my experience. He does not say in his writing how disappointed they all were when the Korean War ended, which was the reason for their call-up. It poses an interesting question to me though. How would I have felt? Would I have been disappointed if Vietnam have ended rendering all my bloody hard work to prepare for war irrelevant? I cannot be sure now, but I hope I would have been thankful. War serves no purpose to anyone.

The standout similarity is Peter's comments on mateship, support for each other and camaraderie. This combination of traits of Australian servicemen's character has existed in all wars. As I said very early in this book, this attitude is unique to the armed forces.

Discipline also is a strong and evident similarity. Peter's training was different to mine, as a Service Corps driver, but discipline existed, most certainly when Corporal Shanks turned up on their doorstep.

Diversity of backgrounds especially within National Service was evident in both intakes. I commented earlier on my intake surmising some additional input by the Army. One might suspect that regular Army volunteers might not be as diversified in background.

I thank Peter for his effort in providing memories of his experiences of over sixty years ago. When I asked him, he said it was something of a challenge. The memories are interesting and are very much like mine. Mateship, camaraderie and Army discipline to the fore.

*

I was in the first intake, January 1956, having been deferred a year while at Teachers College. Having been four years in Army Cadets at school and a CUO (cadet under officer) in the final year, Army routine was much as expected, but the company was different.

Wacol camp was familiar as some cadet camps had been held there, but the big difference was that now I was sharing it with young men from different walks of life. I was placed in G Company, which was the Service Corps, mainly transport. The university students had their own company which worked on Saturdays. They left before the rest of us who did three months, followed by two years of CMF (Citizens Military Forces). Formerly I had been with boys with similar backgrounds and expectations, but now my new mates came from a variety of occupations and sometimes expressed themselves in language which was forbidden both at home, and at school and college. I soon learned to get on with most of them, particularly when they hung two stripes on me because of my previous experience. Our hut was called "Kapyong" from the battle in the Korean War in which many of our trainers had served. One of our "Nashos", who was a commercial artist, painted a sign with the name and the transport logo. I remember he was a big fellow with an English accent, but there was never any discrimination because of that. Another chap read the bumps on your head if you wanted, and a few were lifesavers with fascinating stories of their successes with the other sex— in detail! A fair few had limited education. We did plenty of square bashing at camp as well as driver training in jeeps and Blitz trucks with left-hand drive. The trainers were quite liberal with their descriptions of our performance and much bashing of your hand on the gear lever if you got it wrong. We did a camp at the north coast where I learned that cruising through a sleepy village called Noosa could be made more exciting by turning the ignition on and off to produce a backfire. The artillery boys also made more noise up there at Peregian Beach firing 4.2inch mortars and 25-pounders.

Another adventure was a convoy from Wacol through Warwick and by the back road to Texas, then through Inglewood and back to Wacol. We succeeded in writing off half the trucks mainly through engine trouble, and a couple of crashes as well. It rained quite a bit of the time at Wacol, and we helped in dragging cars out of the flood water near the Oxley Hotel. There were the usual inoculations, usually before leave, probably so we would not get into too much trouble. One of our number succeeded in getting drunk, stealing items from his conquest at a brothel and beating up one of the MPs. We had the honour of guarding him while on battalion guard duty. I often wonder what happened to him as he was a professional boxer. I suppose the main memory I have is that we stuck together, mainly against the Brisbane bodgies when on leave. It did not matter whether he was black or white, educated or not, he was your mate and you stuck by him. This was very valuable when in the teaching game. I met kids and parents from all walks of life and, in the most part, got on with them. On a more personal note, when we just arrived, Corporal Edie "looked after" us. He left after featuring in the newspaper *Truth* as having an affair with the wife of some high-ranking officer. Then we knew why we were asked to wait outside a house at Rosalie while on driver training. His replacement was Corporal Shanks. Thereby began the coincidences with the Shanks family.

At Wacol we were awakened daily by a loud truck horn. Back at home one night a car blew its horn as it came around our corner and I found myself standing to attention beside the bed. On my first day at my first school after nasho, New Farm, the kids were having a music lesson and staff were encouraged to join in. The song was *Do you know John Peel* and I burst forth with my nasho version which had little to do with what the kids were singing and was much more profane. Thank goodness they drowned me out.

CMF was quite different. There was not the same camaraderie at Fraser's Paddock (at Enoggera Barracks). I just went through the motions until 1957 when I was transferred to a one teacher school and had to give it up.

I sometimes wonder how we would have got on in a real war like yours, Peter, but I am sure we would have done our best, as you did.

*

APPENDIX 2:
A POEM BY A SPECIAL FRIEND

A long-time friend wrote this poem when he and his wife visited the Long Tan Cross in Vietnam in 2019. He told me the inspiration for the words was his valued friendship with me and his respect for veterans of the war.

Long Tan Cross replica, Vietnam, 1994. Photo: dy

Appendix 2: A poem by a special friend

The Cross

Rubber trees lined the pathway to the cross.
All was quiet, with a stillness in the air.
Feeling unworthy, in this sacred place,
we joined hands and said a silent prayer.

'Our Father, who art in heaven,
hallowed be thy name.
Hallowed too, these young soldiers
honoured here, without sin or shame.
Rest at ease, you brave young men,
as in the earth's bosom you lie
until reunited with your loved ones,
in the mansions of the sweet by and by.'

Standing there, in the bright sunshine,
where they'd fought in the pouring rain,
and died, side by side, with their mates,
leaving a legacy for those who remain.

Echoing in the silence, the sounds of the
battle, and the last breath of the dying.
Weeping bitter tears for the fallen, there's
no shame in the tears we were crying.

dy

BIBLIOGRAPHY

Australian Government Solicitor (2021) Personal correspondence from Richard Barry OAM, 21 April 2022.

Butler D 'Reflective thoughts, proud moments', in Fairhead, CF (2021), *The history of Sixth Battalion, the Royal Australian Regiment; Vol 1: Vietnam era 1965 to 1970*, Avonmore Books, Kent Town, S.A..

Carew E (1988) *Keating, a biography*, Allen & Unwin Sydney Australia: 95, 111.

Cawthorne N (2010) *Vietnam; a war lost and won*, Arcturus Publishing, London:32.

Childs J (2014) *The Vietnam War*, 2014, Life Books, New York:124.

Defence Honours and Awards Appeals Tribunal (2014) *Report of the inquiry into eligibility for the Republic of Vietnam Campaign Medal*, Australian Government, Canberra:6.

Defence Honours and Awards Appeals Tribunal (DHAAT) (2015) *Report of the inquiry into the feasibility of amending the eligibility criteria for the Republic of Vietnam Campaign Medal*, Australian Government, Canberra:5.

Defence Honours & Awards and Appeals Tribunal (DHAAT) (2022) *Recognising their sacrifice. The report of the inquiry into recognition for members and families of members of the Australian Defence Force who are injured, wounded or killed in or as a result of service*, Commonwealth of Australia, Canberra.

Fairhead F (2021) *The History of Sixth Battalion, the Royal Australian Regiment; Vol 1: Vietnam era 1965 to 1970*, Avonmore Books, Kent Town, S.A.

Hardwick P (2021) *The Toowoomba Chronicle*, April: n.d.

Joint General Staff of the Republic of Vietnam Armed Forces (RVNAF) Directive (1965) *Pertaining to awarding of Campaign Medal HT.655-430*, 1 September 1965:44–45

Langford S (2021) Appendix: The National Service Scheme, 1964-1972, accessed 4 March 2024.

Military Board Instruction (Army) 3 December 1968, in DHAAT (2015) *Report of the inquiry into the feasibility of amending the eligibility criteria for the Republic of Vietnam Campaign Medal*, Commonwealth of Australia, Canberra:102–4.

Monument Australia (2010) Monumentaustralia.org.au/themes/people/military/display/116345-private-robert-jock-buchan/, accessed 13 August 2022.

Pegram A (2015) The Last Post Ceremony commemorating the service of (55613) Private Robert Buchan, 6th Battalion, Royal Australian Regiment, Vietnam War, The Australian War Memorial 3, accessed 4 March 2024.

Pitogo H (2014) Military-historians-desperate-trace-relatives-vietnam-war-hero-robert-buchan, accessed 7August 2024.

Royal Commission into Defence and Veterans' Suicide (2024) 'Royal Commission analysis reveals three deaths by suicide every fortnight', accessed 4 May 2024.

Santayana G. (1922) *Soliloquies in England and later soliloquies*, https://www.oxfordreference.com/display/10.1093/acref/9780191843730.001.0001/q-oro-ed5-00009114, accessed 4 June 2024.

Smith H and McRae T (2015) *Long Tan: The start of a lifelong battle*, Big Sky Publishing Pty Ltd, Australia.

Weir, SP in Fairhead CF (2021) *The History of Sixth Battalion, the Royal Australian Regiment; Vol 1:Vietnam era 1965 to 1970*, Avonmore Books, Kent Town, SA.

GLOSSARY OF TERMS

ATF	Australian Task Force
AGC	Australian Guarantee Corporation
AGS	Australian Government Solicitor
APC	Armoured personnel carrier
AWOL	Absent without leave
BET	Battle efficiency test
BHQ	Battalion Headquarters
CO	Commanding Officer
CHQ	Company Headquarters
CMF	Citizens Military Forces
Crunchy	Foot soldier
CSM	Company Sergeant Major
CUO	Cadet under officer
DH&A	Directorate of Honours and Awards
DHAAT	Directorate of Honours and Awards Appeals Tribunal
Dixie	Small cooking/eating/drinking containers
DJ Letter	"Dear John" letter
DMZ	Demilitarised zone
DVA	Department of Veterans Affairs
ES&A Bank	English, Scottish & Australian Bank
GP	Australian Army General Purpose
GPA	Grade point average
HE	High explosive
HF	High frequency
HQ	Headquarters

Glossary of Terms

Hutchie	All-weather groundsheet/cover
IAC	Industrial Acceptance Corp
IED	Improvised explosive device
LZ	Landing zone
MBI	Military Board Instruction
MP	Military Police
MPC	Military Payment Certificate
NCO	Non-commissioned officer
NVA	North Vietnamese Army
OC	Officer Commanding
OR	Other ranks
PX	The post exchange
PTSD	Post-Traumatic Stress Disorder
RAN	Royal Australian Navy
R&R	Rest and recreation
REMS	Remittance of cheques to other branches and other banks
RAP	Regimental Aid Post
RPG	Rocket-propelled grenades
RSL	Returned Soldiers Memorial
RSM	Regimental Sergeant Major
RTA	Return to Australia
RVNAF	Republic of Vietnam Armed Forces
RVCM	Republic of Vietnam Campaign Medal
Sig	Signalman/radio operator
SLR	Self-Loading Rifle
SOP	Standard operating procedure
SRDP	Special Rate Disability Pension
TAOR	Tactical Area of Responsibility
TPI	Totally and permanently incapacitated
21C	2nd in Command (Captain)
3TB	3rd Training Battalion
6RAR	6th Battalion, Royal Australian Regiment

VC	Viet Cong
VHF	Very high frequency
VVAA	Vietnam Veterans Association of Australia
WO1	Warrant Officer Class One
WO2	Warrant Officer Class Two

www.ingramcontent.com/pod-product-compliance
Lightning Source LLC
Chambersburg PA
CBHW030032100526
44590CB00011B/173